# MOTORING
## in the
# 30s

## GRAHAM ROBSON

 **Patrick Stephens, Cambridge**

**Frontispiece** *Scottish motorists had to share the Connel bridge, near Oban, with a railway service and the trains had precedence. This was 1930 and the car is a works-demonstrator Riley. Today the bridge is still in use (it is the A828, crossing the mouth of Loch Etive) but the railway has been closed, and the rails lifted, for many years* (Autocar).

First published 1979

**British Library Cataloguing in Publication Data**

Robson, Graham
  Motoring in the 30s.
  1. Automobile driving – Great Britain – History
  I. Title
  796.7'0941      GV1021

ISBN 85059 365 4

Text photoset in 10 on 11pt Baskerville
by Type-Spool (Hull) Company, Hull.
Printed in Great Britain on 100 gsm Pedigree coated
cartridge and bound by The Garden City Press,
Letchworth, Herts.
Published by Patrick Stephens Limited,
Bar Hill, Cambridge, CB3 8EL, England.

# Contents

# Foreword

It's a privilege to attempt an introduction to any material of which Graham Robson is the master. Fortunately his book deals with a decade well known to me, containing as it does a veritable compendium of happenings filled with statistics, all of which make attractive reading.

Developments in the later part of the 1920s formed the base of what turned out to be a most useful economical era in the field of passenger cars. For me there is no need to enlarge on the value of the 'thirties' since all its aspects are so fully covered in the chapters which follow, deep full of information for the enthusiast and historian.

My personal pet desire at that time would have been some common standardisation of instrumentation and controls, because one envisaged the motor car fast becoming a machine of general use, motoring becoming a necessary adjunct to family life. In those early days there existed a wide choice of vehicles, so a simplification would have enabled most of them to be quickly mastered by a driver and would add up to the better promotion of road safety.

I much enjoyed the ample coverage of motor sport from every angle. It indeed gives such an honest description of all that happened, from the 'Fastest Ever' and includes the Monte Carlo Rally which was the target of many British drivers.

Graham Robson has produced a book which will be so acceptable as a complete record of what took place in a very interesting and noteworthy decade.

Captain George E. T. Eyston, (OBE, MC, CEng, FIMech E, MASAE (USA)

This Foreword was very kindly given to me by Captain Eyston six months before his death – A.A.G.R.

# Introduction

Too many historians have dismissed the 1930s as wasted years. The miseries of the Depression, and its dragging after effects, made many sensitive people ready to ignore the good features of the decade. Over reaction to these years was to be expected, with derision and scorn heaped on the significant events – whether in art or politics, fashion or sport.

Motoring, and especially the cars themselves, was no more kindly treated. Since the 1930s was a decade sandwiched between two exciting and eventful periods, this was perhaps to be expected. The 1920s have already been made legendary by the 'vintage' movement – a cult, incidentally, founded in the 1930s when a few forthright motoring enthusiasts decided that they did not like the look of the new models then on offer. Neither is the motoring of the 1940s likely to be forgotten. We will always recall the fighting, the personal tragedies, the gloom and finally the great exhiliration of victory. Then, of course, there was the austerity, the rationing, the absence of nearly anything which could give harmless pleasure and what looked at times like a concerted attack on private motoring. But of the 1930s – what should we remember?

This book is an attempt, perhaps the very first, to put the record straight. I hope it might balance the views of the Vintagents, who still think that little engineering of merit ever came out of a British car factory after 1930. I hope, also, that it might explain why so very many cars were sold than ever before – at a time when the country was supposed to be in a desperate economic and social state. There is much more to discuss than the cars themselves. I have not forgotten that although the British were strong in sports cars they were generally weak in sport. We had thousands of active competitors, but not a single Grand Prix car.

The personalities were also as important as the cars themselves – certainly Herbert Austin, Lord Nuffield and William Rootes had as much influence on our motoring as did Stanley Baldwin and Neville Chamberlain. But why did Captain John Black, Spencer Wilks and Percival Perry have more influence than W. O. Bentley, Cecil Kimber and Georges Roesch? If it was not for the quality of their firms' products it must have been something to do with the type of motoring they encouraged.

The Bentleys, Rolls-Royces and Lagondas brought glamour that we can all remember, but it was the Flying Standards, Morris Eights and £100 Fords which were more significant. I hope that this book will show why the often scorned economy cars were so much more important to the world of motoring than the handful of Phantoms, Hispano-Suizas and Mercedes-Benz models which lorded it over them. For if ever a period could have an apt title, it was: 'Motoring for Everyman'. Nothing less than this will do.

Vast numbers of new motorists took to the roads of Britain for the very first time. There might have been many inadequate roads, thousands of traffic black spots and a general lack of services, but to the new motorist it was all very exciting. With new cars costing little more than £100, or less than £50 second-hand, it was easy to graduate from a motor cycle,

**Left** *In 1930 the Depression had yet to bite hard and the Olympia Motor Show was thronged with customers. Isn't it sad that three of the names we can identify – Swift, Standard and Talbot – have now disappeared and that Daimlers are no more than badge-engineered Jaguars?* (Autocar).

**Right** *Leslie Hore-Belisha was Minister of Transport when the first pedestrian crossings were introduced, so naturally the beacons were nicknamed 'Belishas'. This was Cheltenham in 1935* (Autocar).

easy to take pleasure in touring, in motor sport, or even – yes, a growing habit – in one's commuting. Cars were as cheap as they would ever be, as was the petrol, the spare parts and the labour to put them right again. After all, was it not true that living costs actually *fell* substantially during the decade, while wages managed to creep up much of the time? Even though wages and salaries were low, it seemed that everything was cheap. A new semi-detached house of one's own for £300 to £400 in a desirable suburb, full-board in a charming Trust Houses hotel for only 13s 6d (67p) a night, all on an average family income of around £8 a week, is something we will not see again.

The financial blizzard of the late 1920s had a dramatic effect on the cars designed and sold in the 1930s and equally on those machines which no longer found a ready sale. Events led to the disappearance of the independent Bentley, Lanchester, Sunbeam and Talbot names, while Aston Martin, Lagonda and Lea Francis were all badly hit. Humber and Hillman, Riley and Triumph all handed over their destinies to larger groups – was it really so wrong of the tycoons to save these names, if not their loss-making habits?

Many survivors from the 1920s – Crossley, Star, Swift and Trojan among them – disappeared, never to return. There were a few new marques (do you remember Autovia, Burney and Railton?) but few lasted long. Look down an industry list today and you will find only one make still alive which emerged in the 1930s – Jaguar – and even that famous marque is now a part of the British Leyland combine. Jensen is a relatively recent loss. Looking back, it is noticeable that many of the cars revered by vintage and sporting enthusiasts foundered financially, whereas those which they hated so virulently have survived and even prospered. Perhaps this book can explain how and why it happened.

The 1930s was the time for tycoonery, and for badge engineering to evolve. Individual makes huddled together for security. New groups were founded, first of all for security's sake and later to wield enormous power. By 1938 we already had a 'Big Six' and only two

of them were American owned. But if Ford and General Motors dominated Dagenham and Luton, it was Herbert Austin who was Master of Longbridge and Lord Nuffield who personally controlled Cowley. On one side of Coventry the Rootes family had their own burgeoning empire; on the other side of town Captain John Black had his own big ideas for Standard. Triumph had Claude Holbrook and Riley their own founding family. William Lyons *was* SS Jaguar, Cecil Kimber ran MG and the Wilks brothers imposed their high ideals on Rover. There was as much interest in the men as in the products – the motoring press made much of this.

For the tourist there were new road-houses, new hotels and even a few new arterial roads. For a few years there were no speed limits, but compulsory insurance was introduced for the first time; later Leslie Hore-Belisha's pedestrian crossings, the 30 mph 'built-up' areas and MoT driving tests all arrived in a rush. There was no tax on the cars themselves and only a few pennies tax on the petrol. A five-year-old Bentley could be bought for £300, but a new SS Jaguar (which might be faster) cost only a little more. Unit-construction bodies and independent front suspension arrived. Weymann bodies, punctures and road-side breakdowns nearly disappeared. Speed traps faded away, but speed cops came in.

In sport we had many heroes but few successful cars. We had splendid record breakers (men *and* machines) but we only won twice at Le Mans. Trials boomed, then fell back and rallies took their place. For racing we had Brooklands, Donington and precious little else. For racing cars there was ERA – or we bought foreign. We also had an incredible amount of fun and enjoyable motoring.

Technically, the 1930s were more important than the diehards would admit. Many techniques refined since the Second World War were pioneered in the 1930s. We stopped making a few cars beautifully and with care and started making lots of cars cheaply and adequately. Individuality disappeared and 'model cocktails' evolved. We made better value sports cars than any other nation and we have not lost that knack yet. We bought almost any colour of car so long as it was black or another unassuming shade and almost any type of saloon as long as it had four doors and probably a sun-roof. We suffered a weird 'Treasury Rating' of vehicle taxation, which encouraged engines with long strokes and narrow bores, which were quite unsuited to export markets. Yet our motoring magazines were nationalistic and determined to convince us that *all* British cars were best. Strong criticism, it seemed, was only for the disloyal or the anarchists – thank goodness that this attitude, at least, has changed.

In Britain we had the Depression, followed by a strong and steady recovery. King George V died, King Edward VIII abdicated and King George VI took his place. In politics we were led first by Ramsay Macdonald and his cost-cutters, then by Stanley Baldwin, his pipe and his cosy approach and finally by Neville Chamberlain and his appeasers. In Europe we could not escape from Hitler and Mussolini and from 1936 onwards the next war began to look inevitable. Here at home re-armament gave rise to the 'shadow' factories, which the motor industry was asked to run.

All these events had their influence on the cars we could buy and the motoring we could enjoy. It was a fascinating decade that should not go unrecorded. I hope that what follows will fill in many gaps.

Brampton, Cumbria                                                                                    *Graham Robson*
June 1979

# Chapter 1

# Britain and the motor car of the 30s

The first thing I have to do is to ridicule some of the stale propaganda. In Britain life throughout the 1930s, for the majority of the people, was not a continuous round of depression, nor of standing idle on street corners, nor of begging for money from the soulless employment exchanges. On the contrary, many families were happy, contented and became increasingly well-off.

We must also be sure not to accept everything written about the period without question. Most of the social histories and many of the novels were concerned with the real unfortunates – in the mining areas, the cotton mill villages and the shipbuilding towns – where industries suffered badly in a depression which left many people almost untouched. Throughout the country there was often as much evidence of house parties in the Agatha Christie style as there was of hunger marches and doomed communities. The traffic jams on the way to seaside resorts, or to the races, were much longer than the job queues. The fact is that the legend of the depressed 1930s has outlived the realities; people are now more inclined to believe the legend than the facts.

If ever there was a period which might justify the headline 'Britain in Paradox', it was the 1930s. Looking back, particularly at the motoring scene, it is often difficult to comprehend the great difficulty we had, as a nation, in struggling our way through a lengthy and severe trade depression. There is a mass of statistics showing that many of us became progressively better off as the years rolled by and this was not just by comparison with the depths of 1931. At the end of a decade noted more for its gloom and its silly politics than for its cheerfulness and its achievements, more British people owned their own houses, ran their own cars or could spend good money on leisure, than ever before. As far as motorists were concerned, it was a period when motoring for the wealthy was under attack, but when motoring for Everyman arrived.

Getting to grips with the era, to define its scope, is relatively easy. Between 1929 and 1931 the western world, triggered off by events in North America, had suffered a traumatic collapse of business confidence, of sharply contracting international trade, general recession and economic near disaster. After 1939 we were all plunged into the horrors of a Second World War, which brought private motoring effectively to an end for the next six years. In between (and on the surface) the years appeared peaceful and serene, even prosperous and happy for many of the British.

Between 1930 and 1939 there were no General Strikes, no dramatic social changes and no revolutions – at least, not in Britain. In some ways this was a decade of stagnation (some might say it was a decade of drift); any ordinary person put into a state of suspended animation in 1933 might have been awakened five years later on and hardly noticed the difference. No difference, that is nationally, for world events in this fairly placid period were overhung by the manoeuvring of the German and Italian dictators. The spectre of trench digging, sandbag filling and a desperate defence of our shores rose more than once, then receded, before the final descent into war began in 1939.

By 1930 the motor car had been a practicable fact for about 45 years, though there has probably never been a period when the origins of motoring were so freely ignored. Karl Benz's tricycle had run in 1885, the first British 'autocars' had followed in 1895 and the Emancipation Act of 1896 had finally made motoring in Britain both practical and re-spectable. Britain's motor industry established itself at the turn of the century, burgeoned in Edwardian times, in such a way that by 1914 and the outbreak of the Great War the conventional layout of components had virtually been standardised.

Although early motoring was primarily confined to the wealthy, who first had to be weaned off their horse-and-carriage traditions, invariably employed chauffeurs to do the driving and the dirty work for them and had to put up with a great deal of vehicle un-reliability, the motoring 'bug' had bitten so hard by 1914 that there were more than 130,000 cars on British roads.

The Great War changed everything. There were far-reaching social changes – in many people's view, long overdue – and it had given the taste for motoring to millions who had never previously been in a car. Just about every officer who survived the war was keen to spend his gratuity on a new car (as were many of the non-commissioned soldiers) and there were many seductive claims on his loyalties. But at the prices which existed in the early 1920s there was no prospect of the average working man, or even of the skilled craftsman, being able to afford a new car.

Even so, with only 78,000 cars on the roads when the war ended, a large number of small firms were set up to build cars and cycle cars. No fewer than 100 British manu-facturers were represented at the 1920 Olympia Motor Show (of which, incidentally, no less than 59 hailed from the city of Coventry) and a big increase in sales was forecast.

Many of the newcomers to motor car manufacture disappeared as the spurious post-war boom turned rapidly into a sharp depression, but as the 1920s progressed several, already

sizeable, companies continued to expand. North America had already assumed the mantle of the automotive giant, but in Britain it was Austin (at Longbridge, near Birmingham) and Morris (at Cowley in Oxford) who were taking the lead as mass-production car makers. Model rationalisation and mergers were not yet fashionable here, with the result that the growing motor industry became a mass of small to medium-sized concerns, many of whom built their own engines, chassis and coachwork. These were supported more and and more impressively by a whole substratum of companies which were willing to supply anything from spring washers to major engine castings. Birmingham and Coventry, in particular, housed hundreds of tiny metal-working businesses which relied on the motor industry for their very existence.

Although production steadily increased, there was little evidence as yet to show that the transition from the building of hand-finished 'quality' products to the volume production of identical machines was taking place quickly enough. Cars made in the 1920s were still too expensive for most people to buy when new; they took too long to be constructed and needed too many skilled and willing hands in the process for prices to fall. Between ten and twenty companies had dreams, perhaps even made plans, about becoming very important, but few had the capital resources or the vision to achieve them. Billy Morris and 'Pa' Austin were way ahead and realised that nothing less than 1,000 cars built every week was good enough, but who would now credit Bean, Clyno or Swift with the hopeless ambition to rival them?

On the other hand, there were several makers of very fine cars, with neither the financial backing nor the ability to build in any numbers, who relied on the well-to-do or the sportsmen to keep them afloat. Vintage enthusiasts are known for quoting Bentley, Frazer Nash, Lagonda or Lanchester for their technical excellence; none of these concerns was noted for its financial stability.

By 1929 future trends had become very obvious. In Britain, car production had been pushed up rather laboriously to around 200,000 a year, while the United States (which

**Left** *One of the last Olympia motor shows of the 1930s, with crowded stands, hundreds of cars on display and not a sign of the shrugged-off Depression. There were no limits on the way one could build a stand and there was little evidence of mergers at this stage* (Autocar).

**Right** *The highlight of the 1931 Olympia Motor Show was this exhibit, which proved that British machinery was fastest on land, on water and in the air. These craft, respectively, were Sir Malcolm Campbell's Bluebird, Lord Wakefield's Miss England II and the Rolls-Royce powered Supermarine S6B seaplane which won the Schneider Trophy* (Autocar).

had started from scratch several years later than us) made more than *five million* cars in the last frenetic pre-Depression year. To sell more cars the British industry would need the ability to make more (which meant expansion or mechanisation) and would have to offer them at much lower prices than ever before. Quality manufacturers would either have to change their ways, or perish in the wake of progress. All this, and more, might possibly have been achieved in a reasonably organised manner, if the thunderclap of a world depression had not suddenly exploded. Mass production of simple cars, at low prices, in factories where cost accountants would be more important than design engineers, suddenly became essential to survival. It was with this urgent new stimulus that motoring in the 1930s began.

At this point, the motoring historian who is interested, not only in the product, but also in the conditions for which it was made, must pause to consider the sort of nation which was evolving. Social changes had as much to do with the development of the motor car in the 1930s as did the vehicles which preceded it. The Great War had signalled a gradual bridging of the gulf between the leisured and moneyed classes and the mass of working people; thanks to the imposition of income taxes, death duties and other financial changes the gap between 'them' and 'us' was narrowed. British business steadily became more modern and complex and to serve it an entirely new section of British society, which for want of a better term we will call the middle class, developed. These people had educated themselves and worked their way out of the lower orders and had aspirations to upper class behaviour and values. Now, for the very first time, many of them found that they had money to spend on things other than sheer survival. In many cases they decided that the most desirable area for 'optional' spending was housing and motoring.

Unavoidably, therefore, we must now look at a few statistics. The first batch tells us something of the plight of those who could not find jobs for much of the time, the second of the way in which regular incomes were largely being spent.

In the United States, the economic 'crash' at the end of 1929 eventually affected commercial activity all over the world; in Britain the problems began in earnest in 1931. Business suffered as trade (home and overseas) slumped and of Britain's 44 million population, the number officially unemployed shot up to a maximum of 2.8 million in 1932. As this figure was only quoted for the official 'insured' working population, the sum total was probably much higher. Between 1923 and 1929 the average number of people out of work had been 1.2 million, less than it has been in the late 1970s, but still a long way above any acceptable figure, although considered quite reasonable at the time.

Although never less than three-quarters of the working population had jobs in the 1930s (and most of the time this proportion was a lot higher) some areas were hit harder than others. Local tragedies were enacted at places like Jarrow, Brynmawr and Greenock (where about three-quarters of the men were out of work even as late as 1934) while areas like London, Coventry and Oxford were booming and expanding mightily with only six or seven per cent looking for jobs.

Although things were grim, the absolute bottom of the trough came in the autumn of 1932, after which economic activity slowly and steadily began to increase. Even so, unemployment did not fall below two million until the end of 1935 and it could be no comfort to peace-lovers to know that re-armament then had a lot to do with the continuing improvement. The number of jobless averaged over 1.5 million until the outbreak of war, but plummeted thereafter. The motor industry had much to do with the recovery, building 159,000 cars in the depths of the 1931 gloom, but buoyantly pushing this up to 379,000 in 1937. There were 321,000 people working in the industry of 1931, but seven years later this figure had risen to 460,000. At the beginning of the decade about a million cars were in use on British roads, but by 1938 the two million mark had been passed.

Whatever we may conclude from the statistics, there was no doubt that 'motoring for the masses' had arrived.

The Depression, therefore, was serious, but it did not by any means have the same effect all over Britain. Many areas in the Home Counties and the Midlands were scarcely affected, which may explain why successive governments, living as they did in prosperous areas, did not seem concerned enough to take drastic action. To be fair, Britain battled throughout the Depression better than almost any other industrial nation. While the United States once suffered nearly 14 million jobless and Germany six million, Britain's highest figure was just less than three million. Our recovery was helped by a phenomenon which we might find impossible even to understand these days – for the great majority of the period the actual cost of living in Britain steadily *fell*. At the same time wages and salaries at least held their own and in many cases tended to edge upwards. We therefore had a situation where the general standard of life, in what an economist would call 'real terms', was probably 20 per cent higher at the end of the 1930s than it had been in the depths of the Depression and yet salaries had barely risen. As John Stevenson and Chris Cook so rightly point out in their book, *The Slump*:

'For many salaried people affluence began not in the 1950s but in the 1930s, when it became possible for the average salaried person to buy his own house, usually on a mortgage, run a car and begin to afford a range of consumer durables and household goods hitherto considered out of reach . . ..'

All this is not meant to imply that the new motoring classes were very highly paid. Because of the way inflation has hit Britain in the last thirty years, many of us can truly understand the level of prices current in the 1930s. To get anywhere near late 1970s prices, the sums quoted below should be multiplied about 12 times. A useful survey, carried out in 1938, when conditions were as favourable as at any other time in the decade, found that the average British *family* income was of the order of £450 a year (nearly £9 a week) and that middle-class families might be earning between £550 and £600 a year. However, more than 22 million individuals earned less than £5 a week, the average industrial wage was only £3 a week and only 1¾ million earned between £5 and £10 a week.

To compensate for this, of course, was the cost of the cheapest British cars (a 1936 Ford Eight 'Popular' could be had for £100) and 80 octane petrol selling for only 1s 7d (8p) a gallon (of which 9d was duty). The average price of a new semi-detached house was between £400 and £500, which necessitated a down payment of only £25 and payments on a mortgage with a mere 4½ per cent interest rate. Other prices which also make us gape in disbelief were 2s 5d (12p) for a good seat at the cinema and less than £3 for a new suit from Burtons. At the same time direct taxation averaged only 14 per cent of earnings, holidays with pay were extended from 1½ million people in 1931 to more than 11 million in 1939 and personal expenditure on motoring was no more than 9s (45p) a week. This rubs in the low cost of everything from tyres to petrol, from repairs to insurance.

However, this bald statement of prices does not give us a completely clear picture. We must also remember that there was no National Health service yet, nor free dental treatment. Many other expenses had to be borne which are now dealt with by the machinery of government and which are now extracted from us in the form of taxes or rates.

However, great industrial changes had hastened a very important social development. By 1938 there had been created a substantial lower middle class, whose bread-winners worked in the offices of large business and industrial concerns. In the wake of this new-found stability, the urge to spend money on one's own house became overwhelming; there was an explosion of private building in Britain, particularly in the prosperous south-east. Almost all the new houses were on the outskirts of towns and cities. The result was in-

**Above** *The Staples Corner/North Circular Road was much less built up when the 1930s opened. This shot was actually taken at the end of 1928; Staples Corner (where the North Circular Road crosses the Edgware Road, A5) is in the top right of the frame, the North Circular Road itself (towards Wembley and Ealing) runs across the picture and that is the Welsh Harp reservoir at the top of the frame. The factory on the corner at Staples Corner was, of course, owned by Bentley Motors* (Aerofilms Ltd).

**Below** *Suburban sprawl well and truly in progress. This was Hendon in 1932, when the private-housing boom was under way. The airfield (now covered by local authority housing) is top left, the St Pancras – St Albans railway line runs alongside it and the centre of Hendon had a large roundabout at the crossing. This shot is looking north, Barnet is just over the horizon. Nowadays the M1 runs alongside the railway and there are thousands more houses* (Aerofilms Ltd).

variably a centrifugal drift – while the numbers of people living in city centres remained the same or even declined, all the real growth took place in the suburbs. Nowhere was this more drastically shown than in and around London; between 1921 and 1938 the population of the centre fell from 4.5 to 4.1 million, while the outer conurbation surged ahead from 3.0 to 4.6 million. More than a million people moved into London from other parts of the country and there was a net inflow to the Midlands. More than 60 per cent of Britain's inter-war population increase became housed in the south-east of England.

Personal mobility, and one's own little car, had much to do with this. In London, though, one other very important contributory factor was the spread of the new tube trains and the Southern Railway's electrification. Sir John Betjeman has already immortalised the Metropolitan Line and its 'Metroland', which dragged London's suburbs out to Rickmansworth and beyond, but we must also remember that the Northern Line virtually created Golders Green, Hendon and Edgware, unaided, in the 1920s, while the Southern Railway takes much of the credit for the square miles of housing in Orpington, Croydon, Sutton and Kingston, which followed upon the completion of their new suburban electric services.

Look now at the houses, their environment and the roads which feed them, for more evidence of a life style which came to depend on private cars. The shopping areas and the leafy avenues, long distances from a bus service or a train, all cried out for private transport and the occupants of these smart little villas were determined to have it. Cynical commentators of the period suggested that to these people the Baby Austin in the garage was more important than the baby carriage in the hall and who can blame them?

This trend did not only occur in the cities. The life of many villages within 20 miles of any reasonably busy town was also to be revolutionised by transport developments in the 1930s. Many such villages, particularly in prosperous south-east England, were turned into a kind of rural suburb beyond the suburbs. It had become possible, for the very first time, for people born, bred *and* earning in towns to live in the country. The man from Mars landing in Sussex in mid-afternoon would often have been hard-put to muster a group of adult males and would have wondered where they all went until supper time.

Not that public transport was going to give in without a struggle. The railway system, certainly, had become smug and, because it had held a monoply of mass travel for half a century, was slow in modernising its image, but was intent on doing so. Over long distances the trains were still the quickest way to travel, even if their smoke and their riding conditions should already have been banished to museums. Looking back now from the late 1970s when (industrial strife permitting) we enjoy a very fast and efficient railway service in Britain, with trains which are modern and usually clean, it is not easy to realise that then there were no main line diesel or electric services. The steam locomotive was still god of the main lines.

The railways, nevertheless, faced up to the challenge of the motor car with wholesale acceleration in their express services. During the 1930s the LMSR introduced 66 new services with start-to-stop schedules of 60 mph and over and by 1938 the LNER had no fewer than 107 trains scheduled at more than 60 mph. Special timing and lightweight trains allowed Edinburgh and Glasgow to be brought no more than six hours from London (this was *much* faster than could ever be achieved by private car) and other star trains like the Cornish Rivera Express and the Cheltenham Flyer could put up startling speeds with limited accommodation.

Although more people travelled on the railways because of the dazzling publicity generated and because of their growing prosperity (1,800 million journeys in 1937 compared with 1,570 million in 1933), we should not be dazzled by such isolated flashes of high performance, as the railways mainly dealt in mass travel at fairly leisurely speeds and at

**Left** *Surely this is a country lane? But no it was a particularly nasty section of the A1, the Great North Road, near Hatfield. That is an original-type Morris Minor on the road, with a small Ford parked in the lane* (Autocar).

**Right** *Could this be the* Great *North Road in 1939? The Bentley 4¼-litre model is beautiful, and at least the road north of Baldock is arrow-straight, but what about the width! Between London and New-castle there was not a single mile of dual carriageway on our premier highway* (Autocar).

fairly low rates. Although cross-country buses charged only 1d (0.4p) per mile, third class train travel was much to be preferred at 1½d (0.6p) per mile. The big seaside resorts, especially in the North, fed unashamedly on railway traffic. Blackpool, for instance, had abysmal road access, but could support three thriving stations and even Morecambe, which was much smaller, could sustain a couple. Blackpool had seven million visitors in 1937 (half a million of them over the August Bank Holiday alone) who arrived in 50,000 cars and no fewer than 70 special trains. Thinly-patronised country branch lines were everywhere, their trains often carrying only the proverbial 'three men and a dog' – it would be years yet before the private car would really make them redundant.

One consolation for the motor car salesman was that there were many practical incentives for passengers to avoid buses and trams. Local examples were, almost without exception, slow, noisy, cramped and uncomfortable, although the long-distance express variety were much more advanced and attracted quite a lot of traffic. It is significant that during the 1930s the number of cars on the roads doubled, while the total population of buses rose only from 50,000 to 53,000. At least by the early 1930s the upper decks of double-deck vehicles had grown roofs and windows, with enclosed access stairs. The bad old days of the solid-tyred charabancs (known as 'charas' by one and all) were over, but the name stuck when the coaching boom of 1928–32 had subsided and for many more years would be applied to any private-hire coach.

Trams were throwbacks to Edwardian days, when they had had a certain new-fangled technical interest, but by the 1930s the many corporation-owned networks were in full retreat. If it had not been for their high maintenance and running costs, that phenomenon of the 1930s – the trolley bus – might have made even more startling advances. A trolley bus, which was really an omnibus with electrical traction, was both lively and refined, even if it never became socially acceptable. (Some old-fashioned people looked down on trolley buses and their overhead wires, suggesting that it made a neighbourhood 'non U'). It picked up its power from overhead wires just like the noisy old trams, which theoretically meant that it could directly replace them, but because of this it was still not able to divert

in case of accidents, road works or changes in planning. It was also, unavoidably, an urban phenomenon.

For long distance travel, certainly, there were several healthy discouragements to using one's own car. It might have been relatively cheap (though the relative cost of petrol was a little lower than it was in the late 1970s, when cost-of-living indices were considered) but the big deterrent was the state of the road system itself. Although most of the road surfaces were now satisfactory (which was a welcome change from those normal in Edwardian times – even if some critics now though they had become *too* good and so had influenced our car makers to design weak little machines unsuited to export markets) they still tended to follow age-old alignments. With very few exceptions, our roads were two-lane and two-way. Britain's premier highway, the Great North Road from London to Edinburgh, was an anachronistic disgrace; like most others its alignment had been established one, two, or even five centuries earlier, when the pack horse, the bullock cart and, latterly, the stagecoach had been the principal road users. Truly, G. K. Chesterton's 'rolling English drunkard' had built the 'rolling English road' – and modern progress on lengthy trips still suffered accordingly. During the 1930s there was some improvement, miniscule by modern standards and we shall study this in greater detail in the next chapter.

The rich were abandoning their fast cars in some instances and taking up flying instead. Small sporting planes arrived on the scene with a vengeance and there seemed to be aerodromes and flying clubs everywhere. To the well-heeled, a Tiger Moth was just as useful and enjoyable as a Lagonda or a Bentley and was far simpler to maintain. The era of 'build-it-yourself' flying machines was once promised though such notorious little planes as the Flying Flea sustained several unexplained accidents which led to all of them being grounded.

There were already commercial aviation services far and wide. Imperial Airways linked London's Croydon Airport to the Empire with their safe but stately HP42s, while trans-atlantic services finally became a reality just before the outbreak of war, when Boeing flying boats began a regular schedule. There was a large domestic network, with no less

*One great touring innovation of 1936 was the* Twickenham Ferry, *operating between Dover and Dunkirk, which accepted trains and cars on a roll-on/roll-off basis. The sister ships were* Hampton Ferry *and* Shepperton Ferry; *each charged £2 5s 6d (£2.27) for a single vehicle crossing and had space for 25 cars each* (Autocar).

than 95 aerodromes in use by 1935, but few could afford the fares, which varied between 3d (1.2p) and 9½d (4p) per mile. 16 companies, operating 76 separate services, were in existence by 1938, but average load factors were rarely more than 35 per cent, and many companies struggled to make profits. Although only 3,250 passengers were carried in 1932, this figure rocketed to 161,500 by 1937. Although London's principal airfield was at Croydon, Heston was also important; both have now been built over. Heathrow did not exist, while Gatwick was a small field with a grass strip. Hendon (also nearly obliterated by modern 1970s housing developments) was the RAF's showpiece at Air Display time and there were small fighter fields being developed at Biggin Hill and Kenley.

Britain had a fine Navy, which caused many people to suggest that no one would ever dare to declare war on us in the future. The Fleet Review at Spithead was always a major public occasion and the 'send a gunboat' mentality was still very much alive in the land. We British also had to rely completely on ships for overseas transport of cars. Aeroplanes were not yet big enough, strong enough, nor versatile enough to carry cars and tourists contemplating foreign travel had to use cross-Channel ships. Dover or Folkestone to Calais or Boulogne where the principal routes, as they still are today, though ships with a drive-on/drive-off facility did not arrive until 1936.

For many the most exciting – or nerve-racking – part of a foreign motoring holiday was to watch Southern Railway cranes swinging one's precious car from dockside to ship by means of precarious-looking slings. As war clouds gathered towards the end of August 1939, the scenes at Calais and Boulogne can be imagined, with hundreds of frantic tourists clamouring to be taken back to safety; many had to abandon their vehicles and cross the channel without them. At least one irreplaceable car – the aerodynamic Rolls-Royce Corniche prototype – was subsequently destroyed by enemy bombing.

It is often said that fashions in motoring accurately reflect fashions in clothing, architecture and the like. It is not easy to make a direct comparison for the 1930s (after all, skirt lengths, house designs and household equipment were not subject to the Government's horse-power taxation system!) but there were some similarities. The motor car, of course, now became the single most desirable 'extra' after the purchase of the house and took on the guise of a status symbol. Gadgets and gimmicks were the order of the day, a trend which seemed to affect everyone's possessions. If cars were often simply minor variations on basic designs, so too were the houses. Among the hundreds of thousands of new semi-detached dwellings thrown up in the new suburbs, there were few basic differences. They were so identifiable as to type that Osbert Lancaster dubbed them 'By-pass Variegated' and they had decorative details which were instantly recognisable.

New public buildings leant heavily on the '1930s Odeon cinema' type of styling, but an increasing number of factories, mansion blocks and even private houses adopted the smooth 'Modernistic' style which was so popular for a time. London's Great West Road, as well as Southall, Hayes and other parts of West London, all offer prime examples. Almost everyone cites the Hoover building in Perivale as the classic example, but in motoring circles the new Hooper coachbuilding factory on Western Avenue, near the crossing with the North Circular Road, was equally distinctive.

The car, of course, was the great status symbol, but in the home it was sometimes rivalled by new and sophisticated household equipment. Except in remote country districts, everyone who wanted them could now enjoy electricity, gas, water and mains drainage. The National Grid was virtually complete by 1933; in 1920 only one house in 17 had had electric lighting, but by 1930 this had risen to one house in three and by 1939 to two houses in three. In the late 1930s new consumers were being added at the rate of 700,000–800,000 a year.

Central heating was newly fashionable and it was a poor home which did not boast a gas or electric cooker of some sort. Washing machines and refrigerators were still rare and the domestic deep freeze unknown. Electric shavers had still to arrive from North America, though the 'safety' had finally overtaken the 'cut-throat' razor. Man-made fabrics and plastics were not yet common. Nylon garments were a delight destined to arrive along with the American troops in the 1940s; only rayon, still in an early stage of development,

*Overseas touring was on the increase, as was interest in the Monte Carlo Rally. Whatever the purpose, however, cars crossing the channel at the beginning of the 1930s had to be hoisted on board ship at Dover. The car in the sling is Colonel Loughborough's Lanchester and the year is 1933* (Autocar).

*An ultra-modern style with single garage matching the opposite side of the house and connected by a covered passage.*

*(Below) A built-in garage to which a door from the hall could be arranged.*

ground is situated on an incline.

It seems significant that only one of the eight designs has more than two reception rooms, while only two have accommodation for two cars. The house with three reception rooms is in the ultra-modern style, but its garage is only 10ft. wide.

There can be little doubt that a garage built in with the house is in every way superior to one that is detached. It is warmer, it can be heated conveniently from the house central heating, and so help to keep the car in good condition by avoiding excessive changes in temperature, which is the enemy of all pistons and cylinders.

Let us first take the house illustrated in the heading of this article. Here we see the doors of the double garage ranking as equal to the front door to the house. This is essentially a motorist's home. Note the communicating door between hall and garage, a feature so seldom seen that it is possible there are objections to it in spite of its many obvious advantages. Probably memories of garages with oil puddles and dirt have caused owners to decide that a communicating door would mean the transference of dirt into the house by the feet of the family or guests. But there should be no oil puddles in a garage; there should be trays filled with sand to catch any drippings, while dirt should be as rigorously excluded from the

A 27

**Left** *In 1935 The Autocar ran a splendidly evocative series of articles on 'The motorist's house', which told us a lot about prevailing architectural fashions and about the sort of houses the prosperous middle class was demanding* (Autocar).

**Top** *It is difficult to recall how exciting the prospect of a brand new exhibition hall at Earls Court was in 1937. At the time, too, it was the epitome of modern design* (Autocar).

**Above** *As the Depression eased, Hooper, the 'Royal' coachbuilders, opened a new factory on Western Avenue, near the crossing with the North Circular Road. It has changed hands several times since its completion, in truly typical 1930s architectural style, in 1933* (Autocar).

August 16th, 1935.                    305

## DECCA

The Decca Home and Car radio was fully described in *The Autocar* in the issue of July 12th. The feature of this receiver is the fact that it may be used in any place where there is a power plug of 200-250 volts, whether it be in a house, hotel, or of 12 volts in the dashboard of the car. There is no switching, as the appropriate connecting cable automatically arranges the correct supply. When used in the car a rotary converter supplies the HT current.

There are two models—a four-valve receiver at 15 guineas and a de luxe 6-valve model at 18 guineas. Both are superhets and

deliver an output of 3½ watts.

As this receiver is intended for carrying in and out of the car it is not fixed, but placed either on the front passenger's seat when the driver is travelling alone or between the two passengers on the back seats.

The case measures 13½in. by 15in. by 7½in., and is covered with leather.

There is only one knob for tuning, which is divided to control volume, change wavelengths, switch on and off, and tuning.

It is claimed that it consumes no more current than a head lamp bulb.

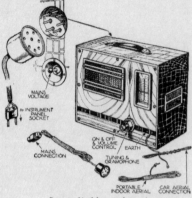

MAINS VOLTAGE · to INSTRUMENT PANEL SOCKET · MAINS CONNECTION · ON & OFF & VOLUME CONTROL · EARTH · TUNING & GRAMOPHONE · PORTABLE INDOOR AERIAL · CAR AERIAL CONNECTION

*Decca combined house and car set.*

*C.A.C. car radio.*

## G.E.C.

The General Electric Company's car radio is self-contained in one case, including the receiver chassis, loud speaker and rotary converter. This case, however, is only 15in. long by 7½in. and 7in. The controls are, of course, separate, and may be mounted on either the steering column or the dashboard, as desired. There are two knobs, one for tuning and the other for volume. The dial is of the "speedometer" type. A Yale lock controls the set and the choice of waveband. A yellow pilot light is used to indicate when the set is "on."

The 5-valve superhet circuit uses

13-volt valves and has been specially designed to exclude noises from the car electrical equipment, and on the receiver case are two switches, one for controlling the tone and the other for limiting the sensitivity when it is desired to cut down the "background" noise from trams or power station.

An unusual feature is the plugs which are provided for an extension loud speaker for use when picnicking or in a caravan.

The output is 3 watts and the consumption about 4.5 amps or 54 watts.

The price, including suppressors, is £19 19s.

## MOTOROLA

There are several Motorola receivers, ranging from a 6-volt set at £16 16s. to a 12-volt de luxe model at 26 guineas.

The most popular model is the 6-valve receiver with the chassis and loud speaker contained in the same case. The circuit includes very careful screening and filters, and therefore no resistors are required for the ignition system of the car. Another important feature is the remarkably low drain on the battery. With a 12-volt accumulator this is only 2.75 amps., which is one of the lowest on the market, and even with the 6-volt set the drain is only 5.5 amps., or 33 watts, or slightly less than the normal head lamps for an Austin Seven. The advantage of this feature cannot be too strongly emphasised, especially when intended for use with some of the

cheaper cars. The price of the 6-volt model is 18 guineas, and 19 guineas for the 12-volt model.

It should also be mentioned that the cheaper model receivers have even lower consumption. The more expensive model is in three units: (1) The 5-valve receiver; (2) the six. loud speaker; and (3) the control panel with master key. The output of this receiver is 4½ watts absolute, and there is a continuously variable tone control fitted to the control panel. Both medium and long wavebands are covered by all Motorola receivers, and it is possible to receive from 35 to 50 stations.

One of the special features of the Motorola is the fact that the chassis is plugged into the case so that it can easily be removed for inspection without disturbing the case.

## LISSEN

Lissen car radio is built exclusively for Ford cars. Whether other models will in future be available for other makes of cars depend no doubt very largely on the result and form of the impending regulations.

The main feature of this receiver is the fact that, inclusive of fitting it only costs £10. It is a 5-valve superhet, covering both long and medium wavebands. The valves are the 2-volt type and HT current is supplied by a dry

battery, while the energised field of the loud speaker is arranged in series with the valve filaments. The current is easily the lowest on the market, being only 1.2 amps. at 6 volts, or a consumption of 7.2 watts.

The receiver, loud speaker and controls are mounted in one case, which is designed to fit into the glove box of the car and resembles in appearance the face of a domestic receiver, with the addition of a master key.

## MARCONI

Marconi car radio, which will be on sale on September 1st, is in three units. The circuit is a five-valve superhet, while another valve is used to rectify the HT current from the vibrator.

The control unit is clamped on the steering column and contains two controls, one for switching on and off and for volume, and the other for tuning and for changing from long to medium wave length. The dial has a large "speedometer" face and is illuminated when the set is switched on.

The receiver chassis is carried in a steel case, which is mounted by means of a single hole fixing. The chassis can be removed from

its case for inspection without disturbing the mounting.

Vibrator and loud speaker are carried together in a separate case and can also be examined without disturbing the fixing. The vibrator has triple electrical screening and is sound-insulated with felt.

An electro magnetic cut-out protects all condensers and other components from the surge voltages which normally arise when switching on car radio.

The consumption from a 12-volt battery is 5 amps. (60 watts).

The price, including suppression equipment, is 20 guineas, but excluding the aerial, and the minimum charge for fitting is £1 17s. 6d.

*A neat Motorola arrangement.*

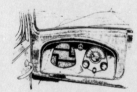

*The Philco dash control.*          *Lissen set for Ford cars.*

*By 1935 it was possible to buy car radios for in-car entertainment. This reprint of one of* The Autocar's *pages shows the state of the art. 'Superhet' circuitry was all the rage and – in round figures – £20 for such a fitting was by no means cheap* (Autocar).

was in wide use. Car seating, incidentally, was usually covered by leather, or by cloth in the most expensive models; dreadfully poor-quality 'leather-cloth' was often found in the cheapest cars. The only structural plastics seen were derivatives of bakelite or celluloid, neither of them renowned for their durability or strength.

The world was effectively shrinking as communications improved. Radio, still known almost universally as 'the wireless', had matured in the previous ten years, since the first BBC broadcoasts in 1922. Receiving sets had improved enormously since the first 'cat's whisker' outfits were sold and the modern 'superhet' sets were now readily available. Prices tumbled as production expanded and radio advertising boasted of the large number of valves and other special features. Sets became available for cars, though manufacturers rarely made any provision for them to be installed neatly; in the early days a motorist had to stop and sling an aerial over the nearest tree to achieve good reception. Interference from the ignition system was serious, so that one really had to park at the roadside in order to listen in. Back in the home, there was the arrival of television – which really *did* look like a haunted fish-tank in those days! John Logie Baird's system had been transmitting experimental programmes for some years, but London's Alexandra Palace station finally started commercial broadcasting in 1936. Viewers with sets were a very select little band – there were only 50,000 of them by the end of 1939 – screens were tiny and no one living far outside London was able to pick up the signals.

For much of the time, in spite of the dramatic events unfolding in America and Europe, the national mood was one of smug isolationism. The British, and their rulers, tended to think only of themselves. Politicians reacted to foreign influences sufficiently to preserve our place in the world, but rarely for the good of others. The archetypal 'man on the Clapham omnibus' would rather not be bothered with events in Italy and Germany – his office job was safe, he had just moved to a smart little house in the suburbs and it was time for another cricket series against Australia – so why should he?

To an equally obviously degree, our motor industry was almost entirely isolated from the rest of the world of motoring. There were several reasons for this. Overriding everything was the British tax-man's love of the annual 'Treasury Rating' (or horse power tax) method of licencing motor vehicles, which almost by definition forced British cars' engines to be narrow-bored, long-stroked and lacking in sheer horsepower. Secondly, at the start of the 1930s our industry was still almost completely geared to supplying the home market and although the importation of foreign cars was not actively discouraged, the existence of the horse-power tax deterred most of them later in the decade. Nevertheless, our exports increased steadily throughout the decade, from 19,000 cars in 1931 to 78,000 in the peak year of 1937, though in the latter year only 18,500 foreign cars were imported. Our relatively well-maintained road system meant that the cost accountants in the car factories could have a field day saving money from suspension systems and it is a sad fact that most of our 'Colonial' models were failures.

Not that this seemed to discourage the typical British motorist, or – more accurately – the vast horde of people who became new motorists in the ten years leading up to the Hitler war of 1939. Once again, I can let statistics speak for themselves. In 1930, with production of quality-first motor cars beginning to tail off in favour of the simpler (some say nastier) types, there were just over a million vehicles of all types on Britsh roads. Eight years later, in spite of the Depression and its dragging aftermath, there were 2.5 million in all. Production of private cars alone shot up from 170,000 in 1930, through 257,000 in 1934, to 379,000 in 1937. By comparison with today's figures – there are perhaps eight times as many vehicles on the roads at the end of the 1970s as there were in 1938 – it does not look much, but at the time the motoring explosion looked positively staggering. Truly, it signalled the start of 'Motoring for the Masses'.

**Chapter 2**

# Who motored and how much did it cost?

There were fewer than a million cars on British roads in 1930 and about double that number in 1939. Throughout the 1930s Britain's population crept ahead from 44.5 to 46.5 millions. Perhaps half of them could be thought of as potential car drivers, but probably not more than four or five million ever actually were. Even though motor vehicles – cars and motor cycles – had long since progressed from the status of expensive toys to that of everyday working machines, there were generations of habit and serious financial barriers, to be overcome before the British could be persuaded to convert themselves whole-heartedly to the use of cars. In North America the process was almost complete, as that 1929 figure of five million cars produced confirms. In one year, therefore, more cars were made in the United States than had been built in Great Britain since the end of the Great War.

Of course, in Britain there was also the question of supply limitations to be considered. Apart from a year here and there (the early 1920s were shaky times for some) there was rarely a time when large concerns like Austin and Morris were working below full capacity. From 1934 certainly, the British public bought as many cars as they could lay hands on, pausing only to reject the most obviously badly-designed, bizarre or over-priced models.

There were, it is true, plenty of inducements. It was so very easy to start motoring. In the regimented and computerised 1970s we have come to expect our activities to be controlled and monitored by state and private influences. It has not always been so. A would-be motorist in the 1930s could quite literally walk into a showroom to buy a car, pay over what now looks like a ludicrously small sum of money – especially if he was choosing a tatty

*The picture which headed* The Autocar's *correspondence columns in January 1935 tells us a lot about traffic density in rural Oxford (this is Burford high street) at the time. The sports car is a P-Type MG Midget and only four other motor vehicles are visible* (Autocar).

little machine built several years earlier that had no real right still to be in existence – and
drive it away. At first the law did not require him to be competent to drive, nor did the car
have to be insured, neither did it have to comply with many stringent safety standards; it
was enough that the Treasury should get its annual licence fees and that HM Customs and
Excise should get its cut from petrol sales.

Incredibly enough, there was no compulsory driving test before March 1935 – before
then anyone, without ever having previously sat in a car, could walk into a Post Office and
fill in an application for a driving licence. Even after that date there was no requirement
for established drivers to undergo a test to prove their competence. Even though accidents
did not soar after the overall 20 mph speed limit was swept away at the beginning of 1931
(less people were killed in road accidents in 1933 than had been killed in 1930, for example)
evidence of poor driving on the unlimited streets of towns and cities led the government to
impose a scheme of compulsory testing, after a year of voluntary testing had produced
little response. Even so, there were millions of drivers then and many thousands *still* driving
today, who have never passed, nor even attempted, a driving test.

Class conventions and a man's expectations, were then very different from today. The
great mass of British working people were not yet used to making their own way anywhere.
Bicycles, or perhaps motorcycles, were used for short trips, a bus or a local train was used to
get to and from work and in most cases special excursion trains were organised for holiday
travel. Most people had not even sat in a car, let alone tried to drive one and most were
still prepared to be patient with the slow and inflexible methods of public transport. The
dustman is still a dustman, in spite of a different job title, but still has a dirty job and still
carries bins. These days he probably gets to and from work in a car; even in 1939 this
would have been unthinkable. The majority of car workers in Birmingham, Coventry or
Oxford would know a great deal about their company's products, but would not expect
to own one – go along and look at factory car parks today and see the revolution which has
taken place.

The type of person who became a motorist had altered dramatically since motoring in
in Britain began in the 1890s. At first cars were purchased by the wealthy and invariably
driven by their chauffeurs. The sportsmen took up the new hobby of motoring, became
owner-drivers and ensured that by 1914 they were already in the ascendant. Immediately
after the Great War, the vast majority of motorists in Britain were from the upper classes,
or were what we might call 'professional people'.

Even in those days, however, the spread of motoring was uneven. At the beginning of the
1920s, for instance, it had still been possible for a Scottish Member of Parliament to state
that he did not need to have sympathy with cars or motorists as 'no one who voted for him
yet possessed one'. In the 1920s, when volume production was really becoming established,
there were many people who could not bring themselves to believe in popular-style
motoring and it is amazing to realise that a large proportion of the speculative-develop-
ment houses built between the wars, in the newly-fashionable suburbs, were originally
constructed without provision for a garage.

The millions of would-be motorists, who made their intentions clear in the 1920s,
showed that although 'vintage' motoring, in fine and largely hand-built cars, was all very
well and good, it could not possibly allow them to afford the pleasure of being mobile.
Some way would need to be found to bring the lower rung of motoring down within the
reach of the middle classes. Not only would the cars have to become cheaper, but the
means of financing them would have to be made easier. Perhaps it was William Morris
who formalised the touchstone of this type of motoring; at the beginning of the 1920s he
cut the prices of his Oxfords and Cowleys to stay in business, found that sales rocketed and
never had to revert to his original price levels.

**D.L. 23.**

**N    00001**

Ref. No.

Road Traffic Acts, 1930 to 1934.

## CERTIFICATE OF PASSING OF TEST OF COMPETENCE TO DRIVE.

Name... Mr R.E.C. Beene.

Address... 44 Kensington Hall Gdns

...W.14. Kensington

has been examined and has passed test
of competence to drive

THE BRITISH SCHOOL OF MOTORING LTD.

...

prescribed for the purposes of Section 5 of
the Road Traffic Act, 1930, or Section 6
of the Road Traffic Act, 1934.

L.J.U.Brougham

Authorised by the Minister of Transport
to conduct tests.

.23.

Date 16.3. 1935

[SEE OVER.

**Left** *The very first Driving Test 'Pass' certificate for Mr Beene of Kensington, West London, in March 1935. Before then, anyone could drive a car in Britain without attempting any form of proficiency test (Autocar).*

**Below** *A fashionable item of equipment on middle-priced cars was a built-in jacking system. Those standardised on this 1936 Morris 25 were hydraulic and less prone to corrosion damage than cruder mechanical types (Autocar).*

**Below right** *H. S. Linfield, The Autocar's noted chief road tester, at the wheel of the interesting, but unsuccessful V8-engined Riley 8-90. Like the similar Flying Standard V8, it failed because of the heavy annual taxation imposed on such engines (Autocar).*

Towards the end of the 1920s, the cost of motoring, along with the general level of prices in Britain, began to come down. In spite of generally gloomy times and the bitter situation created by the General Strike of 1926, the nation's apparent prosperity increased, especially among the newly-important (important, both socially and economically) white-collar office workers of the fast-expanding middle class. Demonstrably, they wanted to have the privileges and accoutrements of the upper classes, even if they had to go into pawn to achieve it.

The sort of car which began to sell in huge quantities as the decade progressed (huge, that is, by late 1920s standards) differed considerably from the true 'vintage' cars. Every motoring tycoon worth his salt, his top hat and his chauffeur-driven limousine, realised that increased sales and long-term prosperity could only be achieved by marketing cheaper and cheaper products. Eights, Nines and Tens proliferated, sometimes taking over complete production lines and factory buildings from the Fourteens and Sixteens which had held the limelight, years earlier. However, unlike the stalwarts of the vintage years, the new breed of motorists were not at all keen on doing a lot of maintenance or of tinkering with their new toys. If it were possible, they would have liked a car which needed no service and one that would be extremely simple to drive. To satisfy this demand, therefore, designers in the 1930s spent a lot of time trying to make motoring more effortless and all manner of semi-automatic clutches, overdrives, free wheels and self-change gearboxes brought out in the period are indicative of just one approach. Built-in jacking systems and the grouping together of greasing points were two others. Some of the fittings developed were little more than showroom gimmicks – the built-in jacks, for instance, were often good in theory but poor in practice, particularly after rust and road dirt had taken their toll.

A look through the motoring magazines of the day tells us much about the social class of motorists who dominated the scene. Columns by members of the peerage were by no means unknown and rarely a week went by without the latest example of coachbuilt Rolls-Royce or Bentley being displayed. Even as late as 1939 the gossip columns still assumed that many of their readers would still be employing a maid (one notable incident, for example, talked about the road-holding qualities of a tea-trolley and made it quite plain that the mistress of the household was not accustomed to steering it) and that many were thinking about building their own fashionable new houses with conveniently located garages. Much was made of the merits of middle class standards, middle class touring and middle class cars. There was continual interchange of information between readers and staff over the merits of hotels and services. Editors tended to be well-to-do and expected their readers to be at one with their life-styles. In the 1930s, for instance, G. Geoffrey Smith, Managing Editor of *The Autocar*, always ran a Bentley of the latest type, changed it regularly and sometimes commissioned special and expensive coachwork for his new car.

Yet all this is a somewhat distorted picture and should be corrected at once. Many of the new motorists could only afford about £150 for their cars – new, or second-hand – and the appropriate type of motoring to go with that sort of machinery. Although it would be nice to be able to write an entire book of nostalgia without ever having to mention money, in the context of everyday life and motoring in the 1930s, this would be quite impracticable.

To get a feel for the mass of motoring which evolved in the decade, I must first talk about the general level of prices and only then consider the earnings necessary to support private motoring and the ways in which cars could be purchased. The cost of everyday things – from houses to holidays, from petrol to beer – was so low and tending to get even lower for much of the time, that it is almost a pleasure to record them, though I must once again emphasise that wages and salaries were also much lower than we are now used to seeing and it is a fact that the general standard of life was way below that which we obtain today.

One of the most significant fixed costs of motoring was that of the annual Road Fund licence, which was disproportionately much higher in the 1930s than it ever has been since. Because of this and because the fee depended on the particular model chosen, it had a great effect on the type of cars which became popular. Few of us have ever motored under any other system than the flat-rate annual licence method, whereby anyone owning any-thing from a Mini to a Ferrari has to pay the authorities the same amount of money (£50 at the time of writing) for the privilege of using that car on British roads. It may still come as a surprise to many to realise that until the late 1940s our cars were taxed according to a rather nebulous 'horsepower' rating.

Variously known as the 'RAC rating', or the 'Treasury rating', this annual tax varied enormously from model to model and could be a very significant item in one's annual motoring budget. It had originated in the early days of motoring, when the government had enlisted the advice of the Royal Automobile Club to settle on a 'fair' rate of motor taxation. At that time, it should be noted, there was no Customs and Excise duty on petrol. For good or bad, it was eventually decided that an owner should pay an annual tax on a sliding scale, which would depend on the notional power output of the engine.

The government and RAC eventually agreed on a system which would calculate an engine's power output solely on the basis of its piston area! This tacitly implied that all engines had the same degree of operating efficiency and that their actual *developed* output had nothing to do with the length of the piston's stroke, nor with the speed of rotation the engine was capable of sustaining. Such decisions could have been prompted by complacency or by ignorance; they would, in any case, bedevil British engine design for

decades. The RAC formula, for what it was worth, laid down that the horsepower rating
for any engine would be calculated as follows:

$$\text{Horsepower} = \frac{D^2 N}{2.5}$$

— D being the cylinder bore in inches and N the number of cylinders

In the good old (Edwardian) days when the formula was devised, and to some extent
even in vintage times when the motoring classes were generally more wealthy than they
were to become in the 1930s, its implications were not thought very important. Up to 1921,
after all, the formula had had a top limit which allowed the really large-engined cars to get
away with a tax of no more than £25 a year. By the time the first ultra-cheap 'baby' cars
were being designed and motoring for 'Everyman' was being considered, the ratings began
to assume great significance.

No self-respecting baby car *was* a baby unless its rating was 8 hp or less, while an aristocratic Daimler, Rolls-Royce or Hispano-Suiza was happy to admit to a rating of 40, 50 or
even more horse power. Since the road fund tax was levied each year at a flat rate of so
much per horsepower (a figure raised or lowered according to the government's need for
for funds), it became critical for an adequately powerful small car engine also to have the
lowest possible rating.

This was a tall order, but not impossible to the industry's resourceful designers, who
soon learned that their new engines would need to have rather singular dimensions. For
any particular model, a certain power output and an acceptable form of torque delivery
would be needed and along with the desired level of fuel economy and a specified ease of
manufacture this usually defined a certain basic size. However, to 'cheat the chancellor',
new engines were invariably designed with hidden reserves of capacity 'stretch' and it was
important that the smallest version built should have small cylinder bores (to keep down
piston area and therefore minimise the tax rating) with long strokes to produce the
desired engine capacity.

It meant that, once knowledge of the system had matured, the British 'standard engine'
needed to have what we would now call very 'undersquare' cylinder dimensions, which
usually meant that engines were taller and slimmer than their continental counterparts
and that while they might be able to produce good low-speed torque and slogging power,
they were usually deficient in good breathing and top end power.

An obvious side effect of this was that to make a particular car's potential obvious to its
public and to place it securely in an obvious sector of the market place, it was often dubbed
a 'Ten', 'Twelve' or 'Fourteen'. Later, as the public became a little more cynical about
such things and a lot more knowledgeable about the actual potential of engines, models
sometimes gained double-barrel titles, like Wolseley's 18-85, where the '18' referred to its
treasury rating and the '85' to its actual (claimed) power output.

In a way this made it very easy for a customer to compare like with like, especially as all
the volume-production manufacturers adopted the same approach to naming their
models. Most 'Tens', for instance, had engines of a similar size, laid out in a broadly
similar way, had similar performance and usually had very closely competitive prices.
There were, however, many anomalies. If one maker was keen to angle his new model
towards a market sector just that bit higher than normal, he might christen it – say – a
'Big Nine' instead of merely a 'Nine', while if a particular car was thought to offer really
splendid value for money and perhaps had fuel economy rather better than average, it
might actually be called a 'Heavy 14' while actually being taxed as a '16'.

Where more than one model cocktail was sold of the basic design, things could get confusing and almost insulting to the customer. At one point in the mid-1930s, the Daimler

*'Prefect' was one of Ford's few attempts to snob appeal. The famous 1,172 cc model, with transverse front and rear springing like all its ancestors at Dagenham, was introduced in 1938 and was built until 1953. This is a 'cheat' picture, as this particular version was being built in post-war years; original Prefects had painted, and not chromed, grilles* (Ford Motor Co).

group were selling one model in two versions – as a Lanchester it was known as an Eighteen and as a Daimler it was a 'Light Twenty', yet the engine size was actually 2.6-litres and the treasury rating was 19.3 fiscal horsepower! Triumph, too, for no better reason than the fact that they were trying to push their car upmarket, changed the Triumph Super Seven to an Eight at the beginning of the decade and Rover indulged in similar advertising gymnastics as their cars progressed towards the end of the 1930s. They were not alone.

Such a regimented system almost always placed imported cars at a disadvantage. In countries where no such repressive measures were in force, an engine was designed solely for efficiency and according to the latest trends; as the years rolled by this meant that operating speeds were steadily increased, strokes shortened and cylinder bores were increased to allow the use of overhead valves and encourage better breathing. In countries where petrol was still very cheap (in North America, particularly) little effort went into producing any sort of small engine; from year to year the average American engine tended to be enlarged, often by the simple expedient of boring out the cylinders to an even greater dimension. An imported car, therefore, might be offered to the British customer at a superficially attractive price, which was then marred by a disproportionately high tax rating.

The anomalies were often ludicrous. The classic example of North American indifference to this system had been with the legendary Ford Model T, made for many years at Ford's Trafford Park factory near Manchester. This had a four-cylinder 2,982 cc engine of no great modernity and was certainly no powerful performer, but was rated at an unbelievable 22.4 hp. Compare this then, with a $4\frac{1}{2}$-litre supercharged Bentley, where there was absolutely no comparison in the performance or the type of motoring offered and consider that it was rated at only 24.8! 

In addition, the regulations made no concession to fractions of a rated horsepower, even though the factual distinction between – say – an 11 and a 12 might be no less than 120 cc of engine size. Anyone interested in buying a car rated at 11.1 hp would still have to pay

*Lancia's Aprilia was technically exciting and had advance styling, by the standards of 1937, but did not sell very well in Great Britain. Later it became the standard by which most small car handling was judged* (Autocar).

the same tax on an 11.9 – both were taxed as '12s', but if the engine of the larger car was then bored out to make it a 12.1 its rating would immediately jump to that of a '13'. A natural consequence is that engines were usually trimmed to be close to the top of an appropriate group.

One obvious result of this was that it encouraged the quantity-production manufacturers to market ranges in a tidy and comprehensive manner. It made good sense to offer a line-up of models, with the obligatory 'Eight' at the base and running right up by easy stages to whatever top level it was thought the marque could achieve. In 1939, for instance, Wolseley were offering 10s, 12–48s, 14–60s, 16–65s, 18–85s, 21s and 25s; but for the outbreak of war they would have rounded this off nicely with an 'Eight' as well. Austin who were market leaders along with Morris, had 8s, 10s, 12s, 14s, 18s and – a big jump, this – 28s. Even Rover, selling only 11,000 cars in a year, had a 10, a 12, a 14, a 16 and a 20 hp model.

Engine dimensions were never forced to the ludicrous extremes imposed on Grand Prix cars by the piston area limits of 1908, but on the other hand there was absolutely no question of a mundane unit even remotely approaching the 1:1 bore/stroke ratio that was already thought to be desirable. In 1938, for instance, the Flying Standard Eight was introduced, with a 1,021 cc engine rejoicing in the grotesque cylinder dimensions of a 57 mm bore and a 100 mm stroke. The car was proudly advertised with this stirring statement: 'Five months ago a Chancellor spoke – decreeing still more burdens on an already heavily-taxed population. An era of THRIFT began: But the Standard Motor Company, ever alert to future trends in public demand, were already building a new series of cars *dedicated to ECONOMY!*' Standard, however, were not anxious to point out that this 'Eight' was an underbored version of the 'Nine' and 'Ten' units, which had 60 mm and 63.5 mm cylinder bores respectively.

Let's compare the effect of this much-vilified tax on modern engines. A 1938 Rover 16, of 2,147 cc, for example (Bore and stroke 67.5 x 100 mm) compares with today's Rover 2300 (81 x 76 mm, 2,350 cc) rated at 24.4 hp. At bargain basement level, a Ford Ten's

1,172 cc was produced by 63.5 mm x 92.5 mm; today's Escort 1100 (1,098 cc, 81 x 53.3 mm) lines up at 16.3 hp.

There were, of course, many variations on such extremes. Most makers offered a range of engines all machined from the same general design. A study of Morris and Wolseley models of the late 1930s (see Chapter 4) shows a complicated relationship between narrow or wide bores, four-cylinder or six-cylinder layouts, and side-valve or overhead-valve breathing – enough to make a historian's eyes gleam, but make a production manager's spirit wilt. In the pursuit of such minor commercial advantage the Triumph company in Coventry once had no fewer than four different piston sizes between 59 mm and 63 mm available within two years!

The treasury rating was the instrument of taxation, but the rate at which it was levied was also important. For many years the tax had been set at a straight £1 per horsepower – which meant that an Austin Seven buyer would have to fork out £120 for his new car, then £8 every year for his licence. On the other hand, a Rolls-Royce customer might pay £2,500 for his car and £44 annually for his licence.

To inflate demand and add to industrial recovery from the Depression, the tax was slashed to 15s (75p) per horsepower from January 1935, but the onset of re-armament and the need for extra revenue caused the policy to be reversed in 1939. In its budget that year the government announced that as from the beginning of 1940 the tax would be raised to no less than 25s (£1.25) per rated horsepower. They were then naively amazed to discover that people immediately began to turn their attention to smaller cars at the expense of large-engined models. There was even some evidence to suggest that total demand had also been depressed by this very unpopular move, though the prelude to the European war cannot have helped much. As war broke out in September, before the tax could be introduced (and as almost all privately-owned cars were taken off the roads within months) we have no way of knowing how the balance of the industry would have been affected in the medium term.

Although the apparent price of petrol was quite low, when related to other prices and earnings levels it was at least as expensive as it became again in Great Britain in the mid-1970s. (In 'real money' terms, petrol was probably at its cheapest in the late 1960s). Then, as now, there were Customs and Excise duties on petrol, which were modified persistently and cynically by a government which had more of an eye on the national balance sheet than on the motor industry's happiness. (Some aspects of our lives, it seems, never change).

Even when petrol was for sale at 1s 2½d (6p) a gallon, it was not thought to be a particularly good bargain, as prices had been lower in the 1920s. There had been fuel taxation even before the Great War, but these were removed altogether between 1921 and 1928. A tax of 4d (1.7p) per gallon was then imposed, doubled to 8d (3.3p) in the economic crisis year of 1931 and (to finance armament spending) raised to 9d (3.75p) in 1938. Surprisingly, in retrospect, there were no further tax changes throughout the Second World War, probably because almost all fuel was being consumed by the armed forces, or by 'essential' users.

It is worth noting that even when petrol was selling at only 1s 2½d (6p) a gallon (equivalent, at late 1970s prices, to perhaps 14s (70p) or even 15s (75p) a gallon – not very dissimilar from those we actually were paying in 1978) *The Autocar*, in an editorial, suggested that oil companies' own prices were being kept artificially low to sustain demand.

They certainly took care to keep their prices as low as possible (we must remember that there was a world surplus of the stuff and that the Arabs did not then control the destiny of the crude oil under their territories) and the untaxed price was generally around 10d (4.2p) a gallon. The quality of the best grade, which might include dashes of alcohol or 'benzole', (which was distilled from coal tar) to boost the octane ratings, was much below present-day levels. A really good petrol would have a rating of 80 or perhaps 82 (today's 4-star spirit is never less than 97 octane) but the evil-smelling 'Pool' which arrived at the outbreak of war in 1939 could only boast of about 70 octane. The name 'Pool' arose because at first all the oil companies pooled their resources during the war so that wasteful competition could be eliminated.

Diesel-engined trucks and buses began to proliferate during the 1930s, but no production-line diesel-engined car was ever built in Britain. In Germany, of course, Mercedes were world pioneers with the 260D model of 1936. Need I say that the moment our political masters saw any sign of diesel units becoming popular they instantly raised the duty – from 1d to 8d (3p) a gallon in 1935? Or that 8d (3p) duty was then 200 per cent of the cost of the fuel, which was extremely cheap at 4d (1.6p) a gallon?

During the decade, the yield from taxation rocketed and protests multiplied. In 1931, which was the low point in every way, vehicle taxation yielded £28.1 million, while petrol duty raised £29.3 million; at that time the point was rightly made that Britain was *the* most highly taxed motoring nation. By 1934, before the horsepower tax was reduced, the two yields had risen to £31.5 million and £38.3 million respectively (a total which was no less than 9 per cent of the country's revenue) and by 1939 that £70 million total 'take' had forged ahead to nearly £90 million There has been no respite ever since.

*September 1939 and the end of peace-time motoring. The only petrol available was 'Pool', which was severely rationed. Whitewall tyres and painted bumper blades helped beat the rigid blackout which was imposed. But just look at the price of petrol – 1s 6d a gallon!* (Fox Photos).

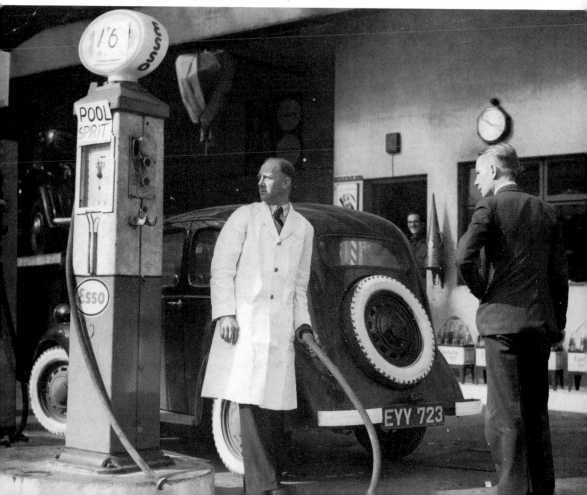

Insurance, too, was none too cheap. Third-party insurance cover had become compulsory in 1931, at the same time as the 20 mph overall speed limit was finally abandoned and most motorists contented themselves with the minimum required. It would have cost them about £10 or £11 to insure a £200 8 hp car comprehensively and perhaps £17 to £18 for a £450 20 hp model. Considering the simple nature of most machines, their relatively low performance and the empty state of many of Britain's highways, this was no bargain.

Sometimes it was quite cheap to borrow money with which to buy one's car. As the majority of 'new motorists' were from the staid and respectable middle classes, they tended to do this by raising a loan at their banks. To generate trade after the Depression, the government set the Bank Rate at an all-time low of 2 per cent in 1932 and maintained that figure until the outbreak of war in 1939. Clearly this meant that normal borrowing rates could be kept down to around 5 per cent for favoured customers.

Although there was a good deal of hire purchase activity even at the beginning of the 1930s, it was always a rather hole-in-the-corner and furtive way of raising the money. Somehow (and such were the fiscal standards of the day) hire purchase was always considered to be a 'not quite nice' way of financing one's purchase and it was never talked about. Usually it was necessary to put down 25 per cent of the value of the car for a deposit. One of the most important firms, United Dominions Trust, did me a great favour by digging into their archives and producing original documents of the period for study; UDT had only been founded in 1919 and found most of their 1930s expansion with traders and wholesalers rather than with private customers.

Payments could be made over one year, 18 months or two years, and – over 18 months, say – a retail customer probably paid about 10 per cent total interest, an effective loan rate of only about 6 per cent. It is interesting to recall that the words 'hire purchase' were played down (in view of the 'not quite nice' reputation) and purchase plans were dubbed to be 'Out of Income' systems.

Coupling these prices with the cost of spares and accessories still produced an agreeably low annual cost of motoring, which more and more people felt they could come to afford. Once the car had been purchased (and a two-year-old Ford Eight rarely fetched more than £40 to £45 – it might be run on a successful shoestring for between £50 and £70 a year and enjoyed to the full if there were no unexpected mechanical disasters. The equivalent figure for a 16 hp/20 hp model might be about £105 a year or just £2 a week.

Even something as lordly as a 3½-litre Bentley could be run for less than £150 in a year – insurance would be about £30, the annual taxation £19.50 and petrol costs less than £40. This is a level of prices quite unfamiliar to most of us, but it has to be related to the wages and salaries being earned at the time. These, too, are considerably out of line with modern comparisons because of much lower levels of taxation. The cars themselves, of course, were not subject to any form of taxation. The hated Purchase Tax was not introduced until the Second World War period, as a deterrent to the manufacture and purchase of all luxury goods (but it continued, thereafter, as a revenue raiser) and it was to be levied at the most savage rates, up to 66⅔ per cent in some cases, during the late 1940s and early 1950s. There was no Value Added Tax nor Special Car Tax. All 1930s car prices should be compared with the *basic* prices of today.

The mass of new motorists were from the middle classes, who found that they needed to be earning £6, £7 or £8 a week before they could afford to motor in any comfort, even if it meant starting with a £25 or £30 'bargain' which was at least four years old. It is an interesting comment on social and financial changes and on the movement of wages and prices, that some 'marginal' motorists of the 1930s discovered that, in the same job, they could no longer afford to indulge in motoring in the 1940s. It took a few years more, and a return to national prosperity in the 1950s, for the situation to be stablised.

Social behaviour was much more conventional and predictable (some would also say it was dull) in the 1930s, so it was often possible to consider a particular profession, or geographical location and have a fairly good idea of the type of cars which would be in evidence. One could take a stroll down any suburban Acacia Avenue on a summer Sunday morning and find a predictable group of cars being washed and generally admired.

It would never have done, for instance, for a respectable bank manager to be seen in a sports car and certainly he would never even have considered any type of imported car. On the other hand, one somehow expected to see the well-off son of the local gentry running an MG or Riley sports car or tourer; he was not likely to be seen in anything mundane with saloon coachwork unless it was a very dashing sports saloon of the rallying variety; never, ever, would it be a Morris or one of the smaller Austins (but a larger Austin – say a 16 hp – was quite acceptable if you were not interested in performance or style) and certainly it would not be one of those nasty Americanised Fords or Vauxhalls.

The gentry, if not the nobility (who could get away with almost any social deviation and allow it to be known as eccentricity) were almost bound to be seen in Armstrong Siddeleys, Daimlers, Bentleys, Lanchesters, and – of course – in Rolls-Royces. When the Prince of Wales bought himself a special-bodied Canadian Buick it caused considerable controversy. Never, but never, would they be seen in SS Jaguars, Railtons or Humbers. SS Jaguars, for example, had a most unfortunate and unfair reputation, which was not at all substantiated, of being flashy cars favoured by bookies and shady traders; for years they were known as 'Jews Bentleys' and it was only the racing success and Royal accolades of the 1950s which completely killed this nickname.

The question of social convention, allied to brand loyalties and the tendency of people to trade more and more up market as their income and position improved, was something neatly exploited both by Lord Nuffield and by the Rootes family. They reasoned that if they could catch a motorist at Morris Ten or Hillman Minx level and keep him happy, they could – if they were lucky – hold his allegiance while he progressed to Wolseleys or Humbers, MGs or Sunbeam-Talbots. It was a successful process which made Ford and Vauxhall jealous and was one reason for John Black's purchase of Triumph (for Standard) in 1945.

Then, as now, the accessories market was booming and there was always something on the advertising pages which was taken up as a 'craze' by the average motorist. At one stage, for instance, a 'sprung steering wheel' was *the* thing. Spokes were mounted in 'live rubber' (whatever that might have meant) and the word 'Brooklands' was worth at least another 10s (50p) on the price. But at around £2 they were reasonable bargains, even if a car's original wheel was often not as ugly as they have since become.

The really practical accessories were those which could keep cars or occupants warm in winter. No sooner had a new car, or more accurately, a new radiator shape, been revealed, than several suitable radiator muffs were on offer. Fans were not universal, neither were water pumps and engines that were kept cool by vast radiators in summer suffered from over-cooling in winter; a roll-up muff was the answer here. At 10s to 15s (50p to 75p) they were a bargain.

Battery chargers? Very popular, for batteries were not the long-lived fit-and-forget items they are now. Cars often had six-volt electrics, which were notoriously short lived and dynamos were not powerful enough; alternators, of course, were completely unknown. The average price of a charger was more than £3 – superficially not much, but when this is converted to current prices (between £35 and £40 perhaps) was it worth it?

Lubrication additives? Whatever the oil companies might have said (and, to defend their reputations, they said quite a lot) their products could not guard against cylinder-bore wear indefinitely, nor against carbon build-up in combustion chambers. Upper

**Above** *Just one page from a 1935 motoring magazine shows the astonishingly low level of prices which prevailed after the Depression had taken its toll, and the sort of accessories which were in vogue* (Autocar).

**Above right** *Two Rytecraft scooter cars, registered for road use, but no doubt breaking some Construction and Use regulation. These machines were developed from fairground vehicles. The £120 Ford Eight in the background was much more practical transport, even for one!* (Autocar).

cylinder lubricants, or 'shots' added to the petrol, was one popular item, colloidal graphite additives were often used in the sump, and (especially for the sportsman) a can of pure benzol was often carried in the boot to boost the commercial petrol's octane ratings.

The 'bolt on goodies' business thrived, especially with an eye to the 'sporting driver' market. What was fashionable could also be effective, but there was also a fair range of rather unseemly but flashy gimmicks. No self-respecting Wolseley Hornet buyer seemed to be satisfied until he had plastered his car with a sprung steering wheel, a 'Le Mans' petrol filler cap, an outside exhaust system with guaranteed 'Deep Note' and Brooklands-type fishtail silencer. Alta made special cylinder heads for Austin Sevens and side-valve Morris Minors for as little as £3 12s 6d (£3.62), while Derrington marketed special carburettor-and-manifold kits for anything from the most humble £100 Ford Popular to the most lordly Lagonda or Talbot. Supercharging was definitely the 'in thing', even if some models converted in this way became petrol burners *and* were unreliable into the bargain. Even so, these were fashionable enough for George Eyston to design and develop his own Powerplus variety and for Pomeroy and McEvoy nearly to bankrupt themselves in marketing their own types of 'blower'.

But was a 'hurricane pipe' a motorist's necessity ('Every motorist should possess one') and how legal was a 'genuine American Police siren' ('with VARIABLE POWER making this signal suitable for both town and country use')? Should we have been surprised to see Dennis lawn mowers advertised in the motoring press, or even 'road tested'? The Autocar, in fact, tested a 30 in cut 'sit upon' Dennis mower in May 1938, which was marketed at no less than £78, which would also have bought a very good year old 8 hp car.

Weathershields could supply slip-over upholstery covers for both front seats for upwards of 15s (75p), which looked like a bargain, but the cost of a Champion sparking plug at 5s (25p) did not. Sun-roofs, when ordered from new, rarely cost more than £5 and car radio fittings sold for the relatively high price of £15 to £16, which compares very badly with today's prices.

All this, of course, has now changed considerably and many would say it was for the better. When cars became available again in the mid-1940s, prices had rocketed, another social revolution was under way and for a time it looked as if it was unpatriotic to want to go motoring for pleasure. Most of us looked back then, and still look back now, to the 1930s, when motoring was a predictable and very enjoyable business. Will it ever be the same again?

## Chapter 3

# What sort of motoring?

Nowadays we don't have to make such a *performance* about our motoring. If we get a sudden telephone call and need to make a 300 or 400 mile motoring dash, we merely pack a bag, fling in a map and set off. The car will need petrol and perhaps some oil, but we do not worry over much about the weather. Unless there are blizzards or blankets of fog the journey should be predictable. How long should it take? We can bet on something like 45 mph average on ordinary main roads and as much as 65 mph on motorways. We should arrive tired, but warm and comfortable. In the 1930s things were very different; we could not possibly have been so casual about it all.

It was true that motoring had long since shrugged off the aura of pioneering and most of the uncertainties and breakdowns of the early days. With few exceptions, cars had become pleasant and willing workhorses. Even so, they were not always as predictable as we would like. The many examples which survive now have the benefit of modern conditions, modern lubricants and usually a lot of loving care and attention to keep them going. When they were new, however, the motoring was by no means as care-free a business as it has now become. Cars needed much more frequent maintenance. Tyres, petrol and lubricants were all inferior to today's products. There were very few high-speed roads, no motorways at all in Britain, only a sprinkling of dual carriageway roads, or by-passes and no segregation of traffic. In short, all major trips had to be planned and the car prepared.

Let's look back to that sudden journey again and consider its implications in the 1930s. One's car was by no means as rapid as a 1970s machine – not even if something exotic like a Bentley or an Alvis lived in the motor house – and because of this even a 300 mile journey became a major undertaking. Something like a Hillman Minx or a Morris Twelve could only be expected to cruise at about 50 mph and even then no sensitive owner would want to flog on for hours at a stretch in case of engine overheating or related protests. The roads themselves, especially if the journey was to be across country rather than to or from London, would not be fast. Hardly a town or village had been by-passed when the decade began, though this situation improved later. Police activity to enforce the new-fangled 30 mph speed limit in built-up areas would be strict.

Although on the open roads traffic densities were much lighter than they are today, even main highways tended to be narrow and to follow the centuries-old alignment of tracks first established by horses and carriages in bygone days; their surfaces, at least, had been improved dramatically since the 1920s and were now the envy of almost every other European nation. Even so, in a family car it was rarely wise to plan on achieving anything better than a 35 mph running average, unless the trip was to be tackled at night;

**Right** *Castrol's lubrication chart for the Austin Seven – showing the very short intervals between oil changes and the multitude of points needing regular attention. This, by the way, was one of the simplest cars in the world* (Castrol).

# SEVEN
## LUBRICATION CHART
### EXPLANATION OF SYMBOLS

WAKEFIELD PATENT CASTROL XL in summer, WAKEFIELD PATENT CASTROL AA in winter. High quality motor oils recommended for the Austin 7 engine.

WAKEFIELD CASTROL HI-PRESS GEAR OIL. A special heavy duty lubricant for Rear Axle and Steering Gear Box lubrication.

WAKEFIELD CASTROLEASE HEAVY. Recommended for the wheel bearings, and wherever grease is indicated.

**WARNING** Do not ask for "XL" when you require CASTROL. Ask for "PATENT CASTROL XL" and see it drawn from a PATENT CASTROL container.

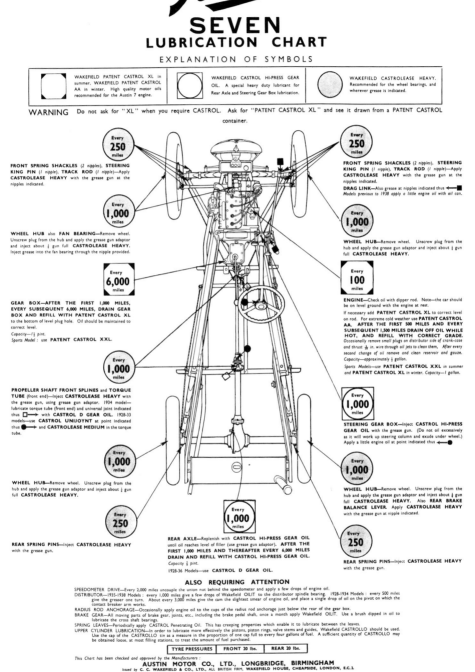

**FRONT SPRING SHACKLES** (2 nipples), **STEERING KING PIN** (1 nipple), **TRACK ROD** (1 nipple)—Apply **CASTROLEASE HEAVY** with the grease gun at the nipples indicated.

**WHEEL HUB** also **FAN BEARING**—Remove wheel. Unscrew plug from the hub and apply the grease gun adaptor and inject about ½ gun full **CASTROLEASE HEAVY.** Inject grease into the fan bearing through the nipple provided.

**GEAR BOX—AFTER THE FIRST 1,000 MILES, EVERY SUBSEQUENT 6,000 MILES, DRAIN GEAR BOX AND REFILL WITH PATENT CASTROL XL** to the bottom of level plug hole. Oil should be maintained to correct level.
Capacity—1½ pint.
*Sports Model*: use **PATENT CASTROL XXL**.

**PROPELLER SHAFT FRONT SPLINES** and **TORQUE TUBE** (front end)—Inject **CASTROLEASE HEAVY** with the grease gun, using grease gun adaptor. 1934 model—lubricate torque tube (front end) and universal joint indicated thus ☐➤ with **CASTROL D GEAR OIL.** 1928-33 models—use **CASTROL UNIJOYNT** at point indicated thus ●➤ and **CASTROLEASE MEDIUM** in the torque tube.

**WHEEL HUB**—Remove wheel. Unscrew plug from the hub and apply the grease gun adaptor and inject about ½ gun full **CASTROLEASE HEAVY.**

**REAR SPRING PINS**—Inject **CASTROLEASE HEAVY** with the grease gun.

**FRONT SPRING SHACKLES** (2 nipples), **STEERING KING PIN** (1 nipple), **TRACK ROD** (1 nipple)—Apply **CASTROLEASE HEAVY** with the grease gun at the nipples indicated.
**DRAG LINK**—Also grease at nipples indicated thus ■ Models previous to 1938 apply a little engine oil with oil can.

**WHEEL HUB**—Remove wheel. Unscrew plug from the hub and apply the grease gun adaptor and inject about ½ gun full **CASTROLEASE HEAVY.**

**ENGINE**—Check oil with dipper rod. Note—the car should be on level ground with the engine at rest.
If necessary add **PATENT CASTROL XL** to correct level on rod. For extreme cold weather use **PATENT CASTROL AA. AFTER THE FIRST 500 MILES AND EVERY SUBSEQUENT 1,500 MILES DRAIN OFF OIL WHILE HOT, AND REFILL WITH CORRECT GRADE.** Occasionally remove small plugs on distributor side of crank-case and thrust ⅟₁₆ in. wire through oil jets to clean them. After every second change of oil remove and clean reservoir and gauze. Capacity—approximately ½ gallon.
*Sports Models*—use **PATENT CASTROL XXL** in summer and **PATENT CASTROL XL** in winter. Capacity—1 gallon.

**STEERING GEAR BOX**—Inject **CASTROL HI-PRESS GEAR OIL** with the grease gun. (Do not oil excessively as it will work up steering column and exude under wheel.) Apply a little engine oil at point indicated thus ●➤

**WHEEL HUB**—Remove wheel. Unscrew plug from the hub and apply the grease gun adaptor and inject about ½ gun full **CASTROLEASE HEAVY.** Also **REAR BRAKE BALANCE LEVER.** Apply **CASTROLEASE HEAVY** with the grease gun at nipple indicated.

**REAR AXLE**—Replenish with **CASTROL HI-PRESS GEAR OIL** until oil reaches level of filler (use grease gun adaptor). **AFTER THE FIRST 1,000 MILES AND THEREAFTER EVERY 6,000 MILES DRAIN AND REFILL WITH CASTROL HI-PRESS GEAR OIL.**
Capacity ⅜ pint.
1928-36 Models—use **CASTROL D GEAR OIL.**

**REAR SPRING PINS**—Inject **CASTROLEASE HEAVY** with the grease gun.

### ALSO REQUIRING ATTENTION

SPEEDOMETER DRIVE—Every 2,000 miles uncouple the union nut behind the speedometer and apply a few drops of engine oil.
DISTRIBUTOR—1935-1938 Models : every 1,000 miles give a few drops of Wakefield OILIT to the distributor spindle bearing. 1928-1934 Models : every 500 miles give the greaser one turn. About every 3,000 miles give the cam the slightest smear of engine oil, and place a single drop of oil on the pivot on which the contact breaker arm works.
RADIUS ROD ANCHORAGE—Occasionally apply engine oil to the cups of the radius rod anchorage just below the rear of the gear box.
BRAKE GEAR—All moving parts of brake gear, joints, etc., including the brake pedal shaft, once a month apply Wakefield OILIT. Use a brush dipped in oil to lubricate the cross shaft bearings.
SPRING LEAVES—Periodically apply CASTROL Penetrating Oil. This has creeping properties which enable it to lubricate between the leaves.
UPPER CYLINDER LUBRICATION—In order to lubricate more effectively the pistons, piston rings, valve stems and guides, Wakefield CASTROLLO should be used. Use the cap of the CASTROLLO tin as a measure in the proportion of one cap full to every four gallons of fuel. A sufficient quantity of CASTROLLO may be obtained loose, at most filling stations, to treat the amount of fuel purchased.

| TYRE PRESSURES | FRONT 20 lbs. | REAR 20 lbs. |
|---|---|---|

*This Chart has been checked and approved by the Manufacturers :*
**AUSTIN MOTOR CO., LTD., LONGBRIDGE, BIRMINGHAM**
Issued by C. C. WAKEFIELD & CO., LTD., ALL BRITISH FIRM, WAKEFIELD HOUSE, CHEAPSIDE, LONDON, E.C.2.

L.O. 8K. (38—38)—1/38—10m & 4 m.i. *Everett, Gibson & Moore, Ltd., S.E.1*

**AUSTIN SEVEN**

Every **250** miles
Every **1,000** miles
Every **6,000** miles
Every **1,000** miles
Every **1,000** miles
Every **250** miles
Every **250** miles
Every **1,000** miles
Every **100** miles
Every **1,000** miles
Every **1,000** miles
Every **250** miles
Every **1,000** miles

then, of course, there would be the serious problem of finding petrol stations open during the night.

A 300 mile journey could take at least eight or probably nine hours, compared with perhaps six hours or less today. If you were a new motorist, financially confined to owning a Morris Eight or a Ford Popular, you would probably cruise at little more than 35 mph. To you, Great Britain would have seemed to be a mighty big place; it would have taken you virtually all of a long day to get from London to the West Country or to the Lake District. A major trip from London to Scotland could not be tackled at all without a major re-think about eating and sleeping arrangements.

Even in a large, fast and expensive car, journeys could seem interminable. One magazine feature of 1938 concentrated on a journey from London to Northumberland in nothing less than a Rolls-Royce Phantom III, using the Great North Road (A1) all the way and leaving Marble Arch just before 11.00 am. Bamburgh was not reached until almost 8.00 pm, although only 54 minutes were accounted for by stops. This represented a running average of only 40.9 mph and was thought to be a terrible indictment of the roads and the traffic. The Phantom III was cruised at 80 mph wherever possible.

Major service intervals, even of the more expensive cars, occurred at least every 1,000 miles (some grease points even had to be looked at every 500 miles), at which point the engine and gearbox oils had to be changed; in view of the current state of lubricant technology it was never wise to overstep the mark by too much. There were no multi-grade oils which could last for 6,000 miles and there would be a positive forest of nipples to be pumped with grease. In winter there would always be worries over the cooling system. Anti-freeze was already on the market, but was not yet free of corrosion tendencies and most motorists still preferred to drain off the radiator and engine water every night. A rug or an old blanket would be flung over the bonnet at night to preserve engine heat and under-sump paraffin heaters were considered essential. Batteries could not be relied upon to start an engine, especially if it was a large one, because the engine oil would be thick and draggy. Starting handles were always provided on British cars and were often needed.

It is still fashionable to deride the modern motor car and to toss off a derogatory remark like: 'They don't make them like they used to in the old days.' I would immediately retort that it is a good thing too and settle down to list the chores which no longer exist. When we took delivery of a car then, we had to set about the tedious business of running in. Something of the sort persists today (but did you ever consult the Owner's Handbook of your latest car to see how easy a process it now is?) but it is no longer a rigid ritual. A really pernickety customer could demand to pick up his new machine from the factory (a modern computerised delivery system can no longer cope with this) and he would usually be made welcome. That way he could control the speeds from the moment his car left the gates of the plant.

The penalties of over-speeding at an early stage would be rapid cylinder bore wear, excessive oil consumption and the need for re-boring and de-carbonisation after little more than 10,000 miles. For the first 500 miles at least the proud new owner was ordered never to push his new car beyond 30 mph. This was done because it was cynically (and correctly) thought that most drivers could only understand the speedometer and because an engine rev counter was rarely fitted to cheap cars. On the other hand, sensible advice about not labouring the unit, about changing down early on hills, was rarely given.

The first service – and what an important occasion this was – took place after 500 miles, when engine oil would be flushed out along with an amazing accumulation of tiny metal particles. (The magnetic sump plug came into prominence during the 1930s and was very popular.) Even after 500 miles one was not free to go quickly. Most handbooks suggested caution at least until the 2,000 mile mark had been passed and a further filter and oil change was recommended before then. Until that point cruising speeds of 45 mph were considered adventurous, full throttle was still discouraged and hill-climbing still led to much gear-changing unless the owner was quite insensitive to protesting noises.

Cars rarely lived out in the open, although – as I have already pointed out – relatively few modern houses were actually being built with their own garages. In the beginning, it should be noted, the great 'motor houses' used by the pioneers had usually been converted stables. The mass of new motorists were therefore beguiled with advertisements for build-it-yourself sectionalised garages, some of which could be squeezed into the back garden where a garden shed had once stood, or which could – with luck – be added to the side of the house. Sir William Morris, who was never likely to pass up a good commercial opening if he saw one, began to sell garages at £9 15s od (£9.75) a time, while there was a big choice in the £8/£9 bracket. The 1930s also saw the arrival of the lock-up garage. Waste lands all over Britain began to grow a rash of sectionalised buildings, converted hen-huts, rebuilt railway wagons and the like. Most towns and villages still have them.

There was always the problem of keeping a car's occupants warm. Built-in car heaters are essentially a post-war phenomenon and in the 1930s the only car to be offered with 'air-conditioning' as standard was the 1940 model SS Jaguar, announced in July 1939 and promptly put out of production by the declaration of war! Accessory manufacturers tried to fill the gap with a variety of add-on kits which either tapped hot water from the cooling system or relied on electric power. Neither was windscreen demisting standardised until offered in SS Jaguars in 1940; previously the most normal way to ensure a clear screen was to open it (this was a feature still found on many family cars of the day) or to invest in an

*Servicing in the open air – do you recognise the place? It is still there in Park Lane, London, but has been re-styled, and the exterior ramps removed* (Autocar).

electrically-powered strip heater which fastened on to the inside of the glass with rubber suckers.

When pressed steel bodywork, jig-built to improve the accuracy of fit between panels, spread from Morris to other makes, it also brought the benefits of better draught sealing. Coachbuilt cars with loose floorboards and especially when equipped with many and various levers and pedals sprouting from the floor, were not the most draught-proof, even if they were expensive, so when pressed-steel floors arrived, matters improved at once. But if the water-filled foot-warmers of Edwardian days were no longer needed, warm clothing, gloves, hats and rugs most certainly were. The combination of through-flow ventilation and efficient heating has made travel in shirt sleeves quite possible, even in an average British winter; 40 years ago even an autumn drive might necessitate overcoat, hat and gloves for the driver and probably a travelling rug for the lady passengers. No mature lady, even those considered 'fast', would be seen motoring in trousers.

The atmosphere for private motoring changed considerably between 1930 and 1939. The decade opened, of course, with a universal 20 mph speed limit still theoretically in force and ended with severe war-time restrictions being introduced and all private motoring about to be banned. The 20 mph overall speed limit – in city streets, on the open roads, or even in the uninhabited wilds of Scotland – had been on the statute book since 1903. It was none too generous even then and by the 1920s it had fallen into complete disrepute and ridicule. The police, with their ridiculous 'speed traps' (handkerchief-waving, stop-watch timing and painfully-measured distances) were pilloried by the motoring press for their activities and the mobile scouts of the motoring organisations had their own special ways of warning members of the existence of such traps. Even the ultra-cautious government and its civil servants eventually listened to the perpetual complaints and in 1930 were proposing to do something about it. Not only were they proposing to abolish the limit on open roads, they were prepared to legalise high speeds in towns too!

The great day arrived on 1 January 1931, when *The Autocar* felt it necessary to say, in a thundering editorial:

'... motorists need scarcely be warned again that this does not give anyone the right to drive fast where circumstances do not fully justify speed ... Anxiety has been expressed lest magistrates throughout the country will take unreasonable advantage of their powers conferred by the new Act to inflict heavy penalties for reckless, dangerous or careless driving ... Should it happen – we do not anticipate that it will – that considerable numbers of car owners or motor cyclists misuse their new freedom, magistrates will undoubtedly alter their methods in the direction of stiffening up the penalties inflicted and trivial offences may be met with harsh punishments . . ..'

Hopes of restraint were in vain and it was soon clear that unlimited town speeds were potentially dangerous. Police were often not able to bring in convictions for 'dangerous driving'. The consequence was that in 1935 – actually on March 18 – the new 30 mph speed limits were introduced for 'built-up' areas. Thus the years 1931 to 1934 go down in motoring history as the only ones in which there were no general speed restrictions of any kind on general motoring – and it seems impossible to hope that they will ever again be experienced. Pedestrian crossings had been introduced in 1934, though without any easily-defined answer to the priority of motorists or foot passengers.

The road system itself was slowly being converted into a layout which took adequate notice of the modern motor car. The use of warning signs with red triangles (in advance of road hazards) was recommended in 1930. The first electric traffic lights (called traffic control 'robots') were installed in London in 1931 and the first-ever 'cats' eyes' followed in 1934. But traffic lights were by no means common even in 1939 – it is a fact, for instance, that no lights were installed on the Isle of Man until the 1960s.

*Front . . . and rear of the new-fangled 30 mph speed limit signs. 1935 saw the end of the motorist's speeding freedom. Towns limits were re-introduced after a few years where there were no limits at all on British roads (Autocar).*

We are now completely accustomed to open-road speed limits, even (though we might hate it) to a 70 mph maximum on our motorways. It should not be difficult, therefore, to realise what a great freedom was being conferred in 1931. With so much less traffic on *all* roads than there is today, it was usually possible to choose one's own cruising speeds. Lifting the overall restriction, however, did not instantly transform British drivers into speed-crazed maniacs.

In 1931 not many people had cars capable of cruising much faster than about 45 mph (maximum speed on an Austin 7 was only 47 or 48 mph, while even the larger-engined machines would be struggling to top 70 mph) and since they had been used to driving at up to 35 mph even in 'speed-limit' days the relaxation made very little difference.

The clamp-down on town speeds in 1935 was predictably followed by an outcry in the motoring press, particularly against the police, who had declared their intention of using unmarked squad cars to help enforce the limits. Sir Malcolm Campbell was one of the first to be 'gonged' for speeding and expressed himself delighted by this. Sporting personalities like Raymond Mays made something of a new name for themselves by the sheer number of times they were caught. There were no fewer than 108,571 speed limit summons in 1935 alone.

Many local authorities took unfair advantage of the new restrictions (they had never agreed with the removal of the archaic 20 mph limits anyway) by spreading the new limits as far out into the countryside as possible. Much of the time in the opening months – in the summer of 1935 – was spent in argument about the scope of the limits and many were eventually clawed back in on the towns they surrounded. It was at this time that the bench mark of lighting posts and a minimum distance between them, was introduced to show that a given road was 'built-up'.

Our road system itself, though now mainly endowed with fine surfaces, was nothing of which to be proud. Europe's two dictators were well on the way to encouraging the completion of new motor road networks even before the British expansion schemes could get started. Mussolini's first *autostrada* (from Milan to Turin) had been finished in the 1920s, even though it did not have divided carriageways. By 1933 Adolf Hitler had authorised the first of Germany's new *autobahns*. These were unashamedly intended to help the German army to move about just inside the country's borders and their construction also served to ease unemployment, but even so they made every other country's ideas of new roads look positively Victorian in concept.

We had entered the 20th century with a road system not seriously improved since the Middle Ages. Although notable engineers like Telford had designed turnpikes between important commercial centres, their surfaces (often of water-bound macadam) were abominable and whole tracts of London's streets were surfaced either with stone setts or slippery wooden blocks. Following Lloyd George's proposal to introduce graduated scales of vehicle taxation and to exact a duty on petrol, a Road Board had been set up to spend the revenue on new roads. This money was to be funnelled in to the Road Fund and was supposed to be entirely for the motorist's benefit. In nine years of operation the Board did not promote a single new road scheme, but the money was channelled to local authorities to resurface roads, to buy materials and to acquire new machinery.

Benefits in the 1920s, therefore, had been a progressive (and necessary) improvement in road surfaces and maintenance. Tarred macadam (a phrase quickly shortened to 'tarmac') began to be used and by 1930 the general condition of our roads was excellent. Winston Churchill, however, when Chancellor of the Exchequer, had made his first 'raid' on the Road Fund in 1926, so that less and less money became available for spending on new highway expenditure.

Not that the motorist was starved of new schemes (as opposed to actual building of new roads) to talk about – far from it. Motorways (or 'motor roads' as they were first known) had been proposed even as early as in Edwardian times and it is interesting to note that these would have been toll highways. Charges would have been about ½d (0.2p) a mile, in order that construction and maintenance should be self-supporting. Nothing ever became of these grandiose schemes, especially at a time when the only traffic congestion was found in the large cities.

County councils became responsible for the building of all new roads in 1937, but central government took over the trunk road programme in April 1937. Until then, however, there was no co-ordinated national plan for road construction and each council fought bitterly for its share of the Road Fund. Councils were usually short of cash for capital spending; in 1931, when the economy took such a tumble, almost every capital scheme in the country was stopped for a time. Road schemes actually in construction were often frozen for years at a time and some were never re-started before the outbreak of war.

A browse through the motoring magazines turns up the first evidence of major schemes only finished in recent years. The Hull Corporation was offered £200,000 towards a new Humber bridge in 1930 (it would then have cost £1.75 million) – even at the time of writing that bridge is not finished. From time to time the possibilities of a Channel tunnel were mentioned – there had been a 'vintage' revival in 1924 and the schemes re-appeared briefly in 1935. Surveys for a Severn road bridge were carried out in 1935 but nothing further transpired, even though a 75 per cent Road Fund grant was offered. A by-pass for High Wycombe was first mentioned in 1936. The inventive Lancashire County Council not only built one of the country's few completely new highways (the East Lancashire road, 27 miles long, between Liverpool and Manchester, opened in 1933) but also laid down detailed plans for a Manchester ring road which is now part and parcel of the M62/

**Above** *Crossing the Firth of Forth took time in the 1930s, for the road bridge was still only a pipe-dream and the Queensferry alternative was a leisurely business. The year was 1938 and the most modern of the three cars being loaded is a Hillman Minx (Autocar).*

**Below** *One of the biggest civil engineering jobs completed during the decade was the original Mersey Tunnel, linking Liverpool with Birkenhead, which was opened with great pomp and ceremony by HM King George V in July 1934 (AP).*

**Background photograph** *Traffic jams at weekends, on the way to sporting events and at Bank Holiday periods, could be horrendous. This hold-up was on the A2, near Rochester, bound for the sea-side in 1937. How many popular cars of the day can you recognise? Starting from the front in the centre of the road there is a Singer Coupé, Morris Ten/Twelve SII, a Ford Eight, another Morris SII, a Hillman Minx 'Magnificent', a later-model Ford Eight . . . there was a lot of variety available to the family motorist (Fox Photos).*

**Inset** *In spite of severe budgetary problems in the early 1930s, the British government managed to commission some good stretches of new dual carriageway road, including this length of the A24 around Mickleham, not far from Leatherhead (Fox Photos).*

M63 complex west of the city, and drafted schemes for a new road from Warrington to Preston in 1937 which eventually became an integral part of the M6 motorway.

St Albans was also to be given a by-pass, costing about £1 million and this matured in the late 1950s as the southern section of the M1 and M10. The Ministry of Transport, having taken over trunk road responsibility in 1937, proposed by-passes for Darlington, Staines, Maidstone and Burton-on-Trent in their 1938 programme. Most important of all, however, was Sir Charles Bressey's monumental Highways Development Survey for London, which appeared in 1938 and had taken three years to produce. Among other things it proposed three concentric ring roads around the capital – a cencept not finally abondoned until the 1970s, although one complete ring (M25) should be completed in the 1980s.

It was a great time for schemes, but it was not a completely quiet period for construction itself. Motorists should be glad that work started before 1939 on roads like the Maidenhead and Ashford by-passes was later completed to a much higher standard. New roads and by-passes built in the 1930s are usually still recognisable by their layout and features. A good give-away is the provision of cycle tracks (Coventry still has good examples), the narrowness of their dual carriageways, a multitude of roundabouts and a lot of trees planted originally to help blend the new roads in the surroundings.

There was a lengthy hiatus in construction during and after the onset of the Depression, but thereafter new roads were opened with some regularity. By 1933 government statements claimed 220 by-passes in Great Britain, totalling 326 miles (though cynics had to scratch their heads to locate some of them). London's North Circular Road was finally completed in 1934, by which time the new Glen Coe Road, the Hogs Back road west of Guildford, the Morecambe to Hest Bank coast road, the Colchester by-pass and the Dorking by-pass had all been opened. These were followed by the completion of the Basingstoke by-pass, new dual carriageways on the Brighton Road at Bolney, the opening of the Mersey Tunnel and the building of by-passes for Crawley, Exeter, Mickleham and Northwich. The Coventry and Winchester by-passes were both officially opened after war had broken out, as was Western Avenue, from the White City area of London to the A40 out towards High Wycombe and Oxford.

In all £22 million was earmarked for new highway construction in 1938/39, though total spending on roads fluctuated fairly narrowly between £50 and £67 million a year throughout the decade. For all that, by 1938 there were only 27.5 miles of dual carriageway on Britain's trunk roads. Not only that, but these dual carriageways seemed to be dotted around with little evidence of overall planning. Will we ever know why isolated patches appeared between York and Malton, or between Preston and Southport, when the important by-passes for those towns or cities were not being built? Flyovers, incidentally, were so rare that when the Winchester by-pass was completed late in 1939 and included two such pieces of modern engineering, it made a major talking point.

In all, more than 1,600 miles of new roads were built between 1924 and 1937, though it seemed to make very little difference to the high accident rates, nor to do much to ease traffic flows. It did not help that the new roads, particularly near towns or cities, seemed to attract new building along their edges, which ensured that congestion was self-generating. A drive along London's Great West Road through Brentford is truly illuminating. The Firestone, Gillette and Pyrene factories and the lengthy rows of modernistic private houses are perfect examples of the phenomenon of 'ribbon building' which grew up in the 1930s. The mushroom growth of building was soon notorious enough to be controlled, for the towns were spreading out into the countryside at a staggering rate, taking their 30 mph speed limits with them. Almost every new radial route out of London – the Southend road, the Great West Road, Western Avenue and almost every highway south of the Thames into Kent and Surrey – all stand as monuments to the Road Fund (abolished in 1937) and to ribbon building.

As prosperity returned in the mid-1930s, however, the British motorist could not wait for the new roads to be built and took to pleasure motoring in huge numbers. The effect on some roads as – for instance – the Great North Road (A1) can be imagined. In 1939 a traveller bound for Scotland had to run the gauntlet of jams in Stevenage, Baldock, Biggleswade, St Neots, Stamford, Grantham, Newark, Bawtry and Doncaster – all before Leeds had been passed. Trains took precedence at level crossings everywhere and even in 1936 there were 1,385 of these across A and B class roads and 4,570 in all.

Nevertheless, the trip to the country, the touring holiday and the 'day out' became fashionable. Invasion of beauty spots and seaside towns might seem like a post-war business to us, but it was rife at the time. Who but Malcolm Muggeridge could have summarised it better in his book, *The Thirties*:

'On bright Sunday mornings the throng of vehicles on roads leading away from London grew denser, an unending procession, slowing down when it passed through towns and villages, then springing forward again . . . The toll of life taken, slowly mounting, caused little anxiety. Speed required its sacrifice like any other deity, though the placid acceptance of the inevitability of this sacrifice may surprise posterity more than larger and more passionate carnage. Petrol pumps, brightly coloured, and Belisha beacons to mark pedestrian crossings, blossomed like flowers; dashboards glowed with a dim, religious light; road houses offered entertainment, dancing and swimming between instalments of mileage . . . How sweet the smell of new leather, how satisfying mudguards' black curves, how exhilirating the sensation of gaining speed . . . .'

J. B. Priestley (in his famous *An English Journey*) had this to say:

'The England of arterial and by-pass roads, filling stations and factories that look like exhibition buildings . . . .'

Muggeridge mentions the road-house – itself not entirely new, but definitely a feature of

*The road house was a new breed of motorist's pull-up. A swimming pool (right, in this example) was a 'must', as was the prospect of dainty afternoon teas, a liquor licence and a place in which to dine and dance. This place is near Dorking, Boxhill is in the background* (Autocar).

**Top** *All the best (or worst?) of 1930s architecture for the British tourist. At one time a chain of 'Knights' was to be thrown up across the Midlands, including this one, the Coventry Knight, built on the A45 south-east of Coventry. The architecture was typical of the period. This hotel has been renamed the 'Ryton Bridge' and is visually unaltered to this day (Autocar).*

**Above** *Speed cops – but how could they do their job in gentle Talbot Ten tourers? These gentlemen were another consequence of the clamp down on speeds in 1935 and were hated by most motorists (Autocar).*

**Below** *They really did build horrific petrol stations like this between the wars – this one was at Langley in outer London, near Beckenham (Autocar).*

the 1930s. Modern motorists, especially the sophisticated, pleasure-loving kind, were not content merely to drive and seemed to want more than the old-fashioned country pub for their halts. To satisfy them a new breed of place, called the 'road-house' was developed, which was really a development of the USA 'motor court'. Their attraction was that they were pub, hotel, restaurant and recreation centre combined – they offered food, drink, dancing, swimming pools, gardens, sports facilities and even accommodation. They soon earned a reputation for charging high prices and for reasons often hard to crystalise they were regularly castigated by the moralists. The ensemble seemed far too attractive and seductive to some observers, so they were labelled as 'fast' – any girl visiting a road-house with her boy friend in his sports car immediately gained something of a reputation.

Because of their size and their multiple facilities, road-houses often hosted the start and finish of major motor sporting events. Places like the Spider's Web near Watford, the Clock at Welwyn and the Ace of Spades, on the Great West Road, soon made their reputations this way. Although the road-house was mainly a home counties invention, passing trade in other parts of the country soon attracted new hotel building. Look around for any example of '1930s modernistic', or 'functional wedding cake' styles and you may be sure it was built about 40 years ago. One prime example stands on a hill overlooking the A1 at Wansford, square, uncompromising (and a great contrast with the nearby age-old Haycock Hotel in the village itself!); the Midlands had their share of 'Knights', a string of identical-looking hotels at Coventry, Hinckley and Leicester. The motoring boom fostered them all.

A motorist's other need, of course, was the petrol station. Let's not forget that pioneer motorists had to buy his fuel from a chemist's shop (and, for long journeys, had to order in advance) and find his spares from a local cycle repair shop or the village blacksmith. Roadside petrol stations were slow to arrive and petrol from underground tanks was not available until the 1920s. By 1930 a rash of dreadfully tatty garages had sprung up and there was already a cry for new buildings to blend properly with their surroundings. In built-up areas the current sharp-edged style was considered adequate, but out in the country the most fantastic confections appeared. Thatched cottages, tudor mansions and baronial castles all doubled as petrol stations, with a few Chinese pagodas and embryo space stations – sometimes in the most dreadful taste. It is interesting to realise that nearly all these horrors have disappeared, though their relics are now highly prized 'collectors' items.

The big expansion in private motoring did not affect the accident rate as much as some road safety fanatics have claimed, particularly when the rise in traffic densities are also considered. 7,305 people were killed on British roads in 1930, while 6,691 were killed in 1931, which was the first year of limit-free motoring. That figure stayed the same in 1932, then rose to 7,202 in 1933, after which government decided to impose speed limits in towns. These figures, however, are nothing to be proud of, for it is true that in the 1970s, when the density of traffic had multiplied by seven times, the number of fatal accidents was no higher than this.

In response to speed limits, therefore, the police became more active. 'Squad car', 'flying squad' and 'Q-car' were all new banners of hate coined by the private motorist who thought (with some justification, it now seems) that he was being persecuted. Not that the police were provided with very appropriate cars in places – those unfortunates driving around in great style in Talbot Ten tourers (which were no quicker than Hillman Minxes, after all) would have been hard put to catch smash-and-grab merchants in stolen SS Jaguars! *The* police car of the period was a big Wolseley, usually an 18-85 – this marque was so popular that anyone buying himself a black Wolseley for private use could almost guarantee obsequious courtesy from every other road user.

**Above** *One idea for minimising injury to pedestrians in road accidents was to sweep them away from the nose of the car. The drum revolved, was geared to the front wheels and was arranged to lift the sack (or body, if we are being macabre) upwards, away from the danger of being run over. It was industrialist Sir Alfred Herbert's idea in 1935 (Autocar).*

**Below** *Traffic problems were rife at holiday times, even with less than two million cars on the roads and this dear little Austin Seven RAC van was kept busy erecting diversion signs in the Carlisle area (Autocar).*

**Above** *The RAC spent tens of thousands of pounds sponsoring a new system of British road signs, most of which have now disappeared. Choose your sign and pick up a bit of instant nostalgia* (Autocar).

**Below** *An SS1 Tourer nears the top of the notorious 'Pass of the Cattle', on its way to Applecross on the Scottish Rally. Cars had to be driven all the way up from sea level, seen in the distance, which is actually Loch Kishorn* (National Motor Museum).

*Motoring in transition. The final pre-war Riley 16 model (2,443 cc 'Big Four' engine) with its war-time headlamp masks. But November 1939 was still the time of the phoney war (Autocar).*

Driving standards were not as high then as they are today and there were no higher-standard driving courses where a driver could compare his driving with those of real experts. However, as the roads were so empty in places this was not often a problem. Holiday motorists venturing to northern Scotland might drive for many miles without meeting another car and a journey to the Atlantic coast could be an adventure in solitude. Even parts of Yorkshire, Lincolnshire and East Anglia could be surprisingly deserted.

Motoring, in any case, was a much more gentle and unhurried process than it has now become. It had to be: tyres were not noted for their wet grip and the performance of contemporary drum brakes often left much to be desired. In winter the only extra aid to traction was to fit chains, which often broke and severely limited speeds. All-weather treads were rare, while studded tyres were still only a rally driver's dream. Autumn fogs were surely much worse then – or is there an element of nostalgia in this impression? There were no Clean Air Bills in force to control smoke and other industrial emissions in towns and cities – a true London (or Birmingham) smog was something fearsome to be remembered.

At night, progress was severely limited by headlamp performance. Even for 50 mph cruising speeds a mass-market car's lights could barely cope and their dipping mechanisms were crude. Double-dipping bulbs had yet to appear; instead the dipping function was often provided by 'dip-and-switch' mechanisms, where the offside lamp was dowsed completely and the alignment of the nearside lamp was changed, often with an auxiliary bulb. MG and Wolseley, however, used the Nightpass system, where the bumper-mounted pass lamps doubled as dipped beams; this was all very well until the bumper bolts began to loosen off . . . Really fast cars like Lagondas and Alvis models needed huge lamps and

*If there was to be no petrol for private motoring during the coming war, a producer gas installation would have to do the job. The alternative was to carry billowing gas bags on the roof* (Autocar).

Lucas's magnificient P100 projector was the best available. Dazzle was still a serious problem and the adoption of polarised glass was often urged.

In some ways cars of the 1930s were more spacious and more comfortable than they are today, but in other ways they were distinctly lacking. Many, even the cheapest family flivvers, had really generous rear seat leg room because seats were positioned above the back axle, but front seat space was usually limited by the body contours. Bodies, in any case, were much narrower than they are today. A Series III Morris or Wolseley 14 of 1937, for instance, was less than four feet wide at front seat level, a space sharply reduced at the toeboard. All doors were rear-hinged, which might not have been ideal in case of accidents (or for accidental unlatching, which few even considered) but made it extremely easy for getting in or out.

If there was any really obvious change in motoring habits in this decade, it was the way in which people came to rely on their cars, to treat them as working tools. The millions of new motorists (there were nearly five million licence holders by 1939) were by no means rich enough to employ chauffeurs and they usually seemed to enjoy doing their own maintenance.

Touring by motor car (or motor cycle) suddenly blossomed and many used cars to explore far off parts of the country (and even Europe) previously unknown to them. New scenic routes in Wales and Scotland became fashionable and the roads had to be improved to cope with the increased traffic. The Birmingham Corporation, for instance, had constructed huge new water reservoirs astride the Elan valley in mid-Wales; these instantly became 'beauty spots' and the dirt road round their perimeters had to be improved. In Scotland the wilderness west and north of the Great Glen was combed by the adventurous.

Western Scotland soon generated its followers and one particular hill – the Pass of the Cattle – became as notorious as any in the country. This was purely because it was as high, steep and sinuous as any other – and because it was remote. Not that it led anywhere – Applecross, on the coast at its western end, was not connected to the interior by any other route until the mid-1970s. The motoring magazines fostered the spirit of adventure; much was made of the discovery of yet another 'worst hill in Britain', 'highest village', 'steepest climb' or 'fastest road'.

But if many were happy to drive further afield, there were some who were still timid. Why else would one reader write to a magazine saying that he wanted to practise his technique and where could he find a hairpin bend nearby? There were, as yet, no 'motels' as such, but many hotels  set out to encourage visits from tourists. The old coaching inns, whose spacious stables had been empty since the last stagecoaches disappeared, found that these were now very useful as garage blocks.

With the rise in tourism came vast expansion in membership of the main motoring organisations – the AA and the RAC. These were intrinsically more simple and more honest in their aims than they have since become. Their principal service was to keep their members' cars mobile and to advise impartially about road and hotel conditions. One great service they provided in the 1930s was to sponsor the production of many thousands of new road signs, which made navigation much easier for all motorists; the first was erected by the RAC on the Basingstoke by-pass in July 1933. The AA, always the larger of the two, enrolled its 500,000th member in August 1933 and was only foiled in its rush to pass the three-quarter million mark by the outbreak of war in 1939.

The motoring organisations did their best to advise their members about road problems and congestion, though the rise in commuting made this difficult. Not, of course, that there was anything new about commuting, but its scale had changed considerably. We must never forget that at the turn of the century there were reputed to be $3\frac{1}{2}$ million working horses in Britain and that upwards of 90,000 vehicles arrived in the City of London every day. Even before the Great War, London was regularly suffering all the horrors of a traffic jam. Congestion, incidentally, was always a major talking point. Even though traffic densities were much lighter than they have now become, the general pace of city traffic was slow, because horse-drawn traffic and the infuriating and inflexible tramcars had to be circumnavigated.

But all this pleasure and business motoring would shortly come to a temporary halt. From 1937 onwards, when Britain began to re-arm in earnest, the spectre of another war was always in the background. In the autumn of 1938, the Czech crises followed by the meetings at Munich brought that spectre right into the open and from the spring of 1939 the onset of fighting looked inevitable. Making a tidy survey of motoring in the 1930s would mean following events right throught to December 31, but by then everything had changed. Peace-time motoring came to an abrupt end during the weekend of September 2nd and 3rd. War was declared on that fateful Sunday morning, though mass evacuation from London had already begun. Plans had been laid well in advance to deal with such an emergency and twin track highways like the Kingston by-pass were rendered one-way to speed the mass exit.

Petrol rationing was imposed within two weeks (on Pool petrol at 1s 6d (7.5p) a gallon) and supplies were extremely limited. A 'Ten' or a 'Twelve' was only allocated six gallons a month (enough for perhaps 150 to 180 miles of travel), while anything of 20 hp or more had to be content with ten gallons and possibly a slightly lower mileage. Extremely restricting headlamp masks became compulsory, forward illumination was almost non-existent and accidents in the 'black-out' began to soar. White patches on car wings, aprons and bumpers were only of minor help. All forthcoming sporting and social events were cancelled forthwith and there was no question of the third Earls Court motor show being held in October.

A few new models, trembling on the brink of being launched, were released on the assumption that the 'duration' would not be a very long one. Some, like the Sunbeam Talbot Two-litre, were never produced in quantity until 1945, while improvements to others (like the 1940 model Jowetts) were never seen again. Some, like Nuffield's new Wolseley Eight and MG YA, obvious developments of existing designs, were suppressed and were not even introduced until after the war.

Some private cars were built until the middle of 1940 and for a time car makers placed reassuring adverts in the press to that effect, but such production was mainly for existing stocks of parts; after the shock of Dunkirk, the war machine was in complete command. Production lines which had fussed over expensive Daimlers were soon filled with Scout cars. Humber Road was more concerned with armoured cars and smaller 4 x 4s than with Snipes and Minxes. Standard went in for aircraft manufacture in a big way, as did Austin. Even MG at Abingdon built its own share of armoured vehicles, to the astonishment of all motoring enthusiasts. A few cars were built throughout the war for 'staff' use, though there were many more Austin 'Tilly' pick-ups than the Austin Tens from which they had been developed.

Before too long, however, petrol for private motoring was withdrawn completely and pleasure motoring was set aside for the duration of the war. By 1942 there were no more than half-a-million vehicles on our roads, which equated with mid-1920s standards of usage. If only we had known it, we would never see the like of this sort of motoring again.

**Chapter 4**

# Cars for Everyman

How should we judge the worth of British cars built in the 1930s? The cars, like the times, were changing rapidly. Their numbers increased as their costs fell. Big-engined and slow-revving tourers gave way to small high-revving saloons. The balance of sales tipped considerably in favour of 8 hp and 10 hp models as the decade progressed. More and more saloons were built than ever before. Fewer and fewer cars had hand-built coachwork. To some motoring historians there is little merit to be found in the cars of the 1930s; to others they represent the ancestry of everything which is modern.

The British cars of the 1930s certainly lacked the glamour of the vintage predecessors. This has affected an impartial judgement of their worth, to the point where many call them dull. By 1939 many models had embraced cost control, mass production and the philosophy of being part of a 'model cocktail' range; the result was that a sameness of character developed and much cheaper motoring was offered than ever before.

Car manufacturers themselves were in no doubt about their policy. If they had persisted with the construction of the 'vintage' type of car into the 1930s they would undoubtedly have perished financially; several tried to buck the trend and failed. The modern car *was* modern, and one has to admit that it seemed to appeal to customers and shareholders alike.

The 'vintage' brigade, well established, middle class and with their engineering values and social standards fixed rigidly in the 'Roaring Twenties', had little time for the modern type of car. Indeed, some were so shocked by the way in which motoring was evolving that they founded the Vintage Sports Car Club in 1934, refusing to consider for inclusion any motor car built after the end of 1930 (and not all those built before) – almost as if design improvements had ceased with cataclysmic suddenness at that time. Later on, in 1949, it must be said, they were forced to modify their extreme views and admitted to the existence of certain later 'thoroughbred' machines, where it suited them.

On the other hand, there was a constantly growing army of new motorists, who readily took to the new designs and voted their approval by marching into showrooms in huge numbers and coming away with the new light cars which suited them so well. Mainly on their side, but trying to be all things to all men, was a very middle class motoring press. Although their staffs might still have preferred vintage cars and certainly sporting machines, they certainly did not admit to this in print. For some time, however, *The Autocar* could not refrain from silhouetting every one of its Road Test cars, week after week, against the background of a lordly 40–50 Rolls-Royce.

In his very detailed study of the cars of the period *(Cars of the 1930s)* that eminent historian Michael Sedgwick had this to say:

'How often do we hear the phrase "the nasty 30s"? Authors have skimmed off the thoroughbreds made between 1931 and 1942 and have lumped the vast majority of the cars of the era into a symbol of degeneracy – mass production, presswork, meaningless gimmicks, ill-braced chassis frames, prolix easy-change systems and nausea-provoking suspensions.

Yet the cars of the period had a character which reflected the restless era which gave them birth . . . If the badge-engineer was at work, his endeavours were well-camouflaged from an uncritical buying public and unquestionably the cars which the man in the street could buy after 1930 were easier to drive and better suited to the tyro than some of their vintage forebears . . ..'

A further comment, inside, makes it even more clear what sort of new driver now flocked to buy the latest cars in such great numbers:

'For the first time, ownership of a motor car was extended to a wider clientele and those who suddenly found themselves able to buy one new . . . lacked the knowledge or inclination to criticise, to slate the unnecessary gimmicks, the lack of steering geometry, the weird gear ratios and the instrument panels which owed everything to the stylist, and nothing to the ergonome or the intelligent driver.'

This summarises the trend admirably. A motor industry content to go on making 'vintage' types of cars in the depressed 1930s would soon have been struggling. On the other hand, companies selling reliable cars in the modern idiom were sure of a regular market – if, that is, the product looked as conventional as possible and sold at the right price.

I have already stated my case. I approve of the philosophy of the cars made at this time because they made economic sense and they introduced a completely new class of people to motoring. Motoring ceased to be mainly a middle and upper class pastime. In fact, for the first time, a car ceased to be mainly a pastime and became a working machine, more and more ignored when not actually in use.

For a time, towards the end of the 1920s, Britain's overall prosperity received a setback and for the motor industry to widen their markets they had to push the motoring threshold firmly downwards. Paying £300 to £400 a car for good vintage transport was quite beyond the reach of most people; to begin offering £150 or £200 models instead required new techniques, new factories and much smaller cars.

The cycle car boom had already vanished, with most of the spidery breed hounded out of existence in a storm of ridicule. With them, for a time, went all the prospects for real 'marginal motoring'. However, the really small cars and the cheap motoring which were to replace them was not purely a 1930s invention and did not arise from its special social conditions. 'Pa' Austin had started it all back in 1922 with the cheeky little Austin Seven (incidentally he infuriated the motor cycle trade by declaring that it 'would knock the the motor cycle and sidecar into a cocked hat and far surpass it in comfort and passenger-carrying capacity') and in 1928 he had been copied by William Morris with his overhead-camshaft engined Morris Minor. Siegfried Bettman also had a yen to join the 'Big League' and announced the Triumph Super Seven in 1927, while Standard's first such offering was the Nine. The start of the small car boom was there for all to see, yet it still had to be backed up by a similar mass of intermediate-sized machines, variants and options.

There was always the sales-worthy attraction of being able to sell a car for only £100 (how unbelievable that seems today!) but in spite of Rover's threat to market the rear-engined Scarab for a mere £89, no other British car has ever been offered for sale for less than £100. Getting down to that retail price, which meant that it had to leave the factory gates for no more than about £85, was an extremely difficult task, if not – as it proved – quite impossible. Only two British cars were ever sold for £100 – the side-valve engined 2-seater Morris Minor Tourer of 1931 and the much more successful Ford 8 hp 'Popular' model of 1935-1937. Such a selling price was only possible if the car's equipment was pared to the bone and if there was virtually no profit in the deal either for manufacturer or

**Above left** *Britain's first £100 car – the side-valve two-seater Morris Minor Tourer of 1931. It was very sparsely equipped and most potential customers were content to 'trade up' to more expensive saloons or tourers* (Autocar).

**Left** *One way to deliver a quantity of Austin Seven bodies from one factory to the next in Birmingham! This was the method sometimes used by Austin in 1934 and only the front car has an engine* (Autocar).

**Below left** *Big and bulbous, with a vast 3,622 cc side-valve V8 engine and lots of urge was Ford's V8 saloon. It cost a mere £220 and could beat 80 mph, which was a considerable bargain. The snag, which stifled many sales, was the 30 hp 'treasury rating' of annual taxation* (Autocar).

**Above** *Ford's very popular Eight – the famous 'Model Y'. A basically-equipped 2-door saloon version was the only British car ever to sell in quantity for no more than £100* (Motor).

retailer. Perhaps this was the first instance of a 'loss leader' philosophy, one which in this supermarket age we have come to accept.

It was no accident that the £100 Minor had the absolute minimum of equipment, a sparsely-equipped open tourer body and a side-valve engine when every other Morris Minor was being sold with a technically interesting overhead cam unit. It certainly attracted people into the showrooms, but most of them left having bought an ohc-engined car, perhaps the De Luxe saloon for £140. Ford's £100 contender of 1935 was much more likely to sell, as its De Luxe equivalent sold for only £110 and both were successful until the model was changed in the autumn of 1937.

A more normal 'bottom limit' for new-car purchases was at the £120 mark, for this sort of money usually bought an Austin Seven (which, though ageing, remained in production until 1939), the better equipped small Ford or Morris and the smallest Singers. Only a few pounds more was enough to secure a tiny Triumph or a Standard, but the smallest Hillmans and Vauxhall of the 1930s were both Tens.

The really small-engined car, therefore, was *not* the 1930s phenomenon, but the method of packing a rather limited range of engines and chassis frames into a number of variations was quite new. The average new motorist, even if he did not possess a great deal of money, could often be persuaded to stretch himself a little by 'trading up' to the next model in the range. With hire-purchase available at attractive rates the prospect of laying out another £40 or £50 did not look too frightening.

This meant that manufacturers serving the mass market had to work hard on their model line-up, a technique which only evolved properly towards the end of the period. It might come as a surprise to some to learn that Ford, of all people, were the least successful in this art; they had no exclusive design for the British market before 1932 and there were usually yawning gaps between the 8 hp and 30 hp limits of their range; even by 1939 they only offered an unbalanced range of 8, 10, 22 and 30 hp models.

In 1930, 1931 and 1932 the maker who had no small car in his range suffered badly. Later on, of course, there would be the pleasurable prospect of getting a showroom customer to 'trade-up'; in the hard times which existed at first it was a matter of getting (and keeping) a customer at all costs. Statistics published at the beginning of 1932 tell their own story. Of all types, the 'Eight' was most popular, followed by 'Twelves', 'Tens' and – surprisingly – 'Sixteens'. In that deeply gloomy year of 1931, 130,700 cars were registered and no fewer than 76,000 of them were in 12 hp or less. Only a couple of years later, however, the swing to small cars had been intensified and more than 135,000 of 186,500 cars bought in the year were of 12 hp or less. In that short time the percentage of 'top people's' cars had shifted sharply from 58 per cent to 72 per cent. By 1938 official figures would show that of the total private car population of 1.8 million, 480,000 had only 8 hp engines 109,000 were 'Nines' and nearly 381,000 had 10 hp units; more than half of Britain's cars, therefore, were in the 'small' category.

Throughout the 1930s this trend was never reversed and although every car maker with a wide range usually topped it off with something in the 20 hp or 25 hp class, the vast majority of all his sales would be of cars costing less than £250 and rated at 14 hp or less. A clever sales department catered for rising prosperity with a range relying on model cocktails and minor variations on a theme and usually managed this very well without too much obvious cynicism. There are many good examples of this and we can do no more than look at a typical year and a typical range. Let us, therefore, look at 1938, at the Earls Court preview of 1939 models, when such policies had been thoroughly refined, and let us compare Austin with Morris.

Austin, with only one marque name, and with all their models being assembled at Longbridge, lined up as follows:

| Austin Seven | £108 to £129 depending on model | Austin Twelve | £215 to £232 |
| Austin 'Big Seven' | £137 to £149 10s | Austin Fourteen | £235 to £252 |
| Austin Ten | £175 to £189 | Austin Eighteen | £350 to £383 |
| | | Austin Twenty-Eight | £700 onwards |

Note that both the 'Sevens' were taxed at 8 hp and the 'Fourteen' at 16 hp. Misnaming a model like this was a common subterfuge practiced by the car manufacturers of the day. As a buyer, one also had to beware of things like 'Big Tens' or 'Heavy Twelves', which usually meant something else entirely. There was only one obvious gap in Austin's armour

**Top right** *The first ever Earls Court Motor Show was held in 1937 and met with great acclaim from the press. No fewer than 66 car makers, and 33 British coachbuilders, had cars on display* (Autocar).

**Above right** *The last of the famous Austin Sevens – the Big Seven – lasted only a short time and had a new design of side-valve engine. The car was replaced by a modern 'Eight' in 1939* (Autocar).

**Right** *Emphasising the strong family resemblance between all Flying Standards is this 1938-model Flying 20, with an entirely different body from the 14, on a longer wheelbase. This car's engine was used (in overhead valve form) on 2½-litre SS Jaguars* (Autocar).

**Above** *How Austins had changed, even by 1937. A current-model Austin saloon parked alongside a 1907 version outside Car Mart's London headquarters (Autocar).*

**Below** *The Morris Eight Series E was announced in 1938 as a successor to the very popular Eight of 1934–1938. It was distinguished by its flush-mounted headlamps – a very brave advance for the period in Britain, although already common on North American models. It was sold in 4-door saloon, 2-door saloon, 2-seat tourer and 4-seat tourer models. A Wolseley 8 and the MG YA models, both based on this car but with different engines (and with independent front suspension on the MG) were introduced after the Second World War (British Leyland).*

**Above** *One of the success stories of the 1930s was that of the Flying Standard theme. This was the Flying 14 of 1937, whose engine would be used until the end of the 1940s and which also formed the basis of the 1½-litre SS Jaguars* (National Motor Museum).

**Below** *Perhaps the very first example of a genuine three-door car, built on the basis of a Singer Bantam in 1936. Standard versions were available with two-door or four-door coachwork, so there was no great difficulty in making this 'one-off'* (Autocar).

– the lack of a truly modern 'Eight' and this would be filled in spring 1939 by a new model, selling for between £128 and £139.

Nuffield, with Morris, MG and Wolseley already integrated in the group and with Riley just having been bought from the receiver, was in an even stronger position. Just look at the ramifications and cross-pollinations of the main Nuffield marques at that same Motor Show:

| | |
|---|---|
| Morris 8 | £132 10s to £149 |
| Morris 10 | £175 to £190 |
| Morris 12 | £205 to £220 |
| Morris 14 | £248 10s |
| Morris 25 | £320 to £345 |
| Wolseley 12–48 | £245 to £256 |
| Wolseley 14–60 | £285 |
| Wolseley 16–65 | £320 |
| Wolseley 18–85 | £325 |
| Wolseley Super 6 '16' | £380* |
| Wolseley Super 6 '21' | £395 |
| Wolseley Super Six '25' | £395 to £775 |
| MG TA Sports car | £222 to £269 10s |
| MG VA Tourer Saloon (12 hp) | £280 to £356 |
| MG SA saloon (18 hp) | £389 to £415 |
| MG WA saloon (20 hp) | £442 to £468 |

*This model was listed when the 1939 range was announced, but soon disappeared from Wolseley's press advertising.*

Morris 16s, 18s and 21s had all disappeared in 1937 to leave the field clear for the more profitable Wolseley equivalents. A Wolseley 10 (based on the Morris 10) would follow in 1939, priced at £215 to £270, though war put a stop to the Wolseley 8 which should have followed. The next MG (the YA, also based on the Morris 8) was also delayed until after the war. It is worth noting how carefully the pricing structure was arranged, so that no model of one make clashed directly with the next model of the same make; even the Morris/Wolseley interface of prices was as logical as possible under the circumstances.

At the same time, the Rootes Group were marketing everything from 10 hp Hillman Minxes at £163 to 27 hp Humber Pullmans at £750, Vauxhall had a big range stretching from Tens at £168 to Twenty-Fives at £630, while John Black's Standard combine had recently rounded off its 'Flying' models, which now started at the 8 hp model (£125, complete with independent front suspension) and finished with the 20 hp saloon at £325.

In the 1930s there were several other sizeable (by standards of the day) independent concerns – a breed which has virtually disappeared from the modern British motoring scene. The biggest of all – Austin, Morris, Ford, Rootes, Standard and Vauxhall – made up the 'Big Six', but other companies like Singer, SS, Jowett and Rover all liked to think that they were important too. And so they were, but none of them could compete with the 'Six' in terms of output, a wide model range or in profitability.

Every car maker, even Daimler and the increasingly aristocratic Rover company, was keen to improve his position in the market place. Almost all of the quantity-production car makers chose to do this by ensuring that their cars were as much alike the opposition's products as possible. Nowhere was this more obvious than in styling trends and the fact that big companies like Pressed Steel were not above selling the same skin panels to more than one customer did not help. The Rover Ten and the Hillman Minx of the early 1930s

*Batch-production of special-bodied Standards in the mid-1930s. Such jobs were usually carried out by specialist coachbuilders – in this case Salmons at Newport Pagnell – on a fairly standard base sometimes shared with other models. The factory, incidentally, is now part of the Aston Martin assembly facility* (Autocar).

were uncannily similar, as were the late-1930s Hillman Minx and the Singer Ten. The Singer Bantam might have had a different body shell from the Morris Eight of 1934–1938, but it needed an expert to tell them apart at twenty paces.

Although there were occasional bursts of idiosyncratic engineering (like Ford's transverse leaf spring suspension) trends were usually well identified and widespread. For a lot of the time popular-priced cars had a none too stiff chassis frame, with half-elliptic leaf springs and beam axles at front and rear, along with long-stroke/narrow-bore engines which minimised the taxman's demands. Three-speed or four-speed gearboxes were controlled by long and willowy levers sprouting from the floor. There were separate front seats, facia styles often in exquisite bad taste and a profusion of alternative body styles.

No self-respecting model range was complete unless it could offer a two-door and a front-door saloon version, and a convertible or tourer. The open body style would usually be farmed out to one of the batch-production coachbuilders like Mulliners, Salmons, Carbodies, Vanden Plas or Charlesworth and if they could also offer a sporting version, then so much the better. Estate cars as we now understand them were unknown; a proper 'estate car' – one, that is, for use on country estates – would be a converted van or light commercial vehicle, rather than the smart version of the saloon we now expect to be offered. With this (and export sales in mind) Morris actually offered a six-wheeler saloon on a Morris Commercial chassis at the beginning of 1931; it was not a success.

As the decade progressed, styling trends encouraged bodies to grow wider and more practical. In small cars of the early 1930s the 'across-shoulder' dimension could have been as little as 40 inches; by 1939 that would have increased by at least five inches, which was a great relief to those who regularly had both front seats occupied. Chassis frames progressed from having channel-section side members, to more rigid box-section members; later they would also be welded to a pressed-steel floor pan, which could provide further improvements in torsional rigidity.

Whereas the decade opened with almost all small cars except the Morris Minor being equipped with simple side-valve engines, new designs usually appeared with overhead valves and more efficient breathing and combustion. Other historians have suggested that cars of the 1930s were more economical than any others built before or since, but I have to say that this was probably due to the low performance, light weights and average driving methods of the day. Some engines, originally with a side-valve layout, were given overhead-valve conversions to keep them abreast of engineering fashions. Standard supplied overhead-valve engines to their customers – SS and Morgan – but kept side-valve versions for themselves. For years Nuffield's engine factory in Coventry was building both types at the same time – side-valve units for Morris, overhead-valve derivatives of the same designs for MG and Wolseley. However, to buck the trend completely, Morris replaced their overhead-cam Morris Minor engine by a side-valve design for 1932, then kept it throughout the decade! (There was also to be an overhead-valve version – for the Wolseley Eight – but this was temporarily killed off by the war).

Independent front suspension took ages to arrive on popular priced British cars, held back perhaps by the fact that road surfaces had improved so much. *The Autocar's* gossip columnist, 'the Scribe', started grumbling in 1932 on these lines:

'I think our motor car designers are getting into a rut. They seem to think the public will not entertain anything that differs from the specification they have always had . . . Where are the independently sprung cars every designer knows must come sooner or later? Is there a single designer who will deny that independent springing, in theory at all events, is a step forward?'

In 1935, 'the Scribe' was still nagging away at British cars' deficiencies:

'I have called it (i.f.s.) an innovation in error. Nearly every car at the Berlin show has independent springing and only a few of the Americans now remain without it . . . .'

Independent suspension, in quantity, first appeared on middle class and middle price cars – not on expensive machines like the Rolls-Royce, Lagonda, Alvis type – and even though it was neither sophisticated nor refined, it was an advance on what had gone before. Vauxhall, Rootes, Singer and Standard were pioneers in the 1930s, but even by 1939 no Austin, Ford or Morris was so equipped. By the last pre-war British motor show (Earls Court in 1938) independent suspension was also found on certain Alvis, Daimler, Lanchester and Rolls-Royce models.

On the whole, however, cars were still very simply engineered and could be assembled Meccano-fashion, so most cars came in for regular model changes, often every year. 'Improvements' could be so confusing and so diverse that even dedicated historians find it difficult to keep up with the whims of the engineers and salesmen. Purely as an example, I have chosen to itemise work done on one long-running model – the Hillman Minx – which was, in every way, a typical product of the period.

The Minx had been conceived in 1929 and 1930, tested in 1931 and was first shown to the public in the autumn of 1931. It was the first true 'family' Hillman to be designed following the onset of Rootes influence at the end of the 1920s, and was so astutely laid out that its general concept did not alter until the late 1940s.

*One of the most significant prototypes ever built – a VW 'Beetle', as conceived by Dr Ferdinand Porsche, and ready to go into production when war broke out in 1939 (Autocar).*

*The car which startled most of the world's automobile engineers – the front-wheel drive Citröen. Introduced in 1934 and soon assembled at Citroen's British factory in Slough, the* traction avant *stayed with us until 1955* (Motor).

Here was a new model still not quite ready for production, but already fully developed. In every way it was a typical 'Ten', with a 63 x 95 mm, 1,185 cc, side-valve four-cyclinder engine developing 30 bhp. Modern touches included flexible engine mountings and hydraulic suspension damping. There was a conventional chassis frame with half-elliptic leaf springs front and rear. A three-speed 'crash' gearbox was fitted. Five body options were offered, starting from the four-door family saloon at £155 and progressing to the plushier 'Club' saloon at £198. This was absolutely in line with the competition.

Rootes were not ashamed to remind the public, in March 1932, that deliveries were only then beginning, as a winter's wait for a new car was quite acceptable at the time; the price of the cheapest version had been raised to £159 before deliveries commenced.

By 1933 the gearbox had been changed – to a four-speed design without synchromesh – but for 1934 this was further refined with a clutchless change and a freewheel on the more expensive versions. In the meantime, the styling changed little, apart from cosmetic details and the lowest price stuck resolutely at £159. However the range continued to expand and now included the sexy little Aero Minx coupé, which had a swept-tail two-

*The car that transformed Humber/Hillman's fortunes – the Minx. A modern picture, certainly, but this 1936 model is entirely original. There were Minxes from Rootes between 1932 and 1970* (National Motor Museum).

**Above** *The 10,000th Hillman Minx 'Magnificent', built at the Rootes Group's Stoke (Coventry) factory, in January 1936. The growth of Rootes production was one of the phenomena of the 1930s* (Autocar).

**Below** *Posed, perhaps, but typical in a way of the advertising scene of the 1930s, where snobbery played a big part. The car was a 1937 Hillman Hawk (which later transmuted itself into the Humber Snipe) with a 3,181 cc side-valve engine, the place was Penshurst and quite a number of such middle class car buyers still employed a chauffeur* (National Motor Museum).

door body which later inspired the Talbot Ten. From June 1934 there was also the Melody at £195 – the first British car ever to be offered with a built-in radio (by Philco) as standard.

Rootes made much of their prospects for 1935, calling it a 'vintage year' in advance; the fuss was mainly to hide the fact that they had little else to talk about regarding the Minx, which was entering its fourth sales year without a re-style. Under the skin, however, was a new four-speed all-synchromesh gearbox and the comprehensive line-up of 14 Minxes and Aero Minxes was led, as ever, by the basic saloon at £159.

Just a year later, however, the Minx was given a completely new body style, which the company dubbed 'Magnificent'. Chassis frames were stronger, body lines were plumper (and constructed entirely from pressed steel) with an enclosed boot for the first time and pressed-steel road wheels. The trusty engine and transmission were not changed and prices were still based on the £159 of the cheapest version.

Even for Rootes, however, who liked annual changes as much as the next firm, this was quite enough for a time and there were no major changes before 1938. Even then the car's shape was not changed, but there was yet another new gearbox, proudly advertised, although Rootes omitted to mention that although the ratios were different, they had also removed synchromesh from bottom gear! Finally, and just in time to be stopped by the onset of war, came a new model for 1940, distinguished by a brand-new unit-construction body shell, but a slightly increased price structure (£165 for the basic saloon).

That, of course, was merely the Minx, but at the same time Rootes were also involved in Wizards, Vortics, Fourteens and Hawks, not to mention Humber Twelves, Snipes, Super Snipes, Pullmans and Vogues, and in the absorption and re-structuring of Sunbeam and Talbot and the development of new 10 hp, 2-litre, 3-litre and 4-litre cars which were called Sunbeam-Talbots. There was never a time when an avid car-spotter could be kept so busy, though he had to have keen eyesight to distinguish between the many marques, models and the years in which they were built.

At first, bodies mainly built on a skeleton of hard wood, with hand-worked panels and flat glass, tended to design themselves. Almost every car of 1930 had square and upright body sides, uncompromisingly rectangular door openings and windows, a vertical windscreen and a completely uncoordinated nose. Radiators were still *real* radiators, square-cornered, tall and upright, with slab-sided bonnet panels behind and with a good deal of chassis mechanism exposed underneath. Headlamps were mounted away from the rest of the body. The only true and artistically shaped curves would be on the front wings and perhaps on the rear quarters. Luggage compartments were unknown; the only place for Everyman to carry his cases was on a let-down rack fixed to the back of the body, whereas a tycoon might at least have a separate but fitted 'boot' which was usually trimmed and painted in the same materials as the rest of the car and blended in with the general lines. At the front, the engine, however long, was invariably positioned well behind the front axle, to give clearance for axle movement and steering linkages.

The arrival of pressed steel bodies and the trend to forward-mounted engines, changed all this. Nowadays, of course, we accept the forward position of engines as completely normal, especially as this automatically releases more of the inter-axle space for passenger accommodation to be provided. In 'vintage' years, however, where looks were thought to be at least as important as accommodation and practicality, the gaping void between the front dumb-irons was neglected.

The short-lived vogue for pint-sized six-cylinder engines spotlighted the problem: the conflict between engine bay space and the passenger footwells, for these were usually required to fit into the chassis and bodies of their smaller, four-cylinder engined, relatives. For several good engineering reasons (and those connected with passenger space) it was

**Left** *Ford replaced the original model by a new 'Eight' later in the decade and in spite of the small engine and three-speed gearbox it was quite a regularly-used rally car* (Autocar).

**Right** *The earliest of all the 'streamlined' British cars of the 1930s was the strange Singer 11 Airstream model. It was created by Captain D. F. H. Fitzmaurice of Airstream Ltd and shown at Olympia in 1933, but was relaunched by Singer in July 1934 as a 'production model'. It combined all the gimmicks of the period – streamlined styling, independent (Armstrong-type) front suspension and fluid flywheel transmission combined with a freewheel. The car was not a success and was dropped after a year, when only 200 examples had been sold* (Autocar).

**Below right** *By no means expensive in North America, the hideous Chrysler Airflow of 1935 was not at all to British tastes. Though it was technically interesting under the skin (it had one of the first types of unit-construction) the British could not come to terms with its looks* (National Motor Museum).

not feasible to move gearboxes back, so longer engines could only be accommodated by allowing the radiator shells to be pushed forward. Wolseley, with the Hornet, were pioneers and once they pushed the radiator position forward by at least a foot to accommodate the 1,271 cc 'six' and the public had become used to a prow which stood up near the bumper blade, the fashion spread rapidly.

The next move was for four-cylinder engines to be mounted further forward, which meant that passenger accommodation could be improved; once independent front suspension had been adopted (and therefore the obtrusive front axle beam was eliminated) there were no remaining problems. Eventually the entire 'passenger box' moved forward, so that although there was no overall increase in space it ensured 'between axles' seating for all occupants and encouraged designers to find space for an enclosed boot.

In due course slab panels and squared-up corners became contoured, screens were raked, body styles were sloped and there was even a suggestion of contoured glass. Radiators gradually turned from being functional components into being no more than decorative panels retaining their traditional shapes; the radiator block itself then lurked behind this grille, in the engine bay. The exposed water filler, which had often incorporated a radiator thermometer, was abandoned in favour of a plinth for motives and heraldic symbols.

Stylists began to look enviously across the Atlantic, studied the excesses of Detroit's styling and imported much of it for 1937, 1938 and 1939 models. Ford and Vauxhall models were usually styled in Detroit and British management had little choice in the cars they were commanded to sell. Up to then the rather awkward noses had accommodated radiator, headlamps, perhaps a spotlamp or two, horns, side lamps, chassis frame dumb-irons and the bumper blade. Sheet metal was wrapped indiscriminately round the ugliest parts and the result was never aerodynamically efficient. Bonnets invariable hinged along the centre line from radiator to scuttle and their lines were usually high, to accommodate an imposing radiator made necessary as thermosyphon cooling was still thought to be adequate.

The first all-enveloping cars had bulbous fronts, to say the least; whereas earlier models could be seen to have been hand-shaped by craftsmen in a workshop, these were quite obviously derived from a clay model in a styling studio. It did not help that one of the first such horrors was Chrysler's ghastly Airflow of 1934, nor that the first straight British copy was the equally awful Singer 'Airstream' (of which only 200 examples were ever sold – no wonder Singer were in financial trouble by 1936). Even by 1938 the Morris Eight Series E had a mixed reception and the praise for the streamlined Bentley prototype's performance was tempered by reservations about its looks.

Mechanical development followed predictable lines for some years, especially if we take into account the taxation barriers, the need for as many variations as possible within basic designs and the need, at all times, to keep production lines busy. The business of what I have already dubbed 'model cocktailing' was really developed to a fine art at this time. However, there was one fashionable period which really needs explanation – the vogue for the 'small six'.

*The trend to streamlining led to some strange shapes, like this SS Airline saloon of 1935. This might have looked smart, but was functionally useless as the airflow would already have been disturbed by the unchanged bluff nose* (National Motor Museum).

This has already been summed up well by Michael Sedgwick in *Cars of the 1930s*:

'The very mention of these vehicles is apt to induce apoplexy in the heart of the vintage fanatic and certainly the thought of a lengthy and relatively complex engine revving its heart out in a chassis designed for a smaller, shorter and lighter four-cylinder unit pre-supposes alarming problems of weight distribution and handling. Cars like the Wolseley Hornet and the Triumph Scorpion do not seem to have been engineered at all. They just happened.'

The fashion is easily explained. A new generation of drivers demanded easy-to-drive machinery, which usually meant that they wanted to spend less time having to change gear. Their ideal car needed to be flexible, yet free-revving and smooth at the same time. Rootes had still to invent the flexible engine mounting ('cushioned power' arrived with the Minx in 1931) and four-cylinder engines bolted solidly to resonant chassis frames could not normally be driven at low engine revs. But if a 'six' was the immediate answer, it still had to be small, in order to cheat the Chancellor of his annual taxes. The result, in all cases, was a puny little engine which was splendidly flexible but almost gutless, developed its maximum power at high engine speeds and was sometimes matched to disgracefully-low gearing.

Such engines had such a doubtful reputation that some firms in the industry were not at all happy. But how about this comment from Wilson McComb's 'MG':

'There was some danger that the MS's new 1,271 cc ohc engine (which was, in fact, made by Wolseley to MG's designs) might be mistaken for Wolseley's own 1,271 cc ohc engine, since the dimensions were identical. Kimber, therefore, 'added' one millimetre to the stroke of the MG engine, calling it 84 mm and making the capacity 1,286 cc.'

These tiny six-cylinder engines might not have 'just happened' but they certainly appeared after the very minimum of development. All of them were existing four-cylinder designs to which an additional two cylinders had been added – this involving machining compromises which could easily be accommodated at the time. Therefore an 847 cc four-cylinder Morris Minor engine (built by Wolseley) was easily converted into a 1,271 cc six-cylinder Wolseley – and in spite of what Cecil Kimber and acolytes might protest, it also formed the basis of the ubiquitous MG unit.

Any enthusiastic home mechanic who stayed loyal to one make of car in the 1930s would have every chance of becoming familiar with some engine design, or family of engines, even if he gradually rose in the social scale and purchased progressively larger and more expensive machines. A casual look at the maker's range year after year, might give one the impression of a multitude of changes and many new designs, but this was rarely so.

Nuffield provided one typical and excellent example of the way one range of engines could be used for more than two decades. In any such family there is usually one obvious recognition point. In this case it was the 102 mm stroke (although never confirmed this was more probably a round figure of 4 in, or 101.6 mm) which was in evidence right from the start. The design dated from 1919, although it was actually a close copy of the American 'Continental' design which Morris had been buying since 1914, and which had a 100 mm stroke, and engines were always built in the Coventry factories. It was always possible to build four-cylinder or six-cylinder engines and as the design evolved it was also possible to provide a multitude of different cylinder bore dimensions. At first these units were fitted to Cowley-assembled Morris cars and were simple little side-valve designs. After Morris had completed their rationalisation of Wolseley in Birmingham, overhead-valve derivatives were supplied to that concern. MGs built at Abingdon between 1936 and 1939 (except for the TB sports car, which used a derivative of the Morris 10 Series M engine) used the same family of engines, and by 1938 the Morris range was also converted to overhead-valve operation. In all that time, the permutations or bore size and number of cylinders were cleverly juggled to give as much choice as possible. I have been able to identify six different bores and piston sizes between 61.5 mm and 73 mm and eight different engine capacities (4-cylinder and 6-cylinder) between 1,292 cc and 2,561 cc.

This practice, of course, was not confined to the large scale producers. Middle class car makers might not have been able to offer as many variants, but they still made prolonged use of existing designs. Rover, for instance, introduced the first of a new range of 100 mm stroke engines in 1933, which ran until 1948, with capacities varying from 1,389 cc to 2,512 cc. Every SS Jaguar was based on the origins of a Standard design with a 106 mm stroke, varying from 1,609 cc to 3,485 cc; the latter unit, in fact, had a lengthened stroke.

The concept of badge engineering – of making a multitude of models from very few basic designs – became a recognised science in the 1930s. Both Nuffield and Rootes were very adept at this, with Standard not far behind. Nuffield could play tunes on the Morris, MG and Wolseley marques, while Rootes had Hillman, Humber and Sunbeam-Talbot.

*The best of SS engineering of the 1930s was to be found in the SS Jaguars which were announced in 1935. This 2½-litre model, the epitome of a good sports saloon, shows off its underslung chassis frame, its six-cylinder engine and its sleek lines* (Autocar).

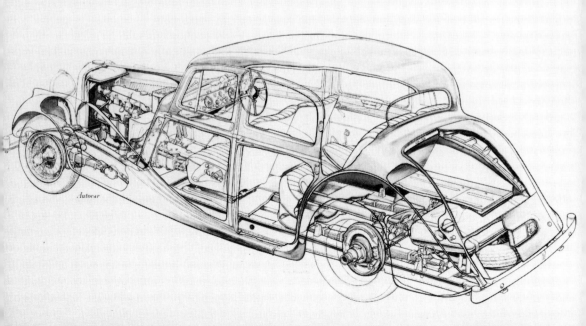

*Miles Thomas concentrated on making Wolseleys graceful in the 1930s. Though they became very closely based on the equivalent mass-market Morris models, the cars from Ward End managed to pack in much extra equipment and usually more performance. This was the 1937 Series II 18–80 (Autocar).*

With the public demanding large ranges, and with only limited quantities of capital and factory space available, such tactics were essential.

Miles Thomas, who was managing director of Wolseley in their most successful period in the 1930s, recalls in his autobiography that:

'We quickly produced a new Wolseley Wasp and a new Hornet', (this was in 1935) 'four-cylinder and six-cylinder saloons of medium and high performance respectively. I discovered that by taking the same fundamental body side panels, but building them wider apart and putting gussets in the tonneau roof and dash we had a body big enough to hold five people in comfort, economical to make and light enough to give a sparkling performance when a 14 hp overhead valve engine was installed.'

So much for the 'new' 14 hp model!

Looking back into the 1920s, it is interesting to recall the fittings a motorist had had to do without. No-one had bumpers, of course, before the later 1920s. Wipers were still something of a novelty and always sold as extras, gearboxes were crude, weather protection often something of a joke, self-starters were not always fitted before about 1923 . . . there seemed to be no end to the 'new' standard fittings which the 1930s might provide.

Once the Depression began to ease, the average car's equipment progressively began to improve. Fifty per cent of cars on show at Olympia had overhead valves by 1930 and this proportion steadily improved thereafter and three-quarters had pump water cooling by 1933. Coil ignition overtook magneto ignition in popularity just as the decade began and by 1935 the transformation was almost complete. Open propeller shafts took the lead from torque tube layouts at the start of the decade, centre gearchanges took over from right-hand change and four-speed gearboxes outsold three-speed versions. In decorative terms, chrome plate had achieved popularity (not without controversy) at the end of the 1920s and consolidated its position in the 1930s.

There was a rush to provide easier gear-changing, sparked off by the successful introduction of synchromesh (by General Motors, on their Cadillacs and La Salles for 1929) and by the arrival of the Wilson 'self-change' epicyclic transmission. GM's British off-shoot, Vauxhall, pioneered synchromesh here, by making it available in October 1931 on their 1932 model Cadet. Rolls-Royce, of all people, were next in the field, with synchromesh being made available on 20/25 models during 1932. Within months the 'Big Six' were struggling to catch up lost ground and by the late 1930s the revolution was complete.

A half-way house to synchromesh changes was provided by the brief vogue for 'traffic top' gearing (which actually meant that third gear was in constant mesh and needed no noisy struggling with sliding pinions to effect the change), which was also known as a 'silent third'. Freewheels, some more complicated than others, made their appearance at about this time, but only survived to the 1940s and 1950s on the Rover range. In spite of press forecasts, however, a clutchless-change overdrive was only offered on one range of cars – the 1938 model Rileys. 1939 model cars built under Nuffield control abandoned this feature which was, incidentally, allied to a freewheel. The 'overdrive' Bentley of 1938/1939 was nothing of the sort; its gearbox had been redesigned with a direct third and a geared up 'overdrive' top, which nevertheless had to be engaged by means of the gear lever and the clutch pedal.

Automatic clutches with centrifugal actions came and went, but the two most significant advances were probably the fluid flywheel (to supplant the friction clutch) and the Wilson gearbox, which the BSA/Daimler/Lanchester combine brought together to produce a remarkably nice transmission. The fluid flywheel did away with any need for dexterity in operating the clutch (always thought to be a desirable feature by new motorists of the period) and gave very smoothly-cushioned power take-up. Armstrong Siddeley had first introduced the Wilson box in 1928, but it was first fitted to a Daimler in June 1930 (the 20–30 hp model). Later the Wilson box, but not the fluid flywheel, came to be fitted to at least a dozen other makes and models, this including the accolade of being chosen for use in the ERA and MG K3 Magnette racing cars, not forgetting the conversion job done on Whitney Straight's GP Maseratis.

Fully automatic transmission was introduced on a few American cars at the end of the period, but they were all forestalled by the weird and complex Hayes transmission in Britain, which was announced as an optional fitment for the Austin Sixteen at the 1933 Olympia Motor Show. The extra price – £40 on top of a £328 price tag for the standard car – was itself a big deterrent, but it seems that the British public was not ready to buy an automatic box (not, at least, on what was a none too popular Austin model). Technically, too, the Hayes box was interesting but apparently unreliable. Only 50 were fitted in the next couple of years, though historians are delighted to know that one or two survive to this day. No other British concern troubled itself to offer an automatic option and it was left to Rolls-Royce, in post-war years to start the proper trend.

Regular lubrication of the chassis and suspension was always a chore (every 1,000 miles, if one was conscientous) and to ease the pain some car makers specified 'one-shot' systems (which are still retained on the current Morgans), or by having a system of grouped grease nipples on a panel hidden away from view by a bumper or body panel, from which pipes led to the points to be greased. This, though laudable, was costly to install, and not very reliable as old grease tended to clog in the pipes and nullify the operation of the entire system.

Built-in car jacks were a good sales feature and were found on many cars during the period. The best types were hydraulically powered, which were usually well sealed and impervious to road filth, though some cars were equipped with mechanical scissor-type jacks bolted to chassis members or axle beams which soon succumbed to corrosion and seized up. Rover, in 1933 (for their 1934 models) were the first to standardise that curious feature, the harmonic stabiliser bumper, which had been developed by Wilmot Breeden. This relied on mounting bumper blades having dumb-bell weights at their extremities, on spring mountings to the front dumb-irons and – in theory at least – helped to minimise the wheel patter and frame vibration problems which intensified as performance and wheel/tyre weights increased. I have spoken to no one who actually knew if these bumpers had been of any benefit whatsoever, but it is a fact that they enjoyed considerable popularity for a time.

**Left** *Was it neat or was it rather ghastly? Most thought it was horrid, but people sold cars with much worse styling for years. Clocks, even on mundane Morris saloons, were normal fittings in those days* (Autocar).

**Below right** *Production cars were bad enough, but VW Beetle protypes looked even worse. No one could have realised the significance of this design when it was first shown in 1937. The prototypes, incidently, were built for Dr Porsche by Mercedes-Benz in Stuttgart* (Autocar).

Although there was a general trend to better and more comprehensive electrical fittings, which included the near-standardisation of 'trafficators', Morris blotted their corporate copybook in 1932 when they announced their 1933 model range with miniature 'traffic light' indicators on the scuttles to act as turn indicators. These flashed red, amber and green when operated by a facia switch, but were soon pronounced illegal by the government's lawyers and had to be replaced, at no charge to the customers, in April 1933.

Even in relatively ordinary family cars, the number and type of standard fittings could be gratifyingly high and it was not until the 1960s or even the 1970s that the modern equivalent was quite so well equipped again. One of my father's first cars was a Morris 12 Series II of 1937 vintage, where little details such as a rear window blind, which was operable from the front seat, were very welcome. Usually there were plenty of instruments (sometimes 'styled' into one grotesque dial), good carpet on the floor and (for almost any car costing more than about £200) real leather facings on the seats. Padded head cushions in the rear quarters, and doortop 'pull' straps were certainly expected on any car in the Riley/Wolseley/SS class.

But there were also many gimmicks, of which one of the strangest and most short-lived feature was the 'Startix' electrical fitting. Once again intended to make motoring easier, the Startix was an electrical box of tricks, designed to operate the starter motor a few seconds after the engine had stalled, without any positive action being needed from the driver. Potentially this was invaluable in heavy traffic conditions or for engines which might not have their idling settings properly set and it should have been a real boon for the novice. An engine would be running, then – for some reason – would stall. Electrical impulses from the ignition circuit ceased, a solenoid was released and this then activated the starter motor circuitry. If all went well the engine would then re-start and the car could be driven away. The snag, however, was that an engine in poor condition could drive the device to distraction and a parked car with its ignition switch inadvertently left in the 'Startix' position could cause the Startix to make the battery go flat in a very short time.

Perhaps the most significant technical advance of the period was the way in which structures were built in large quantities. This was due to the maturing of engineering know-how which made it possible for body shells to be built entirely from pressed-steel panels and later for the chassis frames to be incorporated into the body itself. Morris, in conjunction with the Budd concern of the United States, got together to found the Pressed Steel company in the mid-1920s and this concern, with factory buildings literally across the road from the Morris assembly lines at Cowley, supplied its first all-steel shell in 1927.

It took time, a great deal of effort and some embarrassing disasters before the technique was viable as an economic replacement for bodies coachbuilt by traditional methods, but by the early 1930s most of the 'Big Six' were building their standard models this way. In the mid-1930s the process was taken a stage further when chassis frames began to be welded (not bolted) to the body shells they had to support; the Series II Morris Tens and Twelves were among the first to exploit this.

From there it was only a short step to designing chassis and body as a single unit, which – even in the 1930s – cost a prodigious amount of money in terms of complex press tools and assembly jigs to be manufactured, but helped by saving a great deal of weight and unit costs. Vauxhall, helped by the experience of their parent company, General Motors, were first to announce a British-built unit-construction body-chassis unit. Their pioneering model, the Ten-Four of October 1937, was followed a year later by new Twelve and Fourteen models. At the same time Nuffield joined the accelerating trend with the new Morris Ten Series M (body by Pressed Steel) and Rootes (also with Pressed Steel bodies) joined in with the 1940 model Minx which was stifled by the onset of war. But for that war, several more unit-construction designs would have been in the pipeline.

Although mechanical advance was often found first in the cheapest cars (which might benefit most from cost savings) or in the most expensive (where different forms of enterprise might add to their mechanical prestige with potential customers) in the middle there was an entire sub-industry of concerns which sold on various combinations of quality, elegance, some exclusivity, a touch of class or extra performance – all of which made them attractive alternatives to the products of the 'Big Six'. What was also remarkable, in the increasingly standardised 1930s, was the amount of home-inspired engineering in these cars. AC, Alvis, Crossley, Jowett, Riley, Rover, SS, Singer, Sunbeam, Talbot and Triumph were all independent concerns for much of the 1930s. Most made their own engines, all assembled their own bodies and each had individual designs of chassis frames built for them by industry suppliers.

Each, too, seemed to have something special to advertise. Crossley, for instance, traded

on north-country loyalty with their Stockport origins (and burnt their fingers badly by taking up the Burney Streamline layout for their own Crossley-Burney derivative). SS offered superb styling and extremely low prices. Alvis concentrated on high performance and fine engines. Riley had very interesting engine layouts and a fine sporting record (which eventually helped to bankrupt them). Talbot had the magic of Georges Roesch's reputation. Jowett sold idiosyncratic Yorkshire vehicles which were at the same time crude and appealing. Triumph, for their part, combined a good rallying record with Donald Healey's engineering reputation and fine styling.

Not that the performance of any of these cars was startling, even by the standards of the day. 80 mph was a very creditable maximum which many of the 'middle class' machines could not achieve and anything better than about 25 mpg fuel economy was not usually to be expected. Although each marque was instantly recognisable by the individual touches in its design, there was a general styling trend which can be recognised today.

Our ideal middle class, middle price saloon from such manufacturers would almost invariably have a four-door, four-window style, with a sweeping tail, a long and slim bonnet with instantly recognisable radiator grille and badge, big proud free-standing headlamps and elegant flowing front wings. There was a great deal of mechanical rivalry between owners, most of whom took marque loyalty seriously and were ready to defend their choice in print, or – in mediaeval jousting fashion – on the concours and rallies which became so popular in Britain towards the end of the 1930s.

Over and above the bread-and-butter saloon car market, there was a healthy demand for special bodies, of which tourers, convertibles and coupés were most popular. Unless demand was high (which, by the standards of the day, could mean selling more than 1,000 or 2,000 a year) the car makers rarely built their own special coachwork. This meant a continuing flow of very acceptable work for middle class coachbuilders like Mulliners, Thrupp & Maberly, Salmons and the others who showed so regularly at Olympia and Earls Court Motor Shows. But their task was made much more difficult by the arrival of the unit-construction body shell; it was one thing to produce a special shell on the basis of a separate chassis frame and a simple standard body, but quite another to consider a major re-build of a stress-bearing unit-construction shell. Once unit shells became established, the days of the budget-price coachbuilt car were numbered, but the decline did not truly take effect until the end of the 1940s.

The demand and the market for sports cars and sporting motoring was extraordinarily strong. No matter what criticism can be made of the saloons of this decade, the sports cars were a real revelation. Those built in Britain were so successful and so numerous, that they deserve special study. For one thing is quite certain – when the saloons are forgotten, the open MGs, Rileys and SS Jaguars will live on. The spirit – the real romance of motoring in the 1930s – lies with the sporting cars.

**Chapter 5**

# Cars for the sportsman

The British may have been making boring little family cars, but they built some fine sports cars. Not even the vintage enthusiasts could argue about this. There was some very exciting imported machinery, usually rather expensive, often much more complicated in its engineering and usually rather rare. The continentals, somehow, took time to master the problem of making cheap, enjoyable *and* successful sports cars. Then as now, some of the best-loved sports cars were closely based on the saloon cars of the time. Is it difficult to accept, therefore, that without some of the slow, fussy and gimmicky little family tubs there could have been no successful and nippy two-seaters?

Examples are legion, none more obviously so than the MGs. Here is a marque of sporting car revered all over the world, yet at first they had been very little more than tarted-up 'bullnose' Morrises. By 1930 the popular M-Type was a re-bodied overhead-cam Morris Minor, later models used progressively developed Wolseley engines and the final Nuffield-inspired cars were little more than re-developed Wolseleys. The Coventry approach was just as simple, with Riley, Singer and Triumph all producing attractive little two-seaters which were often little more than open versions of their existing touring cars.

The most expensive sporting tourers – Bentley, Lagonda and Alvis, for instance – were much more specialised, more desirable, but considerably more expensive. But it is a sad commentary on this decade that specialisation and mechanical excellence seldom went hand in hand with prosperity; the finest of all were sunk in the Depression, or by the more pragmatic buying attitudes which followed. In the middle were small-scale builders like Morgan, Frazer Nash, HRG and AC, where interesting styling and rakish lines sometimes hid undistinguished mechanical components. Not that the buyers seemed to mind very much – surely they must have known that Jensen engines came from Ford, SS engines from Standard or that Triumph bought their gearboxes from Austin at Longbridge.

Incidentally, if these were the depressed years, it certainly is not obvious from the catalogues and motor shows of the period. Surely there was a wider choice of sporting machinery than at any time before or since? But how much of this was of thoroughbred design and what were the marketing intentions? The problem, as usual, is that to define a sports car accurately we must descend into motoring philosophy and it would still be impossible to embrace everything.

'Sports cars are those intended for sporting use'. How is that for a definition? But in trials? In rallies? In races? In driving tests? Did a sports car need a good competition record to make it worthy? How can we define the shadowy fleet of machines which were advertised as 'sports', but rarely achieved anything better than a noisy sprint down the High Street or local by-pass? Fashions come and fashions go, too. Today we would probably accept a Capri or an Alfetta GT as sporting, but forty years ago a tin-top just would not do at all. No matter what else had to be included, our 1930s sports car certainly had to be supplied with a lightweight body and a folding hood, the skimpier the better.

**Left** *A brave effort by a well-to-do private owner – this was the only 'racing Rolls-Royce' for many years. Actually Eddie Hall's famous sports car started life as a 1934 Derby-built Bentley and in successively faster and faster form it took second place in the Ulster TT races of 1934, 1935 and 1936* (Autocar).

**Right** *A selection of MG models being finished off at Abingdon in the 1930s. The year is probably 1933, for in the foreground is one of the very first PA models, while beyond the Magna L-Type saloon is one of the last J2s. Two of the unloved and unlovely Magna Continental Coupés are also in line for completion* (British Leyland).

But were all fast soft-top cars sporting? Certainly not. They might have been impressive (how about a magnificent £3,500 V12 Hispano-Suiza, or a long and low Daimler Double Six, for instance?) and they might have been fast, but they were not sports cars. Neither were all the models advertised as sports cars honestly described. Even the splendidly thoroughbred Rolls-Bentley was dubbed the 'Silent Sports Car' by its makers, but only specials built for heroes like Eddie Hall really qualified. Was performance enough? Usually, but even this was not infallible. After all, 100 mph Lagondas with V12 engines might have normal five-seater saloon car bodywork. At the other extreme, too, MG's humble Midget of 1930, with a mere 847 cc and 20 bhp, found getting to 60 mph a struggle in standard form, but no one argued with its intentions. And did not a team of specially developed M-Types win the Brooklands 'Double-Twelve' against formidable opposition?

It was the age-old problem, satisfied in the age-old way. You could look at any particular car and say 'Yes' or 'No'. You would look askance at a sporting Armstrong Siddeley in spite of its magnificent light-alloy engine, smile and turn away with a shrug, but you would inspect a supercharged Squire, a chain-gang Frazer Nash, a Talbot, or a Marendaz Special and have no doubts.

Everyone had a problem in one area, where the purist would be so appalled by the crude engineering he found under a purposeful skin that he might draw back. Such cars, usually grouped together as 'Anglo-American Sports Bastards', tended to have vast engines which ensured a great deal of performance without even a nod in the direction of advanced design. The trouble was that something like a Railton, with its 4.2-litre Hudson straight-eight engine, was faster than nearly any other British car and an Allard was more effective up trials hills than most . . . perhaps performance was enough in these cases?

However, such cars bordered on the exotic, while it was the MGs, Singers and Rileys which really epitomised the age. The raffish young man, with scarf and gloves, hair brilliantined to a glossy sheen, a languidly-elegant girl friend in the left-hand seat, a car snarling in and out of the fashionable road houses, country inns and seaside resorts – that is

what we all remember. The cars would be hard-sprung (*very* hard-sprung, or are we now too old to judge?), starkly styled but well equipped and definitely intended to carry only two people. Headlamps stood rampant even when saloon car lamps began to hide discreetly in front wings, windscreens could be folded and hoods could not only be folded back but usually removed completely. Spare wheels (sometimes two of them) would be exposed, often strapped to the back of a big slab of a petrol tank. There would be dials and knobs galore, separate seats and a fly-off handbrake. Bonnet louvres and twin number plates were in fashion, along with Bluemel 'sprung' steering wheels, pneumatic seat cushions and badge bars. No one, but no one, built sports cars without wire-spoke wheels (when MG turned to pressed-steel for the TD as late as 1950 it caused a real storm of protest) and anything with really effective all-weather protection was considered cissy.

We must also put our impressions of performance, hazed over by pink-rimmed clouds of reminiscence, in perspective. The M-Type Midget already mentioned might be urged up to 75 mph when much modified, but in 1930 it was still hampered by having only three forward gears and in standard tune would be struggling to beat 45 mph in second gear. Fuel consumption, on the other hand, could often be up to 40 mpg, which in the days of petrol at 1s 4½d (7p) a gallon was not bad.

Times, and performance standards, have certainly changed. The Midget thought to be creditable and amusing at the time, could now be matched by the Fiat 126 (arguably Europe's slowest production car of today) and soundly beaten by any other. Yet at the time there were very few small saloon cars which could themselves reach 60 mph and 80 mph was considered to be a most spirited performance. By comparison 100 mph was a speed few had ever experienced and then probably only on a race track. Perhaps in 40 years time, when someone looks back on motoring in our decade they might want to know why we thought maximum speeds of 110/120 mph for a sports car quite so satisfying?

At the beginning of the period there was not a single British-built sports car which could reach 100 mph on road test in standard form and precious few which could beat 90 mph.

The rare 4½-litre 'Blower' Bentleys and Speed Six models were fast, but ponderous, while cars like the 4½-litre 'flat-iron' Invictas were quicker than most. But as the years passed by, performance standards improved and it is worth taking MG as my example to illustrate this.

The M-Type's maximum was soundly beaten by the J2, which was probably good for about 70 mph. With this car, however, MG reaped the awful commercial consequences of submitting a tuned car to the press; their *Autocar* test car recorded 80 mph, which was excellent publicity at first, soon turning sour when retail customers found their own cars to be much slower, or blew them up comprehensively trying to match the figures! Years later, Cecil Kimber had the temerity to write to *The Autocar* stating that MG had stopped submitting cars for road test because of rival cars submitted with 'irregularities which have occurred to our definite knowledge . . .' This august magazine, for their part, merely noted darkly that: 'we know of only one case in a period of years where a non-standard car passed scrutiny . . .', but forebore to mention that this single example had been an MG! Kimber's problem, incidentally, was that the SA saloon was not as quick as the 2½-litre SS Jaguar and he did not want it proved.

The PA Midget kept the 847 cc engine, but its maximum went up to 74 mph and the 1936 TA Midget (bigger, better and with a 1,292 cc pushrod engine) raised this standard to 78 mph. A 1939 TB, in good tune and with the smaller but high-revving 1,250 cc engine, could just reach 80 mph. Thus, in the nine years of tests in the decade, MG had been able to push up their Midget maximum speeds by 17 mph, or by more than one quarter, while average fuel economy had fallen only from 40 mpg to 32 mpg. Prices, on the other hand, had crept up. M-Types sold for £175, PAs, PBs and TAs for £222 and the final pre-war TB Midget for £225. A £50 increase for such vastly improved performance and equipment was quite reasonable.

Sports cars were still treated with great suspicion by the authorities, especially as they were usually driven with far greater abandon on less-crowded roads than we drive our machinery today. We must not forget that there was still a blanket 20 mph speed limit in 1930 and that many of those who sat 'on the bench' had grown up in the 19th century when cars were nearly unknown.

The cars themselves tended to be fairly noisy and many sporting events (like reliability trials and long-distance rallies) seemed to attract hordes of them. But there did not seem to be as many spoil-sports and do-gooders in the country then. There were far fewer cars on the roads and somehow it was expected for a little sports car to be driven hard.

But what of the 'pecking order' of the day? Which make was at the top of the popularity tree? Which was thought the most desirable? And what about the odd-balls and the failures? Should the perspective of history alter any of the judgements of the time?

In Britain, Bentley (who else?) had most prestige at first, even if very few people could actually afford to buy one of the cars. Until the firm collapsed financially in 1931, the five Le Mans victories, countless other sporting successes and the social (anti-social?) antics of the 'Bentley Boys' all helped to top-up the legend, even if it was founded on what were definitely vintage or even Edwardian design principles. Later, their mantle was taken on by Lagonda, whose cars got better and better, more and more expensive, but who also had one Le Mans (in 1935) and a near-miss in 1939, by Talbot (who also, like Bentley, lost their independence after financial problems and take-overs) and to a certain extent by Alvis.

The most desirable of all seemed to be foreign imports – desirable not only because they were so fast and so effective, but because they were rare, costly and therefore exotic. The Alfa Romeos, Bugattis and Delahayes were usually imported by wealthy men for use as racing machines. Lord Howe, for instance, who was nothing if not a patriot, often had to

*The splendid supercharged Alfa Romeo 8-cylinder car, so versatile in touring, sports-racing and outright racing form, in 2.3, 2.6 and 2.9-litre guise. This was a Paris Show exhibit in 1937. Very few of these exciting projectiles ever reached Britain* (Autocar).

put results before national pride to stay competitive. His efforts to get any British firm to build an Alfa-beater were fruitless.

The Alfa-Romeo Type 8C-2300, and its later derivatives, was really the standard by which all other machines was judged, and *The Autocar's* road test maximum of 106.8 mph recorded in 1932 for one of the short-chassis two-seater road cars was to be unbeaten until the late 1940s. If scratch racing, as opposed to handicapping, had been in vogue, more and more hard-earned money would have gone abroad to buy such cars. The Alfas and the Bugattis were in all respects the Ferraris and Lamborghinis of their day.

But if by popularity one means large sales, there could only be one winner – MG. The Abingdon-produced cars had evolved from humble origins in Oxford, under the knowledgeable and dedicated guidance of Cecil Kimber. MGs might, however, have been no more than low-production 'specials' if it had not been for the fact that Morris Garages was personally owned by 'Billy' Morris, whose Cowley factories were already the largest in the land.

The first MGs of all were no more than rebodied and slightly-modified Morris tourers, and the true Abingdon tradition was really founded by the tiny M-Type Midget. MG had had several cramped little homes before moving a few miles south to a disused leather-working factory at Abingdon in 1929. There were old-model MGs running alongside the M-Type for a time, but Kimber was determined to produce better, faster and more sophisticated little thoroughbreds from the Pavlova works. He preferred pure sports two-seaters, but had enough commercial sense to know that four-seaters, coupés and even the occasional saloon should be marketed on the same basic designs.

To be frank, I must point out that as MG's prestige and engineering reputation rose, profits and sales fell. From 1932 to 1935 sales plummeted from 2,400 to 1,250 cars a year and this could not be blamed on the Depression. Other car makers hit bottom in 1932 and climbed steadily out of the depths thereafter; MG sales began to fall when the M-Type disappeared and as the price of special and competition MGs shot up. The tide only turned after Lord Nuffield demanded rationalisation and easier-to-sell cars in 1935.

But technically there can be no argument. The MG was a true sports car and Cecil Kimber always pursued a consistent policy. All his cars would have overhead camshaft engines, simple and rugged ladder-type chassis frames and would basically be suitable for racing, rallies or for sporting trials. He backed this with short runs of special competition cars, works teams and a tuning service (which persists to this day at Abingdon). It was Kimber who personally approved all MG styling, which explains why every 1930s MG had distinctive 'family' features and why the use of his beloved 'octagon' symbols progressively increased.

But as MG was always small (their best sales year was 1937, with 2,850 cars delivered), in sales and in capital backing, they could not afford to design and build their own engines and had to buy in coachwork from a variety of sources. Let nobody state that MGs were throroughbreds because they designed and built everything themselves. In this respect they were no more in control than many of the smallest specialist concerns. Getting chassis frames built to order was easy – there were several competent specialists in the industry – but for engines and transmissions they had to rely on the Nuffield group. There was a design watershed in 1935 – up to then MG engines were very special versions of the overhead camshaft Wolseley units and afterwards they were no more than specially-prepared overhead-valve Morris/Wolseley units. This could have been embarrassing at first, for at the time Wolseley Hornet sports cars, which were among the most hated of all the 'pseudo' machines, were using the same basic six-cylinder engine design. MG went to great lengths to preserve the fiction of having their own unique engines; Kimber was so obsessed about this that for his first Birmingham-sourced 'six' he had the Wolseley engines disguised by adding sheet metal panels on their sides and later he 'added' 1 mm to the stroke so that it differed from Wolseley in the catalogues – in fact there was never any difference and historians puzzled over this one for years.

The M-Type Midget, Minor-based since 1928, gave way directly to the J-Type in 1932, with a more specialised chassis but still with the old two-bearing 847 cc engine. In 1934 this design was replaced by the PA model in which the 847 cc engine was considerably redesigned and had been given a three-bearing crankshaft and by the end of 1935 this had been supplanted by the PB, where that engine had been enlarged to 939 cc.

Lord Nuffield then sold MG to his Nuffield Group, which immediately stopped the racing programme and demanded that the MG company established a much closer and more standardised design liaison with other Nuffield companies. By then, anyway, the overhead camshaft engines were obsolete and not due to be used by any other new Nuffield model being planned. They disappeared completely from the Nuffield scene in 1936. It was at this juncture that the PB model gave way to the new TA Midget, which was a bigger car in every way, had a much modified version of the '102 mm' Nuffield engine from Coventry and for the very first time on any MG (after the first few examples had been built) there was a synchromesh gearbox. This engine was much more tunable than its critics first believed and the car became more desirable in 1939 when – as the TB – it was given the new short-stroke XPAG 1,250 cc engine.

MGs' other late-vintage model had been the 18-80, with its 2,468 cc overhead-cam engine, which was built until 1933, but from 1931 there was also a confusing variety of smaller six-cylinder cars – Magnas and Magnettes, Fs, Ks, Ls and Ns, all related to each other, with the small 'six' which by 1935 was almost pure MG, though manufactured by Wolseley. The same business revolution which removed the PB then swept these cars away, to be replaced speedily by the large SA and WA four-seaters and by the modest little 1½-litre VA model. After 1935 the bigger MGs were not sports cars and were Nuffield-develop-

*A fine Max Millar cutaway drawing of MG's P-Type sports car of 1934. This was the four-seater version, which cost £240, but the two-seater sports car sold for only £225. The PB of 1936 was the last of the overhead-camshaft MGs (Autocar).*

ed at Cowley; on the other hand they had sleek styling aimed unashamedly at the SS Jaguar market.

The little two-seaters might have provided Abingdon's sometimes-precarious cash flow, but it was the competition cars which provided the glamour. To Cecil Kimber, a sports car was not a success until, and unless, it could win races. Up to 1935 he had approved a succession of increasingly-costly and fierce little cars – some of which formed the basis of the legendary 'EX' record cars made famous by George Eyston and Major 'Goldie' Gardner. The C-Type Montlhéry Midget was loosely based on the old M-Type and proceeded to take the first five places (on handicap, admittedly) in the 1931 Brooklands 'Double Twelve' hour race. J3s and J4s were much-modified J1 and J2 production cars with 750 cc supercharged engines, while the K3 Magnettes were the famous 1,100 cc cars which did so much for our sports car racing prestige in the mid-1930s. Just before Lord Nuffield stepped in to shut down the racing operation, Kimber also sold eight Q-Type 750s (which had more than 140 bhp with supercharging – no wonder they got a reputation for being far too fast for their chassis) and ten single-seater R-Type racing cars with backbone chassis frames and all-independent suspension.

The price of such fame and performance was, quite logically, money. A C-Type cost £575 (compared with £185 for the M-Type), a J4 – £495 and no less than £795 was asked for a K3 Magnette. Even at £750 the exclusive R-Type was not thought to be a profit maker. Such high prices could only be justified if the cars were winners and in MG's case there was rarely any doubt about this. There was no sporting homologation problem in the 1930s, so the fact that only 44 Montlhérys, 33 K3s and 31 J3/J4 cars were built was no problem. Their production took up a disproportionate amount of MG's time and development effort.

**Left** *A Singer Nine 'Le Mans' sports car in a sporting trial, probably the most popular type of clubman's motor sport. These little cars were worthy competition for the ubiquitous MG Midgets* (National Motor Museum).

**Right** *Driving tests were one sure way to settle rally results. This was a 1937 1,496 cc Riley Sprite (1937 model), with the controversial 'fencer's mask' type of radiator grille, competing in the 1939 RAC Rally, at Brighton* (National Motor Museum).

Even so, Kimber thought it was all worth it. Knowledge gained at Brooklands and beyond soon worked its way through to the production cars and the customer gained as a result. A PB was vastly better than a J2, even though many components were similar. The final overhead cam 'sixes' were almost immeasurably better than the first Wolseley units, all the improvement, indirectly, having come from racing experience.

MG's continued popularity was partly due to a consistent basic style. One could look at M-Types, TBs, even at K3 racing cars and see similar lines. Radiators looked alike, the same man (Kimber?) clearly influenced wing sweeps and always had his preferences in dashboard layout. Even when Cowley began to interfere, a Midget's purpose never varied; no publicity man ever had to explain its intentions, nor compare its merits with an ancestor. It was an attribute envied by many.

Several competing companies tried – very hard. The principal competition came from Riley and Singer in Coventry and Birmingham – two marques built in factories geographically close together. So if you think you can see traces of Triumph in Singer, or of Riley in Triumph, do not be too puzzled. MG might have been able to keep their new developments well hidden, but in Coventry that was not at all easy. The motor industry in the Midlands was very 'in-bred' at the time, and especially as many peoples' suppliers were the same it took much ingenuity to keep an industrial secret. With well-known engineers and salesmen moving around from one company to another (Donald Healey, for instance, moved from Invicta to Riley early in the decade, then on to Triumph in 1933) the task was nearly impossible.

It was surprising therefore, to find that Singer and Riley were far apart in their thinking and approach to building sporting cars. Riley's advantage was in a family of carefully-detailed and robust engines, all complete with that well-known twin high-camshaft layout and part-spherical combustion chambers, but their prices were high and their cars often far too heavy. Singer had a much broader commercial base; they were not at any time in the 'Big Six' (they also thought they should have been in that exclusive club) but they still relied on a healthy output of workaday saloons showing more and more tendency to copy the large-scale competition from Cowley to keep the money flowing in.

Singer flirted heavily with an MG-style competition programme, particularly when Stanley Barnes (who later came to control the RAC Motor Sport Division) was in charge, but they were never as fashionable as the Rileys. Riley's bonus at the beginning of the 1930s was the Brooklands model, developed by Reid Railton at Thomson and Taylor's Brooklands workshops and much favoured by habitués of the track. Riley built a succession of fast and competitive racing sports cars in the 1930s (which partly explains their bankruptcy in 1938) and Freddie Dixon was renowned for extracting the last ounce of performance from his Dixon-Riley specials (more, indeed, than the factory could find). Later, of course, ERA gave Riley the ultimate accolade by choosing their six-cylinder unit as the basis of the single-seater racing car's engine.

At the end of the decade, however, which Singer survived in some style in spite of more than one serious financial upheaval and in which they did not have to rely on their sports cars too much, Riley independence had gone. In spite of their styling and their racing reputation, the cars were usually too heavy, too thirsty (except for the Nine) and too expensive.

Like MG, Singer sold four-cylinder and six-cylinder sports cars, some of which looked remarkably similar to the Abingdon machines. The Junior was not a true sports car, but the Nine (a four-seater at first) was a real competitor. It became even more of a problem to MG in its Le Mans Speed Special guise and for a time more of these speedy little cars were sold than the equivalent MGs. The Le Mans two-seater was a fine little car, with successes at Brooklands and in the sporting trials which were held all over the country. We must not forget the quartet of very special ultra-light works cars built to race in 1935, but these achieved notoriety at Ards in the Tourist Trophy race when three cars crashed at the same spot with identical steering failures. Before then, however, their little overhead cam engines (972 cc) had proved good enough to propel them at 90 mph and they were definitely as quick as the current PA MGs. But these crashes discredited the model in the public eye and did nothing for the Le Mans model's reputation in general.

Singer also built overhead cam 'sixes' and once again it was the Le Mans version which were fastest of all; they would undoubtedly have sold better if the factory had not run into

*Donald Healey's Triumph Dolomite straight-eight, an admitted (engine) copy of the Alfa Romeo 8C-2300 sports racing car. It was a fabulous car, which never went into production after its launch in 1934 (Autocar).*

financial problems, decided to concentrate on the Bantam saloon (a 'look-alike' Morris Eight competitor) and lost interest in low-production sports cars. They actually announced a 1½-litre four-cylinder car in 1937, but this did not go into production; the engine, another overhead camshaft design, was luckier – HRG took it up for their own models where it achieved fame and, of course, it was the last Singer engine to remain in production, being used in saloons and tourers right up to the Singer (Rootes) Gazelle of 1958.

Sporting Rileys, with engines designed in the 1920s, were already famous when the 1930s opened, as the Brooklands model had already made its mark. The 1,087 cc engine design was more efficient than MG's smaller unit and the factory was equally as keen on motor sport. The Brooklands Riley won many awards – round the Surrey concrete and elsewhere – not least in the 1932 Ards TT where C. R. Whitcroft won the event outright on handicap. Most 'Nines' were saloons and surprisingly fast for their day (much faster than most of the mundane opposition), but the last was built in 1938.

Two larger engines which became even more famous as the years passed were the six-cylinder unit (1,633 cc at first, reduced to 1,486 cc to allow it to fall into a convenient sporting category) which appeared as early as 1928 and the '12 hp' four-cylinder unit of 1,496 cc which carried on into Nuffield-built cars of the 1950s. The 'six' acquired a water-cooled centre main bearing in 1932, which made it even more suitable for tuning and racing. Raymond Mays and Amherst Villiers produced the very fast 'White Riley' around this six-cylinder unit, which led to ERA then adding their own special expertise to the engines. In ERA guise, with cars built between 1934 and 1939 there were much-modified 1100s, 1500s and even the occasional 2-litre versions, all from the same basic design, though Riley themselves never adopted them. There was once speculation about an ERA-engined Riley sports car, but this never came to anything.

Riley models were prolific, but were never produced in large numbers. There were Imps ('Nines'), Sprites ('1½-litres') and MPHs (very rare – with the six-cylinder engine in three sizes), plus sports saloons, coupés and combinations of all three in some profusion. But the company collapsed financially because of all this complexity. The beginning of the end probably came in 1935 when the first of the V8 designs was revealed. A year later the Riley family set up a special factory to build Autovias, which had larger, plushier and more expensive V8 engines. By the spring of 1938 Riley's finances were in ruins and a receiver was nominated; within months the company had been absorbed by Lord Nuffield and began to lose its identity. Yet throughout the 1930s the cars were exquisitely engineered, if heavy, and the two modern four-cylinder engines lived on for 20 years.

Another Coventry company which aspired to sports cars was Triumph, but with one honourable exception theirs rarely had competition-winning potential. At first they sold the tiny Super Seven sports car (a few of them with Cozette superchargers) but from 1932 to 1934 there was also the chunky little Southern Cross. This car, like the Nine saloon from which it was derived, used a Triumph-built 1,018 cc (later 1,122 cc) Coventry-Climax engine and was good enough to give Donald Healey a magnificent third place overall in the 1934 Monte Carlo Rally (with Tommy Wisdom in the passenger's seat) and an important team prize for the factory in the French Alpine Trial later in the year.

Triumph had attracted Donald Healey from Riley to be Technical Manager, to finalise the sleek and elegant Glorias and to prepare new derivatives. His first effort was the Monte Carlo Tourer (really a developed Gloria Tourer) which was followed by the short-chassis four-cylinder (1,232 cc) and six-cylinder (1,991 cc) Gloria Southern Cross sports cars but there was one Triumph for which he will always be remembered. This was the remarkable, near-mythical, Dolomite Straight-Eight.

This car deserves study for the number of ground rules it broke: it was extremely expensive, at a time when such cars were simply not selling, it was mechanically complex, when Triumph were not used to building such cars, it was an out-and-out competition sports car, which could only be expected to sell in penny numbers and finally it was almost a straight copy in many ways of an Italian Alfa Romeo!

*Blue Hills Mine on the Land's End Trial, with John Ferguson's Triumph Gloria Southern Cross scrabbling for grip around the right-hand hairpin* (Autocar).

Lord Howe, the aristocratic racing motorist, had been trying to interest British industry in this sort of car for years – in fact ever since the withdrawal and collapse of Bentley in 1931. Although he personally had no success, his lobbying must have influenced Lieutenant Colonel Claude Holbrook of Triumph to set Donald Healey to designing one. With very little cash and in a great hurry, Healey was not able to design from scratch, so he obtained Alfa Romeo's blessing to making a copy of their obsolete 8C-2300 engine (their chief engineer, Vittorio Jano, was already losing interest in it, in favour of V12s for Nuvolari to race). The Hon Brian Lewis's racing Monza Alfa was purchased (using Tommy Wisdom as an intermediary), the engine stripped and then copied, line for line and bolt for bolt, for Triumph's own use. A well-authenticated Coventry legend has it that there were certain bosses and protruberances on Dolomite engines quite unused – they were unused on the Alfa engine – which Triumph included in the design in case a need was discovered in future use. The only real difference between the two was the carburettor installation and the fact that the Triumph was reduced to 1,990 cc with a competition class in mind.

It was a fascinating project, with a most attractive Triumph-styled two-seater body. If you think there is a passing resemblance to the Riley MPH, you may be right; Donald Healey had much to do with the birth of the MPH when he was with Riley. (Both were inspired by the 1930 Zagato Alfa). In conjunction with its Wilson pre-selector gearbox the magnificent engine should have propelled the car at unheard-of speeds, but Triumph's money ran out and the project was killed off after three prototypes had been built. Healey wrote one off under the wheels of a train in Denmark in the 1935 Monte Carlo Rally, finished eighth in another one (unsupercharged) in 1936, then sold off the surviving bits and pieces to Tony Rolt.

The other well-known Coventry sports car, whose makers never looked likely to run out of money, was the SS90/SS100 series. These, like William Lyon's saloons, were fast, wickedly attractive and gave remarkably good value for money. No one else could match the combination of £445 cost, 3½-litre engine and nearly a 100 mph top speed – very few cars, after all, could reach 100 mph for *any* price. In Britain only the most powerful Lagondas and Alvises were ever timed at such speeds and both were much more expensive. Lyons always professed not to be very interested in sports cars or competitions at that time, and indeed these sports cars had chassis which were no more than cut-and-shut versions of earlier SS1 touring car designs.

The 3½-litre engine, with a Weslake-inspired cylinder head and breathing arrangements, produced more than 120 bhp and since the unladen weight was less than 25 cwt a remarkable performance was assured. Only about 300 were made and in retrospect one can see certain deficiencies in handling and stability, but this has not affected the car's curiosity value. SS100s tuned by Walter Hassan went extremely rapidly at Brooklands and elsewhere and a little-used car was good enough to take Ian Appleyard to the first of his five *Coupés des Alpes* in post-war Alpine Rallies (in 1948).

So far, I have made little mention of Bentley. At the beginning of the 1930s Bentley was *the* British sports car, with a reputation sealed by a series of great victories at Le Mans and Brooklands. But the factory closed its racing department in 1930 and sank into bankruptcy in 1931. The 4½-litre 'Blowers' and the Speed Six machines were designs of the past and the Le Mans results of 1930 and 1931 bear this out. In 1930 the strong locomotive-like British Speed Six won the event at 75.87 mph, but in 1931 the small, slim, spritely 2.3-litre Alfa Romeo 8C-2300 won at 78.12 mph, driven by Lord Howe and Sir Henry 'Tim' Birkin.

Bentley, sunk at the end of 1931, was refloated in 1933 as the 'Silent Sports Car' from Rolls-Royce and actually was nothing of the sort. Invicta, who made big sports cars with

4½-litre engines and reputedly perilous handling, would have loved to fill the gap in the market, but it was Lagonda, so similar to Bentley in some ways apart from using a proprietary Meadows engine, who took up Bentley's mantle of 'big sports car' manufacture.

An Invicta, much modified and very bravely driven by Donald Healey, was good enough to win the 1931 Monte Carlo Rally, even though 'Sammy' Davis was seriously injured in one unexplained accident at Brooklands the same year. Invicta also tried to sell smaller-engine cars, but by comparison with the 4½-litre model these were gutless and unsuccessful. Invicta, like some other small firms, was always under-financed and under-developed, moved out of Cobham (in favour of Railton) in 1933.

Lagondas, built in Staines only a few miles from the Invicta factory at Cobham, were also built by an under-capitalised concern which somehow survived the Depression, but needed more money and a change of ownership in 1935. In the early days there were cars between 2-litres and 4½-litres, one supercharged and one (the 'Selector') with Maybach transmission, along with the tiny twin-cam 1.1-litre Rapier. The Rapier sold reasonably well (as it should have, at £270 chassis price) but was eventually hived off to a separate company in London.

The bigger six-cylinder cars were expensive and fast, as Bentleys had been, even though they did not have quite the same social cachet. The 'Selector' model gained some notoriety in 1932, as gear change arrangements were complex, such that the eight forward gears were also matched by a disconcerting number of reverse ratios! One well-known tester decided to try this feature to the full, accelerating smartly backwards along the Brooklands finishing straight, until at about 40 mph there were loud and complaining noises from the transmission. 'Lagonda', he said, 'were really very nice about it!' The car, at least, would not have to be towed many miles back to the factory.

The big Meadows-engined 4½-litre car was made famous, and rightly so, by its unexpected victory at Le Mans in 1935 while the Lagonda company was actually in the hands of a receiver. Its winning speed, 77.85 mph, was just a couple of mph quicker than Barnato's Speed Six Bentley had achieved in 1930. This Le Mans victory was one important factor in persuading W. O. Bentley to join Alan Good's revived concern. His first job was to refine the existing 4½-litre model (which was achieved in an astonishingly short time – Bentley joined Lagonda in mid-summer and the improved model was shown at Olympia in October), but it was not for this purpose that he had been hired. A year later, and with a new team of engineers around him (some 'poached' from Rolls-Royce), the fruits of these labours were revealed – well before actual deliveries could commence – a brand new chassis, more refined than before and a magnificent new V12 4,480 cc engine to match it.

This was arguably the finest British engine so far built and was more efficient and more advanced than Rolls-Royce's own V12 design, which was, after all, looking to refinement rather than power output and was based largely on existing dimensions and engineering. The Lagonda engine, however, mainly designed for W. O. Bentley by Tresilian and his team, lacked torque at low speeds, which was strange when its undersquare (75 x 84.5 mm) cylinder dimensions and its overhead cam cylinder head layout is considered. No one, however, could argue with the top end power, which was quoted as no less than 180 bhp at 5,500 rpm. This was enough to propel even a two-ton saloon car to a 100 mph maximum speed. Not many people could afford such glorious cars. Saloons cost £1,600 (as much as a Rolls-Royce Wraith, no less), though the sports cars were somewhat cheaper. Lagonda built a couple of special Le Mans cars in 1939 (with 220 bhp engines) which took third and fourth places when running to a strict schedule. Without the intervention of the war the cars might have been further developed, but the engine jigs were subsequently destroyed and the entire project died.

*Definitely one of Britain's fastest and finest Grand Tourers – the 4.3-litre Alvis in short-chassis form with a Vanden Plas four-seater touring body. This was the last and greatest of the six-cylinder Alvises, first produced in 1936* (National Motor Museum).

The old Meadows 4½-litre engine was offered throughout, finally being offered in the latest V12 chassis as the LG6 model. There was no getting away from its agricultural tendencies, but it still made a 90-plus maximum speed possible and the car was more than £400 cheaper.

Alvis was another Coventry concern which shook off the effects of the Depression and continued to make faster, smarter and ever more sporting cars until 1939, losing much of their original 'vintage' reputation on the way, for although Captain Smith-Clarke was still keen on motor sport and its prestige, his refined saloons sold even better. Descendants of the much-loved 12/50 were still being made in 1930, but by the middle years these had given way to a series of fast and elegant six-cylinder models. The family was based on a 100 mm stroke engine at first, in 2.1-litre and 2.5-litre versions, but by 1935 the stroke had been lengthened to 110 mm and there were 2.3, 2.75 and 3.6-litre engines. As a final gesture, with an eye on the very high-speed Lagonda and imported-car market, in 1936 Alvis produced the 92 mm bore 4,387 cc engine, which boasted 123 bhp at a leisurely 3,600 rpm. This was possibly the most powerful British 'six' of the period and in touring form an Alvis could reach 100 mph. Race-tuned Brooklands specials put up most creditable performances.

So far I have only considered the production-line sporting machines, but in Britain in the 1930s there was a group of out-and-out sports car makers who looked on any order for six or more cars as a bonanza, and to whom a weekly output of two cars was quite something. There were HRGs (Meadows and Singer engines, made at Tolworth, Surrey), Frazer Nashes (various engines, made in Isleworth, Middlesex), Atalantas (Gough engines, made at Staines), Altas (with their own engines), Aston Martins (own engines, made at Feltham) and less successful-firms like Marendaz, British Salmson and Squire.

Perhaps the saddest demise of all came in Barlby Road, West London – to Georges Roesch's Talbot concern. Every 1930s Roesch Talbot was powered by one or other of the same six-cylinder engine family, painstakingly and progressively developed by Roesch, finally being enlarged to its 3,377 cc '110' form for 1935. Only a pushrod overhead valve design (at a time when the pundits were clamouring for overhead cam layouts), these Talbots were nevertheless light, efficient and very powerful.

Teams of 90s and 105s performed with great speed and reliability all over Europe and there was one particularly stirring show in a French Alpine trial, but all this came to nothing in January 1935 when Roesch found to his horror that the company had been taken over by the Rootes Group. Rootes had been debenture holders in the Sunbeam-Talbot-Darracq combine and, when that concern defaulted on its loans, Rootes were happy to step in with a rescue.

From then on, rationalisation with Rootes was rapid. The first new model, called a

Talbot Ten, was little more than a modified Hillman Aero Minx with Roesch improvements to engine and styling. The takeover came at a time when Roesch's cars were reaching for new pinnacles of performance, refinement and competition success, and his experiences under Rootes' management broke his spirit. He finally resigned in 1938, when the launch of completely Rootes-style Sunbeam-Talbot models was in progress.

Roesch, however, was always happy to prove the wisdom of his designs and was delighted to see the continued improvement of one famous Talbot (BGH23 – driven by Mike Couper of St Albans), which finally lapped Brooklands at nearly 130 mph. This car was one of the team which had originally performed so well in the 1934 Alpine Trial. But fame is ephemeral; soon after its last Brooklands performance, and with war clouds gathering, Couper offered BGH23 for sale, at a miserable £235.

This car was no more famous than the racing 105s which raced in the early 1930s and whose best performances at Le Mans were third over all in 1931 and 1932. We must never forget, too, that a pair of 90s took third and fourth places at Le Mans in 1930, behind the two victorious Speed Six Bentleys. Several of the most famous cars are now owned by Cornishman Anthony Blight and are regularly seen at vintage race meetings.

Finally, but not because they were of the least importance, I turn to the numerous breed of hybrids known unkindly as 'Anglo-American Sports Bastards'. This phrase was rather unkindly coined to categorise the species of low-production sports car or tourer with American-designed engines, sometimes with American chassis, but with British coachwork and final assembly in this country. It always infuriated the purists that cars built in this way were often very fast and often much cheaper than all-British machines of similar performance. The purists did not approve of (or was it that they did not understand?) the vast engines, softly tuned and almost completely under-stressed and they did not approve of the noise (or lack of it) these cars made.

There were several – the most famous being the Railton, built in the old Invicta factory

*The man and the cars which so nearly took over from Bentley at Le Mans. Georges Roesch is between the two 1931 Le Mans Talbots and their drivers (left to right) are Hindmarsh, Rose-Richards, Eaton and the Hon Brian Lewis* (Anthony Blight)

**Background photograph** *There was still a spirit of chivalry among the sportsmen. When Ian Connell (who owned a 4-litre Darracq) thought that Hugh Hunter's 2.9-litre Alfa Romeo was not the fastest road car in Britain, he challenged him to a race to settle the matter. The 1939 Brooklands 'Invitation Road Race Car' proved that on the day Count Heyden's Delahaye was better than either. Here the cars swing onto the Brooklands circuit in the 'Mountain Circuit' section of the challenge (Autocar).*

**Inset** *A famous and controversial picture! H. S. Linfield of* The Autocar *jumping the incredible Railton Light Sports over the crest of the Brooklands test hill. This car could beat 100 mph and it really did jump so high, though the author now admits he must have been mad to smoke a pipe at the time. The performance secret was a light chassis and a powerful straight-eight Hudson engine (Autocar).*

in greater numbers than that distinguished car and with considerably more financial success. Most Jensens used British-Built Ford V8 engines, but there were a few Nash-engined cars. There were Allards, Brough Superiors (they also built the 'Rolls-Royce of Motor Cycles' – remember?) and a few Atlanta V12s, but the Railtons were the most numerous.

Named after the noted chief engineer from Thomson and Taylor's famous business at Brooklands (who numbered among his successes the later Campbell 'Bluebird' record cars, both of John Cobb's Napier-engined Railtons, the Brooklands Rileys and the original chassis work on the ERA), the Railton production car was certainly not to be grouped at that exalted level. Although Railton was certainly the design consultant and presumably benefited financially from the use of his name on the car, he was not able to get much thoroughbred engineering into the car. Engines were all unmodified straight-eight side-valve Terraplanes or Hudsons from North America and the same firm's rather flimsy three-speed gearbox was thought to be good enough; this was perhaps acceptable only because the engines had such stupendous low-speed torque delivery, but anyone who used his gears hard and often on a Railton did so with his wallet much in mind.

Railtons came in many guises – saloons, tourers, coupés and the occasional sports car – with nicely elegant model names like Cobham and Fairmile, both of which were localities very close to the factory itself. Railtons were always fast, but one of them – the very rare 'Light Sports' – was almost shatteringly so. In acceleration up 60 or 70 mph, no other car sold in Britain could touch it and that includes any of the exotic and expensive machines imported from Europe.

Looking almost too similar to an Invicta – the pedigree was obvious – and with very skimpy coachwork, the road test car lent out by the company was reputed to reach 107 mph on occasion (though *The Autocar*, who were commendably accurate in their findings, were happy to note a mere 98.9 mph, with a one-way best of 102 mph) and it leapt so far

**Below left** *One sure way to get up steep trials hills was to have lots of power. This was F. D. Gilson's Allard Special of 1937 (the very first 'production' example) storming over the humps on Nailsworth Ladder* (National Motor Museum).

**Below right** *Jensen started very slowly in the 1930s, making only a handful of stylishly-built cars which had Ford V8, or American-made, engines. This was their Earls Court motor show stand – with a Nash-engined car in the foreground and Ford-engined cars behind* (National Motor Museum).

*Fiat's cheeky little Balilla sports car was as advanced as any British model in its class, but very few were sold here. Imported cars held a very small market share in the 1930s* (Autocar).

off the ground at the top of the Brooklands Test Hill that readers thought that a published photograph was a hoax. As the driver's hair was well plastered down and he was sucking a pipe one could not blame them, but he subsequently admitted to a lot of grease and thoughtlessness respectively! Whatever the critics might have said, there was no other production car sold here which could beat the Railton's performance and at £878 it was remarkably good value. Good value, that is, except for the high Treasury Rating tax, which had to be paid to enjoy American-engined motoring. The Light Sports, indeed, cost £29 a year before the 1935 reductions and would have been no less than £36 if peace-time motoring had carried on into 1940.

American-engined cars were fun in themselves, but were important as a portent of what might follow in the future. They might have been scorned at times in the 1930s, but who, now, would look askance at a Jensen, Bristol, AC, de Tomaso and Facel Vega built in modern times? It was interesting that the Americans exported their products and their expertise to use in the 1930s, while from 1945 onwards it was our turn to send vehicles the other way. For even by 1939, pure sports cars were beginning to look like an irrelevance, especially as coupés and sports saloons were already a pleasure to own. After 1945 the trends intensified and British sports cars could only survive in production by courtesy of huge export sales.

From Europe, from time to time, tiny numbers of sports cars were imported, but apart from machines like the Balilla Fiats they were exclusive models from Alfa-Romeo, Bugatti, Lancia and Mercedes-Benz, usually intended for competition and often the preserve of the wealthy. Even so, most people who were able to choose how they wanted to motor did it in style and elegance – in a British quality car. If we have to admit that many of Britain's ordinary cars from these years will be forgotten, we can be sure that two categories will survive – the sports cars and those built for the carriage trade.

# Chapter 6

# Cars for the wealthy

In the 1930s there were very few instances of inverted snobbery. If a motorist was well-heeled enough to afford an expensive car, he usually bought one. It was more than likely that he still employed a chauffeur to drive him – at least on business or formal occasions. In the egalitarian 1970s it might be all very well for the Queen's cousin to be seen belting around on a powerful motor-cycle, or for well-known film actresses to drive round in suitably custom-built Minis; forty years ago this simply did not happen.

When Jack Buchanan was at the height of his fame as a musical comedy star, he naturally celebrated by buying the first of the very rare 8-litre Bentleys. The King was loyal to his Daimlers – vast, sedate and always trailing that slight but definite smoke screen behind them, which was a trade mark of the sleeve-valve engine. Top-hatted buinessmen (they really did dress like that, every day) would not be seen dead in the city without their Rolls-Royces. For that matter, they were probably planning on being seen dead in one too – for the Rolls-Royce was just as necessary to a funeral then as it was later. The bank manager or solicitor might find an Armstrong Siddeley quite acceptable, though the nobility and the tycoons were not likely to slum it so far down the social scale. The motoring scene was so ordered, so predictable, that when the Prince of Wales first took delivery of an ugly and new-fangled Burney Streamline and, a few years later, followed it by a Buick, the establishment was shocked to the core.

*Even in times of economic depression, there was no shortage of eccentricities. This was Sir Denniston Burney's rear-engined Burney Streamline, in which the 8-cylinder engine lived behind the rear wheels and the spare wheel was stowed in one of the rear doors. The Prince of Wales bought one, but few other customers supported his gesture. The car was first launched in 1930* (Autocar).

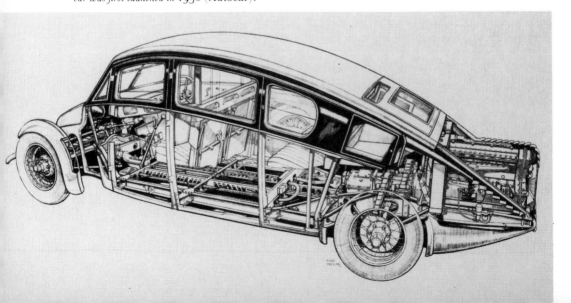

We do not need to define the wealthy, except to point out that in those days there seemed to be be rather more of them around than exist today. Income tax and surtax did not bite nearly as hard as it does now – the House of Lords would never have approved a 98 per cent tax on investment income, neither would the House of Commons ever have proposed it. Death duties had not then struck so deep at the heart of the aristocracy and the land-owners and the top social and financial strata were still noticeably well off in every way. This is no place to comment on the situation – I must merely set the scene.

Even so, the market for the really plushy and expensive car was still very limited. No matter how many people were supposed to have *disposable* incomes of more than £5,000 a year (that would be equivalent to about £60,000 – £80,000 a year in late-1970s terms) they did not rush out and buy a vast new car every year, partly because there was always the tiresome problem of getting rid of the old one and due to the gratifying fact that the 'old' quality car was neither wearing out quickly, nor becoming out of date.

By using the RAC Treasury rating of horsepower as a guide, we might arbitrarily decide to set the lower limit of carriage-trade motoring at 30 hp, but even this would rule out the smaller (20/25 hp) Rolls-Royce, several Daimlers and at least one hopefully upper-class Armstrong Siddeley. Sales figures varied somewhat from year to year, but to get the very worst case we must look at the gloom of 1931, when many a tycoon faced with busi-ness crises put off spending his capital on a new car. In that year, which was something of a disaster for the luxury-car trade (Bentley closed down, Lanchester was taken over and Napier decided not to re-enter the market), only 1,536 cars of 30 hp or more were sold in all. This miserable home-market total had to be shared between 34 car makers, British and foreign.

On the assumption that no real plutocrat could really get by without a 40 hp car at least, we find that only 451 cars were delivered, of which 204 were '44s' which would nearly all be Rolls-Royce Phantoms. When these figures are compared with more than 130,000 cars registered in a depressed British market between November 1930 and October 1931, the limited scope for luxury builders is obvious. Official figures, incidentally, peaked out at the majestic figure of 58 hp, where nine cars were registered – Hispano-Suizas, probably a V16 Cadillac and maybe one Maybach-Zeppelin.

*The bulldog is British, but the Isotta-Fraschini 8ASS is Italian. This splendid sports car was virtually unknown in Britain and Touring of Milan had produced remarkably modern lines for 1931, when it won the Villa d'Este concours* (Autocar).

*An elegant Royal Daimler – a brand-new V12 engined 'Double Six' with Hooper coachwork and that distinctive high roofline – as delivered to the Royal household in 1935 in time for the Silver Jubilee celebrations. This picture was taken in the Royal Mews at Buckingham palace* (Autocar).

Of course, we know that all these famous high-priced cars were being hand-built with great care – in a process which took months to complete. With these registration figures in mind, one might comment that there was really no need for more streamlined methods to be adopted, nor for the cars to be erected in more haste, as the supply and demand situation was nicely in balance. An idea of the way in which the world-wide trade depression and the lack of confidence in spending one's money had affected the carriage trade is that two years earlier – in 1929 – the '30 hp and over' British market was for 2,398 cars, 479 being 40 hp and above.

But what sort of car did the truely wealthy buy? For the moment we can ignore the *nouveau riche* (for they existed, then as now) and the sportsmen who wanted the ultimate in high performance, and we can concentrate on the demand for gracious living, elegance of structure and decoration, fine craftsmanship and the use of the very best materials. Throughout the decade there was little change in the line-up of car makers willing and eager to supply the best of bespoke machinery to the aristocracy and the gentry.

Rolls-Royce, need it be said, held the upper hand at all times, combining an unchallenged edge in prestige with occasional leaps into the vanguard of technical achievement. Daimler, of Coventry, were always recognised as their well-respected rivals (especially because of Royal patronage) and from 1931 they also owned Lanchester. There had been some impressive Lanchesters built by the independent Birmingham-based concern, but financial collapse followed by the Daimler takeover led to the most depressing changes in their model range. By 1936 a Lanchester was nothing more than a smaller, bargain-basement Daimler, with less prestige; worse, there were even cheap Lanchesters strongly related to BSAs of the period.

In 1930 and 1931 Bentley made 100 really outstanding 8-litre cars to back their fast and sporting 6½-litre models before the Depression caught up with them – whereupon Rolls-Royce bought up the ruined company in a sordid court-room auction (their nominees outbid Napier by a mere £20,000 for the assets and trade marks) and effectively killed off

*An exciting, but unsuccessful, car was the American Cord Type 812 model. The car could be bought with or without supercharging and had a complex but effective front-wheel drive layout. The styling was very 'way out' for the period; this is a 1937 Cord Beverley* (National Motor Museum).

their greatest competition. W. O. Bentley was bound to work for Rolls-Royce for a time, but it is entirely appropriate that he later moved on to Lagonda, where his final efforts with a V12 engine could usually rival anything produced at Derby. Bentley was re-born in 1933, a car which was nothing more than a sporting Rolls-Royce – and very nice too, even if every Cricklewood tradition had ruthlessly been expunged.

From abroad there was usually a huge choice of large (always), fast (often) but rarely attractive products. Often there were American cars – usually with the dreadful styling excesses which characterise anything which left Detroit from 1934, in the days of the New Deal – which dominated the price lists in numbers if not in quality. The only worthwhile competition to British cars – worthwhile, that is, in terms of quality and fine engineering – came from France, Italy and Spain. A handful of Hispano-Suizas and Isotta Fraschinis were all that could compete, though Mercedes-Benz did their Grosser (literally) best to keep up. Most experts agreed that a Hispano-Suiza was something special in its engineering, but they also agreed that no one in the world could build a luxury car better than the British. Tradition, it seems, in centuries of the building of fine carriages, counted for a lot. In detailed craftsmanship, styling and in restrained elegance of lines, the British product always excelled.

The secret of this, of.course, lay in the coachbuilding industry, a branch of the British motoring scene which has now almost disappeared. Companies like H. J. Mulliner, Hooper and Freestone & Webb had been established for many years. At first they had built fine coachwork to grace the horse-drawn carriages which took the nobility from their country estates to their town houses. It was natural that when this nobility turned to the new-fangled motor car, the tradition of having coachwork erected by the people they could trust should persist. All early cars had coachbuilt bodies (even if their weather protection at times left much to be desired), which partly explains the high costs and naturally explains the very obvious visual link between Victorian carriages and early limousines.

While it is easy to talk glibly about the expertise of Rolls-Royce in building the best cars

*By the mid-1930s the Bentleys built by Rolls-Royce had gained a splendid reputation. Their advertising slogan –
'The Silent Sports Car' – was only slightly over-stated, as they could reach more than 90 mph in great comfort
and refinement. This is a 1936 model with the latest 4½-litre engine and Gurney Nutting coachwork, and is parked
outside H. R. Owen's main London showroom* (National Motor Museum).

in the world, we often forget the fact that up to the outbreak of the Second World War
Rolls-Royce never built a complete car at all. The excellence and unique performance of a
Rolls-Royce motor car was all confined to the rolling chassis supplied from Derby; the
rest was up to the individual (approved) coachbuilder. Although Daimler and Lanchester
at first relied to some extent on bodies built in their own factories, later they shipped out
all their rolling chassis for the attention of the coachbuilders. Really small-production
concerns could not have survived without them.

Consider, then, the pleasurable process by which a wealthy man – be he tycoon or
land-owner, young or old – set about choosing his new car. He would have little mechanical
knowledge himself and to a great extent would rely on his chauffeur's advice, especially
regarding the reliability record of his existing car. His chauffeur would possibly be asked
to study all the latest designs and would then be asked for his comments. Though there was
little choice of British manufacturers (and after all, no true gentleman would consider
buying an imported car) there was a big array of alternative engines, chassis lengths and
coachwork styles. A leisurely but purposeful visit to the annual Olympia motor show
would follow, where the chassis could be chosen first and the coachbuilder consulted
afterwards.

Chassis were fairly immutable objects (at the time there would be no automatic transmission, power steering or air-conditioning options to be considered) but there were several
requirements which might affect the choice of engines or wheelbase lengths. Clearly,
someone wanting a formal limousine with a division would be likely to choose the longest
wheelbase and the most powerful engine, while a sports saloon or convertible might demand the same engine in a short chassis. A dowager, or a more sedate land-owner, might
place elegance before performance and choose a less powerful engine in the long chassis . . .
the possibilities, if not endless, would all have to be considered. Tax rating differences
between engines was rarely a factor (who was it who first said: 'If you have to ask the
price you can't afford it'?) even though the rest of us had to worry about annual licensing
costs at the rate of £1 per horsepower.

With mechanical details settled, an order would speedily be placed and a round of
coachbuilders started. This was where the mistakes could be made, for among the legions

*Elegant, exclusive and very costly – a Phantom III Rolls-Royce (with V12 engine and independent front suspension hidden under the skin) with Barker coachwork, built in 1936 and originally supplied to Mr. E. Bowater (of the paper-manufacturing family)* (National Motor Museum).

of constructors there were the excellent, the merely competent and the frankly indifferent. Fortunately, Rolls-Royce and Daimler were always happy to let their preferences be discreetly known and in most cases a mention of Barker, Freestone & Webb, Hooper, H. J. Mulliner, Park Ward, Rippon, James Young or Gurney Nutting would be made. These, though certainly the cream of the profession, were neither in a majority, nor did they build the most bodies in the 1930s. *The Autocar's* show number of 1935, for instance, listed 42 coachbuilding concerns exhibiting at Olympia, which was one of the largest attendances of the decade.

Commissioning a new body from a well-known coachbuilder involved a well-established ritual. The customer would first discuss his needs with the directors and designers, and sketches according to these comments would eventually be produced. Further meetings would then be necessary for a final style to be produced, for details to be refined and perhaps for a study of other bodies already going through the workshops to be made. No coachbuilder worth his pedigree would dare to admit to a desire for standardisation, but before the end of the 1930s a styling expert could pick out many structural similarities under the skin of supposedly different and unique styles. Nevertheless, there was no question of tooling fixtures being laid down for a run of identical shells – especially where Rolls-Royce models were concerned – and most of the work was completed by hand, where craftsmanship and years of skill counted more than the use of formers and standard profiles.

One consequence of this was that body styles were occasionally horrid and, at times, grotesque. Very occasionally a reputable coachbuilder would refuse a client's instructions, but more often than not his money spoke louder than the sensibilities could bear – even Hooper and Park Ward can recall the occasional 'lemon' – and Indian potentates seemed to excell in this sort of thing.

With a style agreed, work could begin at a certain pace, but would never be completed in a hurry. Even Royalty were accustomed to waiting months for their new cars, as the hand-building process could not be curtailed. Everything from the forming of wooden supports, to the individual construction of fittings, took much time and the actual erection of the body was a studied and careful business. It was quite normal for a body shell to take up to six months from agreed style to completion – at times, much more. One very good example comes from Bentley. Although the last splendid 8-litre chassis was built in the

**Left** *Even high quality coachbuilders could be persuaded (by money) to build monstrosities! This dreadful Siddeley Special was built for George Wansborough to use in the RAC Rally of 1934, with the coachwork/concours competition in mind. He was unsuccessful* (Autocar).

**Below right** *By the late 1930s Park Ward had progressed beyond the use of a hard wood framework for their coachbuilt bodies. This example is here seen being constructed on a strong but simple steel base* (Autocar).

summer of 1931, limousines gracing the design were still being delivered a year or more later. A mid-1932 8-litre Bentley, therefore, is not an anomaly, but merely an indication of the pace of the coachbuilding industry's operations.

The basis of all the best bodies, at first, was a wooden framework, of the highest quality; thoroughly seasoned ash was ideal for this purpose. This was glued, bolted and screwed carefully together before being clad in panel-beaten light-alloy sheet, or (as often as not) sheet steel. The whole was carefully matched to the complete rolling chassis, which arrived complete with radiator, scuttle and perhaps instrument panel already in place. Several road tests would then be needed for the body to be matched accurately to the none too rigid chassis. Buying a bespoke motor car was rather like buying a bespoke suit – indeed Savile Row and the top coachbuilders had much the same mission in life. Many delicate hours went into the suppression of rattles, squeaks and groans before the great day of delivery to the customer could be fixed.

Although most bodies were clad in steel or aluminium, there had been a short vogue for patented Weymann bodies, where the bodywork was specially built with metal pieces to keep the wooden skeleton members slightly apart (to eliminate the squeaks as they 'worked') and in which tightly stretched and specially treated fabric was used in place of a metal outer skin. Weymann bodies were practical when new and surprisingly refined as as well as light, but did not stand the test of time. An ageing Weymann shell, especially if originally made with less than loving care by a second division coachbuilder, was a tatty sight and did little to prolong the fashion.

During the decade there was little advance in constructional techniques, except that cast metal skeleton 'ribs' began to take the place of wooden ribs where standardisation had actually begun. Styling tended to advance in the mainstream of fashion, perhaps even slightly behind it, rather than by setting trends for the rest of the industry. The convertible, or coupé, which has virtually disappeared now, was a very popular variant, along with other derivatives which rejoiced in the names of Sedanca de Ville, Cabriolet and others. As the times became increasingly more democratic, limousines were later built with an eye to the owner-driver; one advantage of this was that the space allocated to the driver became more spacious and better equipped, whereas earlier cars very definitely imposed a military and erect driving position.

Minor fads ebbed and flowed. There was a time for separate trunks to be carried behind the bodies, which – in time – naturally progressed to become integral boot compartments. Spare wheels were often carried in ostentatious covers let into the flowing front wings and ahead of the windscreen; later thoughts on aerodynamics banished the spares to the rear, in the boot and occasionally behind obviously contoured recesses in the boot lid. Divisions became detachable, so that limousines could be chauffeur-driven or owner-driven. Externally, headlamps increased in size and culminated in those splendid Lucas P100 monsters which are now such prized collectors' items and running boards, though persistent, were eventually faired in to increasingly-smooth styles.

The majority of wealthy people looked no further than a Rolls-Royce for their motoring and Sir Henry Royce rewarded their loyalty by marketing cars which altered little from year to year. In ten years there were to be basically only two new 'big' models and only one new smaller car. When the Phantom III replaced the Phantom II in 1935, it was a very important event. Not only was there a new chassis with a brand-new V12 engine (which finally replaced the venerable 'six' which had steadily been developed from that of the original Ghost) but that chassis was also equipped with independent front suspension. Nothing so dramatic ever happened to the smaller design, except that it grew up from a 20/25 to 25/30 rating and finally to a Wraith (when independent front suspension like that of the Phantom III was finally adopted).

The Phantom II, or 40/50, of the early 1930s was the epitome of luxury motoring. In a word, it was 'Royce all over' and owed nothing to cost cutting or quantity-production techniques. Built with great care and in steady numbers (1,700 in six years) at Derby (where the aero-engine side of the company still survives), it had a massive 7.7-litre six-cylinder engine which was both powerful and enormously refined. Although a Phantom was not outstandingly fast (85 to 90 mph was the best to be expected, even with a relatively compact body) and certainly not very economical (less than 10 mpg was normal, but with petrol at such low prices not many owners noticed those costs), it was beautifully made. That famous 1960s slogan about 'the noisiest part of a Rolls-Royce at 60 mph is the ticking of the dashboard clock' might also be applied to the Phantom, even if tyres were a bit noisier then and sound-deadening to the interior was not as thoroughly understood.

With a chassis price which greeted the 1930s at £1,850 and which slipped down by a nominal £100 for 1932, it was definitely a car for the moneyed classes and no compromise was ever allowed to get in the way of this philosophy. Synchromesh gears were offered

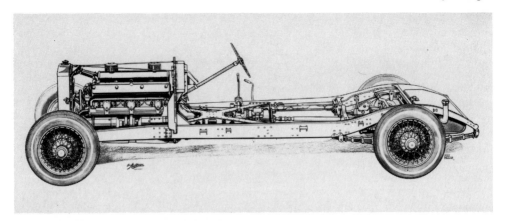

from late 1932 and adjustable shock absorbers during 1933. Yet the suspension was still crude, with simple half-elliptic leaf springs all round and a chassis which was still sufficiently whippy to allow considerable front wheel wobble to set in on certain roads. No matter what the press might say (and in those days the motoring press was a very bland and reassuring body of men) even an expensive car with a solid front axle could suffer alarming bouts at times.

Nowhere is this better illustrated than by W. O. Bentley in one of his own books, in an account of a testing run in one of the new Rolls-Royce designed Bentleys:

'One day some time in 1933 I was putting the $3\frac{1}{2}$-litre saloon through its paces, which meant treating the brakes unmercifully at corner after corner on my own special route to London. Unfortunately, someone had dropped a brick at the side of the road and on the apex of a rather nasty left-hand corner. I caught it with my nearside front wheel and was at once subjected to the most appalling axle tramp. This meant I had no steering at all. So I tried to use the brakes and found that I had none of those either, as they had faded quite away. With neither steering or brakes, I calmly awaited my fate, curious to learn what I was going to hit. My victim was a Wolseley Hornet, approaching innocently and on the correct side of the road . . . .'

The Phantom III, announced in the autumn of 1935, was a much more advanced car, whose V12 engine needed absolutely devoted care to ensure long life and good performance. Rolls-Royce were not anxious to admit that their new masterpiece was based on any other, though its bore and stroke efficiency made it a strong relative of the existing 25/30 and $3\frac{1}{2}$-litre Bentley units. Its V12 unit was unique in Britain at the time, though North American engines of this type were in production. W. O. Bentley, who must have known of the existence of the Phantom III project when he left Rolls-Royce to join Lagonda, capped it with his own V12 design a year later, but there was otherwise nothing remotely as complex built in Britain until the arrival of the Jaguar XJ12 unit of 1971. The independent front suspension was a great advance at a time when most of the British car makers were still firmly wedded to their beam front axles, but it must have been humiliating for Rolls-Royce to have to pay royalties to General Motors in Detroit because of certain features which were common.

By any standard, though, the Phantom III was a magnificent creation, of which Royce would have been proud if he had lived to see it launched. The company never felt it necessary to divulge the power output (one of the longest running of all Rolls-Royce anecdotes, after all, was: 'How much power does it produce?' . . . 'Sufficient'). Chassis price, as for the previous car in 1935, was £1,850 and even the most mundane coachwork would then lift the ensemble's price to more than £2,500. By the end of the decade it was quite possible to spend £3,000 on a complete Rolls-Royce, an astonishing price when we remember that this was, by today's standards, a 'basic' price without taxation. When looking at a 1939 Phantom we are considering the equivalent of today's very exclusive Phantom VI, except that in 1939 a totally individual body style could have been ordered to complete the machine.

Set against these staggering figures (staggering, too, because of the number of people who could still demonstrably afford to buy one) a complete price of around £1,550 for the less ostentatious smaller Rolls-Royce seems positively mundane. Indeed, the chassis price of the last of the 25/30 models was little more than £1,000 and even a completely equipped modern Wraith could be put on the road in 1939 for little more than £1,600. Even so, set against the background of rock-bottom motoring from Ford which started at £100, and good middle-price travel in a Rover for less than £300, it was still very high.

Rolls-Royce had already built an aura around themselves, which led to all manner of unlikely stories about reliability, unquestioned guarantee repairs, sealed engines and the like. The Rolls-buying classes knew better (especially those unfortunates whose chauffeurs did not treat the Phantom III with enough mechanical deference) but to the working classes the anecdote about the car which broke its axle in Spain, was repaired by Rolls-Royce mechanics in a couple of days and whose story was then met with blank disbelief at Derby, had already achieved the reputation of Holy Writ. A Rolls-Royce was reliable and it was beautifully made, but when it went wrong the repair costs were high and were exacted in a businesslike, if well-mannered, way.

Nowadays it is natural to link the name of Bentley with Rolls-Royce, though for a short time in the 1930s the two concerns were deadly rivals. A Bentley never had the tradition, nor quite the cachet of a Rolls-Royce, but once the Cricklewood marque had won its fifth Le Mans race and almost simultaneously introduced its magnificent 8-litre chassis, they closed the gap with an *éclat* which must have terrified the Derby concern. The 8-litre Bentley was splendidly engineered, technically as advanced as any existing Rolls-Royce, could propel even the most upright saloon coachwork at more than 100 mph (no pre-war

**Above left** *The Rolls-Royce Phantom III laid bare. The wheelbase was no less than 11 ft 10 in, and this was the first time that independent front suspension had been standardised on a Rolls-Royce* (Autocar).

**Right** *The patrician nose of an open 8-litre Bentley – W.O.'s greatest masterpiece from Cricklewood. There were no 'real' Bentleys built after 1931, those from Derby being no more than rather special Rolls-Royces* (National Motor Museum).

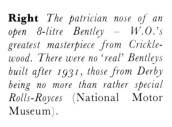

**Left** *The advertising – and the snobbery – of the period, made clear in this Bentley advertisement of 1935. 'The Silent Sports Car' was a very deft, and very apt, slogan by the crude standards of the day* (Autocar).

**Below** *Daimler traded for years on the cachet of Royal approval. Here is a 1936/1937 Straight Eight 4½-litre car with Hooper Landaulet body, with HM King George VI and Queen Elizabeth being driven through the gates of the Palace of Holyrood house after a state visit in Coronation year* (National Motor Museum).

**Below right** *Here is an excuse to show the later Bentley style according to Rolls-Royce and the type of razor-edge coachwork which was in vogue towards the end of the decade. The style was by Freestone & Webb* (Autocar).

Rolls-Royce of any type could ever match that) and was cheekily priced at £50 more than the Phantom II. Nothing else that Bentley were selling – particularly the sporting super-charged 4½-litre cars or the elephantine 4-litres – was in the·same class as a Rolls-Royce; even so the Derby firm were very relieved to see Bentley collapse into financial ruin in 1931.

Later, having absorbed Bentley and all the rights to its designer's talents, Rolls-Royce showed technical jealousy by ordering all 8-litre spares to be scrapped, allowed no more 'proper' Bentley cars to be made and set about designing their own new model. Less than two years later, at the end of 1933, the new 3½-litre car was announced. It was badged as a Bentley, was advertised as the 'Silent Sports Car' and became universally known as a Rolls-Bentley or a Derby Bentley. The new car was closely based on the engineering of the 20/25 model, taking over its 3,669 cc engine with some modifications, the synchromesh gearbox (no 'W. O.' Bentley ever had that feature) and a very similar chassis frame. Although the road behaviour was none too special, the performance was very good.

After a time the weight imposed on it by bigger, better-equipped and more formal bodies produced by the coachbuilders began to hamper the performance and from 1936 onwards the engine size was pushed up to 4¼-litres. Later, for 1939, came the 'overdrive' car which was nothing of the sort, but a name given to the car when fitted with an integral but geared-up top gear. By comparison with the Phantom III and the Wraith, a 1939 Bentley was beginning to looked dated, but the onset of war put a stop to developments which included special streamlined coachwork (the Corniche), independent front suspension and an uprated engine.

Physically the Bentley was slightly smaller than the Rolls-Royces, and the prices were in line with this. Chassis prices started at £1,100 and complete cars could be had for little more than £1,400. The 'Silent Sports Car' could always achieve more than 90 mph, though its performance did not actually improve as the years passed and although this was

quite noticeably down on the old-style Bentleys it was still very creditable by 1930s standards.

In direct competition to the cars from Derby, and in many ways in direct contrast, were the Daimlers from Coventry. Daimler, of course, had lengthy traditions, having evolved from the worst excesses of adventurer Harry Lawson's empire in the 1890s and since the Great War (latterly under the technical guidance of Laurence Pomeroy Senior) had become one of the world's finest, if staid, cars. If a Rolls-Royce was instantly recognisable by its Grecian radiator style, so was a Daimler by its fluted radiator, which had originally been added in the interests of cooling when such matters were little understood.

Even though they never openly boasted about it, Daimler had one great advantage over Rolls-Royce. Even though most people believed the Rolls-Royce to be the world's finest car, it was a fact that British Royalty and much of the allied nobility insisted on choosing Daimlers instead. It was a happy situation of which the Coventry company was justly proud – one which had many years of tradition and presumably, satisfactory experience behind it. There had been 'Royal Daimlers' since Edwardian times and they would continue to reign supreme until the 1940s.

Their reputation and dignity, were such that for the 1937 Coronation no fewer than 150 Daimlers were used (many hired) and an impressive press picture survives to show the Mall full of these cars, without a Rolls-Royce in sight. King George was very loyal to his Daimlers and in the depths of the 1931 Depression he commissioned Daimler (and Hoopers, who always built the Royal body shells) to build five new cars. This was not that he needed them, but so that it would give employment to craftsmen during the coming winter. Also, to avoid any criticism, he made sure that the cars were paid for out of his own private income.

Until the early 1930s Daimler made most of their own bodywork, in styles which were

*All the under-stated elegance of a Daimler straight-eight. This was a 1939 model, with coachwork by Vanden Plas of North London, photographed in the grounds of Chatsworth, Derbyshire (Brian Smith).*

*By the late 1930s, Lanchesters were really budget-priced Daimlers and appealed to the would-be car snobs. This was the 1937 Lanchester 14 and there was a very similar 'badge engineered' Daimler* (Autocar).

noted for being old-fashioned and distinguished, but comparatively ageless and restrained in every detail. But as far as mechanical engineering was concerned, Pomeroy was never loath to push innovations along. The famous Knight sleeve-valve engine design had been used by Daimler since 1909, but the formidable range of V12s – 'Double Sixes' – were Pomeroy's creations. These fearsome devices were for the well-heeled and no-one else; the biggest was a monster 7.1-litre '50 hp' unit, which did not survive for long in the 1930s, but there were three others, the smallest being a 3.7-litre. All these engines were bulky, complex, expensive to build and very heavy. All could be relied upon to drink petrol at a prodigious rate; not even a Phantom, it seems, could boast figures as poor as 5 mpg!

The biggest Daimlers were always marginally cheaper than the equivalent Rolls-Royces, probably because there was marginally less handwork in their construction and because factory overheads were lower due to the considerably higher sales from Coventry, which included a number of buses. For Daimler, in spite of their Royal patronage, were not nearly as exclusive. Not only did the factory at Radford, Coventry, build commercial vehicles (and very fine ones they were too) but the entire model range encompassed a wide span of prices. In addition to Daimlers there were Lanchesters (which were neo-Daimlers after 1932) and BSAs to be considered. Lanchesters became small Daimlers (often with an actual badge-engineered Daimler equivalent) built down to a price rather than up to a standard, while BSAs were even smaller, rather nastier and not at all desirable.

Daimler's policy in the 1930s was to spread its offerings over a wide price/engine size spectrum, which tended to detract from the sheer excellence of the flagships. As the years progressed they began to cater more and more for the middle classes. Whereas the smallest 1931 Daimler was a 16–20 of 2.6-litres and three of the six models had 12-cylinder Double Six engines, by the end of 1938 all the V12s had gone, the largest car was a 31.7 hp 4.6-litre Straight Eight costing upwards of £1,550 and there were Lanchesters down to a 1.4-litre 'Eleven'.

Sleeve valves disappeared in 1935 in favour of conventional overhead poppet valves and at the same time Pomeroy's new straight-eights replaced the V12s. Perhaps it is not quite fair to accuse Daimler of selling model cocktails, but look at this for confusion at the 1936 Olympia show: Daimler had six ranges from 2,166 cc to 6,511 cc (the very last of the Double Six models), while Lanchester had three from 1,444 cc to 2,565 cc. All but one used its own particular engine size, although chassis frames and basic body shells were ruthlessly permutated to keep up the interest.

*The Hon Cyril Siddeley in his Armstrong Siddeley during the 'slow-running test' which decided the 1932 RAC 'Torquay' rally. His car is creeping along at less than 1 mph!* (Autocar).

By the end of 1939, when the factories were turning over to making military vehicles, there had been a confusing number of Lanchesters, Daimlers, fours, sixes, eights and twelves all streaming out of the same doors; to cap it all and to satisfy the wishes of the Duke of York (who became King George VI) they even built large-engined Daimlers with Lanchester radiators and badges. Their greatest asset throughout the 1930s, of course, was the sweet and silky combination of the Wilson pre-selector gearbox with Daimler's own fluid flywheel. This was, without a doubt, the most advanced and easiest-to-drive transmission in the world until the first fully-automatic North American transmissions came along a few years later. These fluid-flywheel installations were standardised in 1932 and were features which Rolls-Royce were quite unable to match.

The other important Coventry 'thoroughbred', of course, was the Armstrong Siddeley, which was never wholeheartedly looking at the upper-crust market alone, but had its faithful adherents. Siddeleys were usually a lot cheaper than a similar type of Daimler – often by hundreds of pounds – and were often marketed with smaller engines. For all that, in terms of quality and of their general ambience they were usually a cut above the rest of the opposition. For some reason difficult to quantify a Siddeley became linked with the military, or – more correctly – with the *retired* officer classes.

Like Daimler, Armstrong Siddeley usually marketed something in the 'bargain basement' category, selling for about £300 and offering very little in the way of performance, but at the other end of their range there was usually a 'Thirty' – a 30 hp model – or, later, a Siddeley Special, to attract the carriage trade. Armstrong Siddeley styling seemed to change very little and only gradually, throughout the decade, except by embracing a general softening of lines and by 1939 the cars were still noticeably staid-looking and upright. Under the skin, however, there was some fine engineering (the hiduminiumalloy 'Special' engine was an engineering masterpiece and the company was, after all, the first to use the Wilson epicyclic gearbox) and lightweight cars in touring form could still pick up their skirts very smartly, as Alpine Trial results proved.

Armstrong Siddeley liked to push their associations with the aircraft industry, which was fair and reasonable, as the cars were erected in workshops next to those involved in the machining and assembly of fine aero engines. They liked, without actually saying so, to give the impression that all the cars were built to similarly high quality standards. They were unashamedly snobbish in their advertising outlook – their 1934 appeal to 'the daughters of gentlemen' has become a motoring legend.

Other British manufacturers had ambitions to join the élite, but none quite made it. Alvis, Lagonda, Sunbeam and Talbot were all in the running, one way of another, but the war nipped Alvis's intentions when their splendid engine and chassis was coming to maturity and the dead hand of Rootes killed off anything which Talbot might have achieved. Only Lagonda, in the last few years, could produce fine engineering, good styling and high performance, but it needed Alan Good (as the new owner) and W. O. Bentley (as the technical chief) to turn a rickety image into something approaching respectibility.

The delights of the V12 and the supersporting machines which it powered, have already been mentioned. By 1939 there were V12s in tourers and saloons (the latter with Lagonda-built coachwork), most of which guaranteed 100 mph top speeds and provided great comfort and independent front suspension into the bargain. Anything up to a formal 7-seat limousine could be supplied and prices varied between £1,550 and £1,850. The war certainly killed off the V12 when its career was young and its reputation was still being made.

One of the most intriguing failures was the straight-eight Sunbeam of 1936 and to understand its engineering we must hark back momentarily to the splendid series of six-cylinder cars produced at Talbot by Georges Roesch and his team. Sunbeam and Talbot (of Wolverhampton and West London respectively) had been taken over (or overtaken?) by Rootes in 1935 following financial troubles in the Sunbeam-Talbot-Darracq combine.

Although Rootes were not really interested in preserving the Talbot traditions (cars built at Barlby Road became progressively more Rootes-modified as the months progressed and eventually were phased out altogether) they were very interested in breaking

*An artist's impression, perhaps a little stretched, but 1930s limousines were usually as nicely trimmed and well-equipped as this. The car was a 20 hp Armstrong Siddeley (Armstrong Siddeley).*

into the real upper class market. Georges Roesch would no doubt have told them that with his existing 110 model and with his plans for that model's refinement, they were in it already, but the Rootes brothers were more interested in producing a prestigious new model. Thereupon they set Roesch to designing the finest and fastest new engine possible – reputedly with an eye to future Royal patronage and to cock a snook at Daimler, Bentley and Rolls-Royce.

Rootes gave Roesch little time to achieve this miracle, which they wanted to be on show at the 1936 Olympia Motor Show. The design was not even sketched out before the summer of 1935, but by using every ounce of his Talbot experience Roesch was able to complete the prototypes in time. The engine was a straight-eight design and a miracle of compactness; even though the car was to be badged as a 'Sunbeam', the engine was in every way a Talbot and used some existing engine components. It also followed the William Lyons dictum – that a powerful engine should also look sleek and purposeful – by having ribbed rocker covers and by having a full-length inlet manifold with a downdraught carburettor at each end. It looked strange and unlikely to be effective, but no one underestimated Roesch's ability to make it work beautifully.

This superb unit displaced 4.5-litres and was rated at 31.4 hp. The chassis, which was no more and no less than the latest Humber Snipe design with independent front suspension, also had a Humber gearbox and transmission and was offered in 10 ft 4 in or 11 ft 4 in wheelbase form – which was ample for the biggest and most spacious of limousine bodies. Several complete cars were displayed at the Show – including Mulliner and Thrupp & Maberly coachbuilt examples – at truly grand prices of around £1,300.

Then, following the original release and predictable paeans of praise from the press – nothing. The car never appeared again, it was never really mentioned again and it certainly never went into production. No one knows what persuaded Rootes to drop such a promising newcomer, unless it was considerations of hard cash, just at a time when the carriage trade was becoming bored with their perennial Rolls-Royce and Daimler offerings. But is it a complete coincidence that the Sunbeam was revealed when Edward VIII was on the British throne and dropped when he had abdicated? Rumours suggest that this was the Royal patronage the Rootes family were aiming for and that they knew that King George VI would remain faithful to his family's Daimlers.

Continental opposition to the British-made carriages for the upper classes and the wealthy was slight. Certainly there were cars which were large enough, fast enough and even grand enough, but few had the panache and social standing to make them acceptable. Of course there were Hispano-Suizas, about which no one could complain, but by the end of the decade production had virtually stopped and the cars were no longer imported to

_Cars for the wealthy_

**Below left** _Probably the most exclusive 'super car' of all time was the misnamed Bugatti Royale. It was originally announced with great pomp in 1926 and this Park Ward limousine version was built in 1933 for Captain Cuthbert Foster. Only six cars were ever built and only three were actually sold by Bugatti, none to customers from any of Europe's royal families. The engine size was 12.7 litres and the wheelbase 14 ft 2 in_ (Autocar).

**Right** _The only real opposition to Rolls-Royce in the 1930s came from Hispano-Suiza. Here is a head-on view of the magnificent 1934 V12 54 cv saloon, thought by many to be the finest car in the world_ (National Motor Museum).

Great Britain. In 1931, however, there is little doubt that the new V12 Type 68 Hispano-Suiza was on a par with the very best of Rolls-Royce products – and considerably quicker. Marc Birkigt had no qualms about asking a huge price for this 9.4-litre monster, and its 'square' cylinder dimensions ensured that the British rated it at a staggering 74.4 hp! Even by comparison with the Phantom II the Type 68 was a status symbol to cap all others. Its chassis price in 1931 was a lordly £2,500, which rose to £2,750 by 1934 and a complete car could easily cost £3,500. The addition of an annual tax impost of £75 (not much less than the cost of a complete Ford Eight car!) must have been the final straw to those attracted by its imposing lines, for a mere handful were sold here. The Bugatti Royale, which was really a 'vintage' extravagance, was even more exclusive and rightly so. Because it was so huge and so special, it must be mentioned, but it was of no commercial significance.

From North America there were Cadillacs, Lincolns, Packards and perhaps one or two Duesenbergs, but none of them (not even the fine Packards or near-vintage Cadillacs) had any real class or social standing. Nevertheless pre-Depression V12 and V16 Cadillacs and the 'proper' K-Series Lincolns with V12 engines were fine pieces of engineering and our Anglophile snobbery was misplaced. Even so, the 57.5 hp RAC Rating for the V16 Cadillac must have been a real deterrent.

Mercedes-Benz, Maybach and other German products suffered at first from post-Great War reaction, which was then replaced by distaste for Hitler's capers. However, in engineering terms we should not ignore the enormous and complex Grosser Mercedes cars, particularly the 1938/39 model with its tubular chassis frame and independent rear suspension. Though the latter car was once priced here (at £3,750!) none was sold, which is not surprising as only 88 were built, for top-level Nazis and their sycophants. The earlier model (built 1930 to 1937) was offered for £2,785 in 1930, but attracted no custom. Later

*Before they relapsed into post-war bad taste, Packards could be smooth and impressive. This 1935 Packard 12 was first owned by Hollywood actor Harold Lloyd, here posing by his new car in 1935. Annual taxation in this country was horrific* (National Motor Museum).

limousines might weigh more than 3½ tons, were more than 20 ft long and, without power steering, must have needed strength to drive. As all were chauffered by willing slaves this was not thought to be important. Almost every Grosser which survives is designated ex-Hitler or ex-Goering, but I doubt this very much.

How, then, should I sum up the top class cars of the period? Craftsmanship in the 1930s was probably no better than it had been earlier, partly because excellence could only be assured by the infinite taking of great pains, which tended to cost more and more money. But it is gratifying and interesting to note that few of the gimmicks which graced cars for Everyman were adopted by the carriage trade. In style and in engineering fashion, the more expensive machines only adapted modern ideas when and if it suited them and their judgement and taste continued to be impeccable. Freewheels, odd-ball accessories and engagingly useless instruments were not be found in the over-£1,000 class; not, unless, the car had been ordered by an Arabian or Indian potentate, when there was no knowing what fittings 'including, on occasion, sumptuously detailed commodes) might be required.

Before the Second World War arrived, an expert could detect the first signs of cost-cutting and use of standard components, but this was always achieved with consummate tact and discretion. These words, perhaps, sum up the approach to building some of the world's finest cars of the day. Although the price might be sky high (one Rolls-Royce might cost as much as five semi-detached villas in Caterham, Hendon or Kingston, after all), the engineering specification breathtaking and the detailing superb, there was rarely any attempt to prove it. Rolls-Royces and Daimlers were linked with country estates, London clubs and the rarified strata of the high life.

No matter what the times were meant to be like, there were enough of the old 'ruling classes' to keep this up. Rolls-Royce, Mulliner-Park-Ward and others might be glad of a pop star's business these days and might even accede with only a wince to some rather outrageous demands, but in the 1930s it simply was not necessary. The present Duke of Bedford could still note this of his grandfather's 1930s motoring habits:

'He kept four cars and, I think eight chauffeurs in town, all eating their heads off. They were responsible for the first part of the journey down to the country of any guests. The town car used to take you as far as Hendon, where you had to get out and join the car which had been sent up from Woburn. You never travelled with your suitcase, which was not considered the thing to do. It had to come in another car, so you had a chauffeur and a footman to yourself and a chauffeur and a footman with the suitcase, with another four to meet you. Eight people involved in moving one person from London to Woburn. This regime went right on until my Grandfather died in 1940. . . ..'

The tycoons might have been somewhat more practical, but they still motored in the grand manner. It was nothing to hear of a chauffeur and a full-time mechanic being employed to look after a stable of fine cars (as was Walter Hassan by Woolf Barnato in the early 1930s) and if the cars were not being used the staff would be found something to do. Taking up the floorboards every morning, cleaning top and bottom, applying metal polish and elbow grease to chassis parts nobody ever saw . . . exercising the family dog by tying it to a door handle and letting it trot alongside at 10 mph or so . . . washing and polishing the entire coachwork *every* day . . . these were standards which were not allowed to slip.

But the war which changed the world in 1939 also changed the whole shape of motoring. The 1930s might sometimes be remembered for their Depression, but the 1940s would surely only be remembered for the fighting and the austerity which followed. Yet another social change, if not a revolution, occurred and afterwards there simply was not the scope for this sort of car any more. In the 1940s and the early 1950s the famous old coachbuilders put on a brave show and their products were as resplendent and well-built as ever. But old craftsmen retired, costs rocketed and the clientele changed. The atmosphere and the 'presence' of a bespoke, individual, carriage was no longer needed and by the end of the 1950s the independent coachbuilder was just about extinct. Twenty years after the outbreak of war, at the 1959 Earls Court motor show, only H. J. Mulliner, Park Ward and James Young were left. A war and just one generation, had destroyed the tradition of centuries. Perhaps we can now look back on the 1930s as the heyday of those fine firms and admire their products for proof.

# Chapter 7

# Personalities and tycoons

In 1931 Malcolm Campbell was knighted for driving a motor car faster than anyone else in the world. In 1930 Sir Charles had become Baron Wakefield for his 'charitable and patriotic services'. Sir Herbert Austin, for all his wealth, used to ride his bicycle round the hills of Longbridge for exercise. Lord Nuffield actually bought a golf course near his home to become a member. A pushing and ambitious young man from Blackpool decided that making cars was a natural progression from making sidecars and special bodies for other makes and founded SS. That distinguished engineer, W. O. Bentley, saw his own creation callously auctioned between Napier and Rolls-Royce after it had struck financial trouble.

It all sounds very romantic and we certainly would not expect to hear of such things today. But in the 1930s the personalities, the tycoons and the adventurers were all very prominent. Somehow it was a very personalised, and parochial, motor industry.

When we buy a car these days, it is all rather like doing business with a computer. There are only four giant corporations, each with their mass of models, their trendy advertising and image building and their gimmicks, but somehow there do not seem to be any *people* involved at all. For all we know those omnipotent computers at Dagenham, Luton, Coventry or Longbridge look after everything – design, development, marketing and manufacture – and certainly some of the machines produced could not possibly have been conceived by human beings. It is not exaggerating very much to suggest that our present-day motor industry is one of faceless men. How many people can name the chief executives of Chrysler or Vauxhall? And how much power do they really have?

In the 1930s, it was all very different. Look through the motoring magazines and newspapers of the period and it is clear that one could identify with a well-publicised chief in every company. It was definitely the age of 'Tycoonery'. With so many more individual concerns, all fighting for sales to keep afloat, the individual charisma of 'The Boss' could work wonders. Although Austin and Morris held more than half of the entire British market at the start of the 1930s, they began to lose ground. Below them Ford, Hillman, Humber, Standard, Vauxhall, Singer and others all fancied their chances of breaking into the 'Big League'. Economically it was a stimulating and completely cut-throat rat-race and the personalities to match these battles had to merge.

Towering above them all were the two masters – Herbert Austin and William Morris. Austin was already 63 at the start of the period and Morris was 53. Austin had personally designed his first car (for the Wolseley Sheep Shearing Co) as early as 1896 and had founded his own business in 1905. Morris had graduated from making and selling bicycles from a modest Oxford building, to his first Morris car in 1913.

The state had already honoured their achievements with knighthoods and Austin was to become a Baron in 1936, while Morris was to be made a Baron in 1934 and a Viscount in 1938. Each had a healthy respect and a business dislike for the other. Even in 1924 they had seen the financial wisdom of bringing together their businesses to make up a large combine of enormous potential (and Wolseley, already struggling to survive, would have been drawn in as well) but there were personality clashes which could not be resolved and the idea was dropped. Austin was reputedly willing to let the younger and more vigorous Morris have the run of Longbridge, but Morris still wanted to keep Morris Motors to himself.

It had been the only time they talked seriously about a merger – indeed, by 1926 they were fighting with some bitterness over the bankrupted remains of Wolseley. The Birmingham concern was finally swallowed by Morris after a sensational courtroom auction which ended when Morris declared: "Whatever you bid, I shall bid £1,000 more". Austin never forgave Morris for this and their relationship deteriorated further after Len Lord abandoned Nuffield to become Works Director at Longbridge in 1938.

Yet a merger had always been logical after the Depression – which hit Morris much harder than Lord Nuffield liked to admit and it was urgently needed immediately after the Second World War, but it was not until the end of 1951 that they finally came together. By then Austin himself had died and Lord Nuffield was failing and ironically enough it was Len Lord who was architect of the final deal. But the two companies which had sold so many cars in competition with each other and whose combined share had sagged to 50 per cent of the British market by 1939, never approached this dominance in later years.

If you rate your tycoons by the league table of their sales, 'Billy' Morris was always on top. In 1930 Morris were undisputedly the largest British car-making business, holding 34 per cent of the motor industry's production (58,436 cars out of 169,669), though Morris's own stubborn marketing blind spots soon let this position drop away to only 20 per cent by 1933. Morris, an absolutely perfect prototype of the self-made man, had started as a bicycle repairer in a shed at the back of his father's house in James Street, Oxford. He was 16 years old, the year was 1892 and his capital was just four golden sovereigns. From there he moved into bicycle manufacture and at length – with the financial backing of an Oxford undergraduate, the Earl of Macclesfield – decided to start building cars. William Richard Morris set up W. R. M. Motors in Longwall, Oxford, just a few yards from the epitome of University learning, Magdalen College and sold his first Morris Oxford car in 1913.

At first, as in later years, Morris was a great believer in letting other firms produce his cars' components, while using his own factories to assemble the parts. The snag in having so many important suppliers was that Morris had to keep nagging away to ensure adequate quality control and if he did not get satisfaction he often finished up taking over the company and adding it to his burgeoning empire. Morris was certainly the first British car maker to embrace the systematic use of suppliers on such a large scale and indirectly he encouraged the growth of a large components industry which survives to this day. It can hardly have escaped the notice of his business rivals that by keeping a tight control on his cash-flow situations (and no one could have been more businesslike in that respect than the parsimonious Morris) he could operate a large business on restricted capital.

By the end of the 1920s, however, Morris (and now we really must begin to call him Lord Nuffield – the name by which he became legendary in the 1930s) had built up an enormous business and a considerable personal fortune. At the time he still controlled every share in his companies – Nuffield did not 'go public' until 1936 – and had moved confidently from Longwall to Temple Cowley, where the tiny military academy building had mushroomed and spread further away from the city, expanding piecemeal each time a major new model or development was needed. His business had survived the slump of the early 1920s by massive price cutting (which worked, and worked brilliantly, against all logical forecasts) but in many observers' eyes the Cowley complex was still a 'dark satanic mill' where machines and products took precedence over the men. It was only after Len Lord arrived from Morris Engines Branch in 1933 that modernisation began; £300,000

were spent in 1934 alone before the first moving assembly line was ready for use and for the Morris Eight to be announced.

But by the 1930s Lord Nuffield was already becoming his own worst enemy. Publically his image as a great benefactor went from strength to strength – during his life he gave away more than £28 million of his personal fortune (*not* that of his business) to medical, scientific and other charitable causes – but in business he was a small-minded man. The paradox was complete. Psychologically there was no doubt that Nuffield was a 'small businessman' at heart, the sort of man who worried about lights being left burning unnecessarily in deserted offices, though he was shrewd enough to have guided Morris Motors to a vast size by a whole series of 'seat of the pants' decisions. But when he got more and more interested in his large public donations and took longer and longer cruises at sea to visit export markets and have a holiday, he ought to have been delegating authority to his directors. Capable executives like Len Lord and Miles Thomas often lacked the authority and the freedom to get things done. Trust was something Lord Nuffield never developed and he has to go down in history as one of the great 'interventionist' owners of his time. Miles Thomas (now Lord Thomas of Remenham) once told me that: '. . . Morris was very stubborn and incredibly parsimonious over detail and the best way to get approval for new models or improvements was to suggest to him that he would not like them! . . . It was a tremendously parochial business there – any innovation like market analysis or financial re-structuring just did not get anywhere. Nuffield had a yeoman's mentality and a most peculiar instinct for getting the right answers for no apparent reason . . . When Oliver Boden died I became Vice-Chairman of the Group but I wasn't allowed to do much on my own. It was at times very restrictive because of the overhanging thought that Nuffield's hot breath might come down one's neck. He said he would leave everything to me, but wanted to retain the power to interfere, not just to advise and guide . . . .'

The 1930s, which were difficult enough for most companies, were very hard indeed on Nuffield. Earlier, when building up his empire, he had neglected new model developments. He did not agree with Austin's philosophy of building as much as possible of the car on one site – though Longbridge was by no means a very integrated place – but he eventually changed his approaches after a flurry of company takeovers.

**Left** *Two of the most important tycoons of the decade,
who managed to work with each other for a short time in
the 1930s. Lord Nuffield (left) was the master of a
growing empire – Morris, MG, Wolseley and (latterly)
Riley – while Len Lord (right) was his managing
director at Cowley for a time. A blazing row between
these two strong-willed characters was inevitable and
Lord later moved into Austin at Longbridge as Nuffield's
bitter rival* (British Leyland).

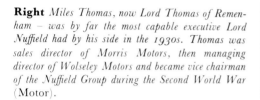

**Right** *Miles Thomas, now Lord Thomas of Remenham – was by far the most capable executive Lord
Nuffield had by his side in the 1930s. Thomas was
sales director of Morris Motors, then managing
director of Wolseley Motors and became vice chairman
of the Nuffield Group during the Second World War*
(Motor).

Apart from the purchase of Wolseley, soon to become nothing more than a thoroughly
'badge-engineered' version of the normal Morris car, he had also allowed Cecil Kimber to
build up the MG Car Co through his private (and completely separate) Morris Garages
concern. To service his expanding group, he annexed Hollick and Pratt (body makers),
Hotchkiss (in Coventry, who made his Continental-type engines,) SU (carburettors),
Osberton (radiators) and several others. He also decided to revolutionise his body-
engineering methods, getting together with Edward G. Budd of the United States to set
up the Pressed Steel company, just next door to his own Cowley factories. Pressed Steel, of
course, were the first concern to supply British car-makers with all-steel body shells, at a
time when most companies were still struggling to make more and more by the traditional
method of cladding wooden skeleton framework with hand-beaten steel or alloy panels.

Morris Motors had good (if stodgy) designers, excellent salesmen (Miles Thomas being
the most notable) and splendid production engineers, but Lord Nuffield often ignored
them all. The result was that his company entered the Depression with unsuitable models
(there was no 'Ten' and only the Minor was a respectably modern design) and the
consequence was that his sales fell alarmingly. In 1933, for instance, when the industry
was beginning to climb out of the Depression, Morris sales dropped by several thousands
and his British market share dropped to an alarming 20 per cent. One must be fair, however, and point out that at this time the American production genius had started to flower
at Vauxhall and was really pushing ahead at Dagenham with Ford. There was also a
growing challenge from the Rootes family, who had grandiose plans for their Hillman-
Humber combine.

Though Lord Nuffield could be very mean and very pernickety over detail, he sometimes made the grand gesture work very well. One which completely misfired was his
appointment of Len Lord as the supremo over his Cowley factory in 1933. Lord was no
more of a diplomat than Morris and after masterminding the renovation of the factory
decided that he was worth more than Morris was then paying him; like any good boss, he
wanted to have a 'piece of the action''. In 1936, when Nuffield turned this down, he left
in a huff. Nuffield later tried to patch things up by asking Lord to administer a £2 million

trust he had set up to assist areas of high unemployment, but would never have him back in his proper place at Cowley. But in 1938 Nuffield's loss was Austin's gain.

The sad fact is that Nuffield was not the genial homespun public-spirited philosopher that his public image suggested. He quarrelled with every one of his senior executives, not least Miles Thomas, who moved on in 1947 after 25 years in his employ. As the years rolled by he made more and more long trips away from his office and his empire, yet was furious if important decisions were then made in his absence. Anyone showing active signs of initiative, or of wanting his job, could soon guarantee to be looking for another post. Worse, Nuffield made no plans for his succession as he got older and up to the very outbreak of war there were no signs that he was ever thinking about retiring.

He was an abstemious man, who earned vast amounts of money from his businesses, but spent very little of it. For some years his personal car was a Wolseley 25 Convertible (and he always used to say that he preferred something much smaller, except that his employees at Wolseley had actually given him this car as a present!) and his house at Nuffield was by no means lordly. Because he had no family or descendants, he had no need to preserve his fortune and spent much of the 1930s giving it away. The Nuffield Foundation, Nuffield College in Oxford and a whole variety of charitable and medical bequests are a lasting monument to a remarkable man.

Nuffield's biggest rival, Herbert Austin, was cast in an entirely different mould. Nuffield was small and once a noted sportsman, while Austin was a big man in every way with little pretension to sporting achievement. Nuffield founded his own concern straight away, while Austin spent ten years turning Wolseley from a maker of sheep shearing machines into one of the largest of the original British car makers. Nuffield never even contemplated his succession, while Austin recognised has advancing years in the 1930s by allowing Captain Arthur Waite, E. L. Payton and – of course – Len Lord, to deal with the day-to-day running of Longbridge. Nuffield, even when elevated to a peerage, was the scruffily-dressed man in a cloth cap, Austin the straight-backed 'boss' in spats and a bowler hat – the latter almost becoming his 'trade mark' as the years passed by.

Herbert Austin, born in Buckinghamshire, had emigrated to Australia in 1883, joined and rose to importance in the Wolseley business, which made sheep-shearing machinery and returned to Britain in 1893 to build up their British offshoot. In 1905, after major

**Below left** *Lord Austin ('Pa' Austin to his many admirers), looking very grave, escorts HM King George VI and Queen Elizabeth along production lines of the new Austin 'shadow' factory in Birmingham in 1939. Len Lord is walking between the royal couple (Autocar).*

**Above** *One of the Nuffield Group's most desirable cars – the Wolseley 25 Drophead Coupé, captured in repose in the Yorkshire hills. The Wolseley cost £498 in 1938, had a top speed of around 90 mph, but could only achieve 16 to 19 miles per gallon (Autocar).*

**Below** *Lord Austin (in white hat), George Eyston and 'B.Bira' in his ERA, on the grid before a race at Donington Park in June 1939. Although Lord Austin was not totally committed to motor sport, he liked to keep in touch with technical change in the racing business (Autocar).*

disagreements with his fellow directors about future design policy, Austin moved on to start his own motor company. The first Austin cars were designed at his home, Lickey Grange and he bought the Longbridge factory after it had been standing derelict and unloved for the previous four years.

Austin, like Lord Nuffield, was a self-made man, having begun motor car manufacture with very little capital, but as his company had originally 'gone public' in 1914 and had temporarily sunk into receivership in the early 1920s, he never had a huge personal fortune with which the gossip columns could speculate. However, within his own limits he was undoubtedly a generous benefactor – as his £250,000 gift to Cambridge University to extend the Cavendish Laboratory confirms. From time to time, too, he held impressive appointments – he was chairman of various hospital boards, of the local Employment committee in Birmingham, of the Cambridge University Appointments Board, to name only a few and he even found time, between 1919 and 1925, to become Unionist MP for the King's Norton parliamentary constituency. It was altogether typical of his approach to life that he later commented: "After my preliminary association with the House, I had no intention of standing for Parliament again. I became convinced that the businessmen of England, including myself, are best engaged in giving their attention to their own particular jobs, thus bringing about a solution to the country's difficulties by material means. The thriving condition of Longbridge [this comment was made in 1929] will do more, for example, to minimise the evil of unemployment than could all my efforts on the floor of the House . . ..' Compared with Austin, however, one could not conceive of Lord Nuffield ever being a parliamentarian, for he would have hated all the conventions, and not trusted his new colleagues enough to associate with them!

Neither Nuffield nor Austin were completely committed to supporting motor sport. From time to time both sponsored their own competition cars. Nuffield told MG to pull out of racing in 1935 when it became clear that Cecil Kimber was spending far too much time and money on it (MG sales plummeted by 50 per cent between 1932 and 1935 when almost everyone else was gaining fast). Austin allowed a trio of very special twin-cam Austin 'Sevens' to be built and used, but later quarrelled with designer T. Murray Jamieson over the expense of it all and sent him packing. The tragedy of it all is that the Austin Twin-Cams were the only modern single-seaters built in Britain in the 1930s. In design even the ERAs, with their Riley-based engines and antiquated suspension, lagged behind.

Austin, though ten years older than Lord Nuffield, had an altogether more friendly reputation. Austin, like Nuffield, could be gruff, abrupt and impatient, but he was not nearly as mercurial in the way he made business decisions and his subordinates could rely on him to operate in a very logical manner. Quite a number of Nuffield's colleagues seemed to hate the old man's guts, but 'Pa' Austin was universally respected. He died, aged 74 and still working as hard as ever, in 1941.

The Austin and Nuffield groups both lost ground in the 1930s as the market blossomed after the Depression and both on hindsight could blame the family of motor trade 'upstarts' who, by 1930, were becoming a real power in the motor industry – Reginald and William Rootes. Reginald was the financier and the administrator, while 'Billy' (no one in the business ever called William anything else) was the salesman, the visionary, the entrepreneur. Rootes, like the other car-making giants, had made their own way in the world of business. The founder, William Rootes senior, had originally opened a car workshop in Hawkhurst, Kent in 1898, and this was followed by gradual and irresistible growth of a sales and distribution network which eventually became one of the largest in the country. By 1930 the Rootes family were established in London, with large and prestigious headquarters in Piccadilly opposite the Ritz hotel and had acquired a considerable financial stake in the ailing Hillman-Humber combine (who made cars next door to each other in Humber Road, Coventry) which also included the Commer commercial vehicle business. Their arrival in the Midlands hierarchy of motor industry tycoons caused about as much commotion as the introduction of a fox into a chicken coop. If Austin and Nuffield were controlling the 'top table' by 1930, the Rootes family were already clamouring for membership. The rest of the decade was certainly going to be exciting for them. As takeover and rationalisation experts, they had no rivals.

Although one must not ignore Reginald, who was always the more modest and retiring of the brothers, it was William who usually made the headlines. He went out of his way to cultivate the press and was a dab hand at publicity wheezes and new-model launches, aided and abetted for many years by the cheerful and inventive Dudley Noble. Hiring the Albert Hall to introduce the Hillman Wizard was something new and made its own headlines, even though the car and its sales record were never anything to shout about. His 'feel' for a developing market was very sound and the Minx project (already being developed in 1930) was entirely to his credit. Throughout the 1930s – indeed, right up to the 1960s – there were few cars more popular, more reliable or more suitable for the British market, and every version was a lasting success.

Throughout the decade, Rootes's fortunes went from strength to strength, even if genuine motoring enthusiasts often hated them for what they were doing to such well-known marques as Sunbeam and Talbot. In their defence, however, I have to ask if any one of the companies concerned could ever have survived as an independent and in what form? It was typical, too, of their enterprise that they probably made the most of the 'shadow' factory scheme, with two ideal sites, one ideal for motor car production in later years. In Coventry there is no doubt that they overtook Standard, Rover and Riley in commercial importance.

If Rootes was not a totally family-owned firm in the 1930s, Billy and Reginald were quite determined to run it as if it was. They certainly had none of Lord Nuffield's problems in sorting out a management succession. Billy was only 36 years old in 1930 and was looking forward to at least another generation of empire building. In addition he had two sons – Geoffrey (now Lord Rootes) and Brian – while Reginald's son was Timothy. All were encouraged to make their way into the firm in due course. There was never any question of nepotism, but the complicated group of manufacturing, sales, credit and holding companies which the Rootes Group built up over the period certainly seemed to contain a large number of the same Rootes names. Colonel Cole, who came into the firm's top management from Humber, must have felt rather isolated at times. Such was the build up of management that later they became universally known as The Family, and no further explanation was ever needed when the phrase cropped up in conversation.

Billy Rootes, like so many self-made millionaires before and since, had neither the time nor the patience to take on the gloss of the upper classes. Though he was later able to match anyone in wealth, fine houses or accomplishments, he was also known (and, at times, feared) for his forthright views on anything with which he did not agree. When Billy expressed opinions on a new car's styling or made snap decisions on some problem, one rarely needed interpret his remarks – the barrack-room language had already made it perfectly clear.

What he proposed to do in the 1930s did not please everyone, least of all the lovers of vintage cars. Hillman never made particularly inspiring cars, even though the company bred a whole generation of accomplished managers who moved on to revive other concerns, though Humber were well liked for their sturdy and nicely-made range in the 1920s. Diehards could not or would not see that Rootes had saved Humber from bankruptcy at the end of the 1920s and never forgave him for the changes wrought to the marque.

By 1935 every Humber was virtually a large Hillman and all traces of the 1920s product had gone. When it came to the enforced changes at Talbot, there were bigger screams of protest. With Sunbeam already broke, Talbot could possible not have survived alone. Nevertheless Anthony Blight (in his monumental history of the Talbot car) tersely described the Rootes takeover as 'rape' and there is every indication that Rootes's lack of engineering finesse broke Georges Roesch's spirit. It was not enough that Rootes then set Roesch to design one more splendid car – a $4\frac{1}{2}$-litre straight-eight 'Sunbeam' whose engine used some Talbot components. After that Talbot's Barlby Road factory in West London was rapidly run down as a car-producing plant and later became Rootes's principal London service depot.

If you measure Rootes by the job-security they provided to thousands at a time when times were hard, then they have to be admired. If you value engineering standards and design pedigree before profitability you will probably not agree. What Rootes did to the traditions of their marques should never be forgotten, but what they did for Coventry should also be remembered. Building up the Rootes group was something of which Billy and Reginald were proud – it was one of the most outstanding automobile achievements of the 1930s in Britain.

Over at the other side of Coventry, another brusque and dynamic leader determined to carve his own name in posterity was Captain John Black, at Standards. Black had started his business career in a patents office, left the Army in 1919 and joined the Hillman company where he had the undoubted good sense and good taste to marry one of William Hillman's six daughters. By 1928 he was running Hillman (jointly with Spencer Wilks) but moved over to run Standard for R. W. Maudslay. A year later he joined the Standard board and by 1933 had become managing director. Although Maudslay was nominally in charge for some time, Captain Black was quite sure that it was he who was really taking the decisions and shaping the future.

Standard's turn-round and vast expansion in the 1930s was mostly to John Black's credit. At first Standard (like Hillman, Singer and several others) was not in the same

*Captain John Black (right), managing director of Standard and his technical chief, Ted Grinham, exchange congratulations over the successful launch of the 1938 Standard Flying Eight. Black was one of the industry's most ruthlessly successful tycoons. He was knighted during the Second World War and led Standard-Triumph until 1954 (British Leyland).*

league as Austin or Morris, but Black was determined to change that situation. To do this he had to shake up the model range, a process which had already started with the Nine just at a time when the presence of such a small car in mass production became essential to success.

Standard's huge expansion (they built 7,000 cars in 1930, but 53,000 in 1939) was urged on by Captain Black's personality, but he certainly did not achieve this by being friendly. Many of his fellow-directors were plainly terrified of his whims and the records show a procession of men promoted, driven too hard and resigning, at times with their health broken. He appeared to have been difficult to work with or for, he was often completely dictatorial, very outspoken and was unlikely to accept any business schemes that he had not initiated himself. Alick Dick sums him up like this: 'No one hit it off with John Black really, and this is nothing against him. He was an individualist. You either hated or loved him. I was his assistant or deputy for years and I alternated between the two fairly often!' In the 1930s his colleagues saw that the best way to keep him sweet was to administer great dollops of corporate praise, in public and private. Such sentiments even appear at regular intervals in the company's records.

Later, after the Second World War, these characteristics became more pronounced, so much so that his Board eventually rebelled *en masse* and demanded his resignation. It is a mark of the man's enormous personality that the Board were very worried as to his response and that they were shattered when he agreed there and then to go. But that was in 1954, many years after the really excellent work he achieved at Standard in the 1930s. Captain Black's character was best summed up by someone who went to see him in his offices at Banner Lane in the 1940s. At first he thought he was on a film set, but later realised that he was standing in a superb copy of Mussolini-type architecture. The urge to be a dictator was so strong that adulation of another dictator's habits had shown through.

He might have been nearly impossible to work with, but the cars he coaxed out of his staff were an enormous success. John Black was also a great patriot and for his theme on the Flying Standards first introduced in 1935 he continued to feature a Union Flag badge. In ten years Standard's share of the British market rocketed from 4 per cent to 15 per cent and incidentally managed to pass Rootes's combined efforts on the way. As war clouds gathered, Standard's offerings represented the sort of range guaranteed to bring smiles to a shareholder's face – there were Flying 8s, 9s, 10s, 12s, 14s and 20s, priced from £130 to £330 and with component interchangeability which gladdened a service manager's heart.

John Black also had a very distinguished relative in Spencer Wilks, who directed the fast-improving fortune of the Rover concern from the beginning of the 1930s. Wilks, too, had married one of William Hillman's daughters, but after the Humber-Hillman merger of 1928 and with the Rootes family involvement becoming obvious, he traded family loyalty for peace of mind. In the autumn of 1929 he moved from Humber Road to Queen Victoria Road in Coventry, to become general manager of Rover.

At that point, Rover were in deep trouble. There had already been severe financial losses in the 1920s – even before the Depression began to bite – which led to changes in management after a shareholders' revolt. The new chairman (W. D. Sudbury) brought in his own nominee, Colonel Frank Searle, as managing director, but soon appointed Spencer Wilks to look after the day-to-day running of the business.

Colonel Searle had opted for an expansion of production at the expense of quality control, which did nothing for Rover's reputation in the trade and he did not survive the mistake of sponsoring the strange rear-engined Scarab which was to have been sold for a mere £89 in 1932 and which, therefore, would have been the cheapest British car of all time. He was dismissed after taking a long trip to view Rover interests in New Zealand, which was historically a dangerous thing to do as the previous managing director had

*'One of Britain's Fine Cars' was Rover's boast in the late 1930s. As the picture shows, they were smart and elegant without being flashy. This was a P2 model with four-door saloon body, but two-door coachwork was also available* (Autocar).

suffered the same fate in 1929! Spencer Wilks and his financial adviser, Howe Graham, immediately took the company by the scruff of its corporate neck and initiated the turn-round.

Spencer Wilks treated the revival of Rover almost as a personal crusade. Having had legal training earlier in his life and being possessed of a finely-honed analytical intellect, he never seemed to lose his impressive calm in any crisis. It was exactly the right approach for a firm which had been buffeted so much in recent years. He always believed in quality before quantity and this belief helped to convert the Rover from a very mediocre machine into the well-equipped and beautifully-made product of the late 1930s.

In 1932 the company came within an ace of calling in the receiver, but by 1939 it was so strong that on more than one occasion it was approached by other firms with requests that they be taken over. By then the company's advertising talked about: 'Rover – one of Britain's fine cars', a claim that would have been howled down in 1930, but which every-one now believed to be true. Spencer Wilk's record of achievement at Rover is impeccable, whether one is considering any period between 1932 and the late 1960s; in the 1930s the changes he inspired were quite remarkable.

There was more, however, to the Wilks family than the patrician 'S.B.' himself. His brother, Maurice, also joined Rover from Hillman at the same time and from 1931 was the driving force behind the new design and development programme. To Maurice Wilks and Robert Boyle go the credit for the steady improvement in design, in styling and to the commitment in later years to such technical masterpieces as the gas turbine projects and the Rover 2000.

Rover, at their low point, needed more than 200 orders every week to keep their opera-tions in profit, were building more than that but were only actually selling about 50 of them. The Wilks approach was to cut waste, to bring down the break-even point and to ensure that 100 well-made machines would both sell and make money. Financial improvements became obvious by 1934, when the vast overdraft was at last wiped out and as production started to build up once more. Under 5,000 cars were built in 1933 (compared with more than 10,000 in the loss-making 1931 season) but this rose to 5,964 in 1934, 7,253 in 1935 – and almost any number that Wilks chose to authorise after that.

By then, to the rest of the directors, Spencer Wilks appeared to be infallible and even looking back at his record from the 1970s one can find little to argue with that. By 1935 there was a queue at almost every Rover dealership for the latest models. It was so reassuring that Wilks would get approval from his board during the summer months for an exact building programme for the coming financial and model year. If one particular model then 'sold out' before the following summer (which often happened) that only made it even more exclusive and desirable for the future. By such subtle and civilised policies, Wilks let production build up very gradually to more than 11,000 cars in 1939, expanding the Helen Street factory in Coventry as and when it was necessary.

Compared with that of his brother-in-law John Black, Spencer Wilks's private and public reputation was almost that of a saint. He was kind, courteous and considerate almost to a fault. His work-force adored him and the long-service list of Rover employees must prove something. There were many unpublished acts of kindness and generosity to company pensioners and widows which were kept discreetly silent.

It is not a cliché to say that for many years Spencer Wilks *was* Rover. The presence and dignified bearing that was his soon began to rub off on his company's products. Somehow one could not visualise 'S.B.' approving of vulgar products and anything which needed backing by lots of loud publicity was turned down forthwith. Spencer Wilks and the Scarab, for sure, were quite incompatible. Government and civil servants loved to deal with him – his approach was like theirs in so many ways – which might help to explain why Rover was the first motor industry firm to operate two 'shadow' factories and why they were chosen to co-operate with Frank Whittle on the development of the new-fangled and still most secret gas turbine engines. It was also no coincidence that when Rolls-Royce, who rarely bent their quality control standards even in war-time, needed to farm out production of their V12 Meteor tank engine (an un-supercharged version of the famous Merlin aero-engine) they chose Rover as their agents.

It is intriguing now to look back on this era and realise that the first commercial links between Rover and Triumph might have been forged in 1932 (for the two Coventry firms held merger talks in that year) but that it took until the end of the 1960s before this actually matured.

John Black, for all his personal failings, also supplied the hardware for another man to make his lasting fortune in the 1930s. That man was William Lyons, who must, by many standards, be nominated as *the* motoring personality of the decade. Mr Lyons (now Sir William and retired from his Jaguar business career) had started by making side-cars for motor cycles in Blackpool, in 1922, before progressing to the manufacture of special bodies for small cars like the Austin Seven and the Standard Nine. In 1928 he and his partner, William Walmsley, moved their thriving little business down to an abandoned Great War shell-filling factory in Foleshill, Coventry and in spite of the business depression, they continued to expand.

In 1931 William Lyons was one of the few men in the motor industry who was actually looking beyond the financial vicissitudes of the day – and astonished the press, the public *and* his business rivals by going ahead with a complete new car of his own – the SS1. The climate for launching a new make could not have seemed less favourable, but this did not seem to deter the ambitious Lancastrian. A modern parallel would have been for a new company to launch a super sports car in the depths of the 1973/74 oil supply crisis – it was something you just did not do. No one, however, seems to have told Lyons about the

**Left** *Not only 'the most remarkable car of the year' but probably the most remarkable achievement of the 1930s, was the way that William Lyons founded and built up the SS marque. This was the first SS advert which started it all on 9 October 1931* (Autocar).

**Below right** *This is how the Lyons-shaped SS and SS Jaguar line progressed during the 1930s. On the right of the picture is a 1934 SSI saloon, on the left a 1935 2½-litre Jaguar saloon and in the centre one of the exciting 3½-litre SS100 sports cars* (National Motor Museum).

national mood and he went ahead anyway – 776 cars were delivered in 1932, 1,525 in 1933 and over 100 cars a week were being produced by 1939.

The SS1 was not even a small and economical car, neither was it modest. It was nothing less than a strikingly-styled coupé designed to appeal to the snob in all of us, where seating space gave way to bonnet length and where comfort came second to the lowness of the roof line. The gamble worked, the SS legend was born and sales raced ahead of production. Lyons's ambitions were high, so that he set his sights on the expensive sports saloon market –and even adopted the telegraphic address of 'Bentley's Second'. But he was not at all content selling cars which used so much hardware from a possible competitor (his engines, transmissions and chassis frames were all supplied by Standard) and his range of SS Jaguars launched in 1935 were altogether more special. It was here that the legendary Jaguar 'value for money' reputation was founded (it would not be destroyed until the mid-1970s), for at the launch party Lyons astonished even his dealers by quoting prices several hundred pounds below their estimates. They thought the new 2½-litre model would sell for £632, whereas its actual price was revealed as £385 – to thunderous applause. In an era, too, where model names seem to come out of a product planning committee's deliberations, or after extensive market research, it is nice to recall that 'Jaguar' was the result of Lyons browsing through a list of bird and animal names.

By 1939 a sports car had been added to the range, Jaguar were designing their own engines and the first racing successes were gained. The business took on a splendid air of permanency. William Lyons was the only person to launch successfully a major new marque in the 1930s and there are many who compare Colin Chapman's modern Lotus enterprise with Jaguar's activities in the 1930s and 1940s.

Lyons was an astute businessman who always made sure he retained full control – when Walmsley left the partnership he took up that shareholding and many years later when he sold out to BMC he made sure there would be no corporate interference unless he wanted it so – even when Jaguar made·a public issue of shares the Lyons family retained more than half of the voting rights. For many years after the Second World War Lyons was reputedly Britain's highest-paid boss, but he made sure that most of the profits were kept in the company to help expansion. Lyons was one of that rare breed of big bosses – neither a financial wizard, nor a brilliant engineer. However, he developed a remarkably fine sense of style and was probably the only chief in modern times who ever personally styled his own production cars. This does not mean that he merely approved personally the shapes prepared by other people, but that with the aid of a dedicated team of carpenters and metal workers who really understood his wishes the final form of a car body took shape according to his sketches.

But he was not a man who dallied in a smart studio with exotic furnishings to get inspiration (neither SS nor Jaguar even had a styling studio until the 1970s). For him the same result could be achieved by commissioning full-scale mock-ups, refined and improved by repeated attention. At Jaguar, even in the 1960s, it was quite normal for the blue-suited Lyons, fresh from a Board meeting, to stride across the factory to Fred Gardner's secret shop, to spend an hour pacing round and round the latest mock-up, accentuating a line here, smoothing out a contour there, or even – it happened often – to scrap an entire project after weeks of effort and to start once again. He was unhappy with his original SS1, for instance, and the 1933 model is vastly different from the 1932 examples.

Lyons was a hard task master and expected his staff to be as hard-working, resourceful and conscientous as himself. Spare time was something he did not seem to need and his working hours spent at Foleshill are still something of a legend at Coventry. Walter Hassan, that distinguished engineer who worked for him before and after the war, said of him: 'I always found Mr Lyons to be rather an austere sort of man, very formal in his business contacts, yet very interested in and very interesting on the question of car design. I never heard him call anyone by their christian names – no one, that is, except Fred Gardner, who ran the sawmill and built all the prototype body shapes for him . . . He was not trained as an engineer, but he always had a very clear idea of the kind of car he wanted to sell. He was always very critical of deficiencies in performance, roadholding, suspension, noise, comfort . . . he would always tell us what he didn't like about anything, but not how he wanted it, and would leave us to sort it out from there. It wasn't what you'd call destructive criticism but he would certainly tell us in no uncertain terms!' Hassan also makes the important point (not quite valid to the 1930s) that when the famous XK engine was being designed during the war years, Mr Lyons made it very clear that not only had it to be very powerful, but 'that it had to look powerful and beautiful at one and the same time.

*The wonderfully-impressive SS100 sports car did great things for SS Jaguar's sporting image at the end of the 1930s. This particular car was built before the war, but attained fame in Ian Appleyard's hands in the 1948 Alpine Rally* (National Motor Museum).

Yet if William Lyons was the most outstandingly successful personal businessman of the decade, there were undoubtedly several more who achieved great things, but never attracted the same sort of adulation. Could it have been a portent for the future that both Ford and Vauxhall chose the 1930s as their springboard to greater things, with remarkably little fuss and without any real 'bossman' personalities emerging?

Ford moved from their relatively small (ex-tramcar body) factory at Trafford Park, near Manchester, to a vast new plant which grew out of the Dagenham marshes, in 1932. From Dagenham the new Ford Eight, a British 'people's car' if ever there was one, was marketed and after that there was little doubt in any observer's mind that Ford would one day become very large indeed in this country. Their *forte* was in organisation, in planning and in efficient production, rather than in flamboyant publicity and sporting machinery and in this they had an excellent leader in Percival Perry to guide the process. Perry had taken the original Ford importing agency in 1907, had set up the Trafford Park factory for Henry Ford in 1911 and had soon got involved in Ford's expansion into Europe and into Ireland. Knighted in 1918, Sir Percival quarrelled with Ford in 1919 and resigned, but was enticed back by Henry Ford himself to master-mind the building of the new Dagenham factories.

Even by 1930, Ford's European conglomerate was building more than 100,000 cars and trucks. In 1932 only 8,260 of the important little Model Ys would be built at Dagenham, but the trickle then swelled to a torrent and was soon joined by the fast and remarkably cheap V8 models. Sir Percival's reward as chairman was a Barony in 1938 and he finally stood down in 1948.

Vauxhall, for their part, had come under the control of the American General Motors group in the 1920s (interestingly enough, after GM had been rejected by 'Pa' Austin at Longbridge) and were progressively being converted from small-scale makers of fine

**Above** *Birth of a colossus – when Ford's new Dagenham plant was first opened in 1931. At this time there was more of the notorious Dagenham marsh than factory, but how things have changed in intervening years! The whole area between the original factory and the A13 main road in the distance is now occupied by factory buildings and parking areas* (Ford Motor Co).

**Below** *The first Ford car designed specifically for Europe was the Model Y, introduced in 1932. In 1935, by furious price-cutting and cost saving, it became the Popular and sold for a mere £100, the first and only fully-equipped British car ever to get down to this price* (Ford Motor Co).

*Assembling the Model Y Ford 8 hp car at Dagenham in the mid-1930s, with a 10 hp Model C at the 'body drop' point immediately behind it. More than 157,000 Model Ys were sold and more than 96,000 Cs and CXs. Apart from the Morris Eight, which slavishly copied the Model Y, these were Britain's most popular small cars* (Ford Motor Co).

vintage tourers and sports cars (surely we all recall the 30/98s?) into the British equivalent of GM-owned Opel. The old-style Vauxhall, with their noted chief engineer Laurence Pomeroy, would never have foreseen the Cadets and Twelves, the unit-construction bodies and the 'knee-action' independent suspension which all came to Luton in the 1930s; nor, for that matter, would they have wanted such things to happen to them! Such a change needed brave and logical (if unpopular) leadership, which duly appeared in the guise of Sir Charles Bartlett. Sir Charles was not only an efficient administrator (he had to be, presiding over a concern which made 8,930 cars in 1930, 26,240 in 1935 and more than 35,000 in the last year before the war) but he seems to have been a labour-relations 'fixer' second to none. Luton in the 1930s had the most placid labour relations possible. Sir Charles was also to be in charge of his concern for a long period – he finally retired from Vauxhall in 1953.

In view of their vicissitudes, perhaps it is surprising that Singer bosses received little publicity. Singer sometimes hovered on the brink of the 'Big Time', but were never big enough, nor well-enough financed, to really make it. As it was, they had to undergo one painful financial reconstruction to survive disasters like the Airstream Eleven and tooling costs for the Bantam, but it was not until the 1950s that they finally fell into the arms of the Rootes group.

Coventry, it seemed, was full of firms with high ideals, low sales and desperate finances. Triumph, for instance, came under the control of that most urbane and popular of men, Claude Holbrook, after Siegfried Bettmann, the company's founder retired, but suffered because he wanted to concentrate on middle class machines when the total market for them was contracting. Claude Holbrook rationalised the business, according to his lights, by selling off the motor cycle arm of the company and by moving Triumph to a new factory alongside that of SS Jaguar. He also encouraged the youthful Donald Healey to design (really a copy from Alfa Romeo) an enormously expensive straight-eight sports car which would surely have bankrupted Triumph in short order if it had gone into production. He had an eye for the ladies (it was motor industry rumour for years that Holbrook named his 1933 Glorias after a Selfridges' model girl, even though the name had been established in Triumph history for a generation) and was a great lover of motor sport. His vision of producing 'The Smartest Cars in the Land' (a Triumph advertising slogan of the later 1930s) partially succeeded, certainly in the styling of the later cars, but foundered on the rocks of competition thrown up at all the middle class concerns by the great success of SS Jaguar. It has to be said, too, that Holbrook's financial advisers were less astute than his engineers. Colonel Sir Claude Holbrook, to give his his full and final title, became Triumph's vice-chairman in 1937 and retired in 1939. Triumph failed after two financial upheavals and entered the 1940s in new hands.

Riley, too, was a famous Coventry concern, controlled until the Nuffield takeover of 1938 by the Riley family themselves. They, like Triumph, allowed enthusiasm for new-model engineering (and particularly for participation in motor sport) to come between prudence and financial rectitude. Although it was always delightful to survey the choice of Rileys on the market, it was always a puzzle as to why there were so many of them. Victor Riley, that much respected chairman and managing director of his company, announced very sadly that his company was being put in the hands of the receiver in February 1938 and though he remained at the helm after Lord Nuffield's takeover, his overall control was lost. For a time there had been five Rileys in the business (more, even, than there were Rootes' names in their own group) and the little Nine engine was always said to be the 'PR' (Percy Riley) type.

And of the other big names of the vintage years, what became of them? W. O. Bentley survived his company's takeover by Rolls-Royce after a sordid court-room battle with Napier – but only at the expense of being pushed into a humiliating 'non-job' with his new masters. Later, having served out his contract, he got away from the dead hand of Derby and joined Alan Good to become technical director of Lagonda. Bentley, unhappily, was a better judge of a motor car than he was of a motor company; his own concern had folded financially in 1931 and Lagonda always seemed to be in trouble, finally being swept up by David Brown (to be merged with Aston Martin) soon after the next war. Louis Coatalen's influence at Sunbeam was almost over by 1930 (shortly he was to go back to France and direct the fortunes of the Lockheed concern) – his most famous models having been the S-T-D racing cars and the various record-breaking contenders he inspired in the 1920s. At the other end of the S-T-D group, Georges Roesch's spirit was eventually broken by the philistinism of the Rootes Group and he eventually moved on to join David Brown Industries in Yorkshire.

As far as the specialist motoring press was concerned, the one really famous engineer was Reid Railton. Railton was a thin, humourless, almost ascetic engineer, who had gained valuable experience with Parry Thomas at Leyland, before moving to Thomson and Taylor's engineering workshops in the Brooklands 'village' to become chief engineer. He was down-to-earth and practical and never seemed to step too far into the engineering unknown. With the help of the eminently experienced 'Uncle' Taylor he proceeded to lay

*Two of the most successful men in British motor sport were Reid Railton (wielding the pencil) and Ken Taylor, who between them controlled the fortunes of Thomson and Taylor at Brooklands. Railton was the brilliant designer of the later Bluebirds (a cutaway drawing of this car is hanging on the wall behind their heads), of the original ERA and of both of John Cobb's Napier-engined cars (Autocar).*

out a whole series of outstandingly successful competition cars. Early work on well-known and well-loved machines, like the Brooklands Riley Nine, led to a lengthy improvement and rebuilding operation on the Campbell Bluebird, the mechanical layout of the 1934 ERA single-seater racing car, John Cobb's Brooklands Napier-Railton and finally the design of that most beautiful of all record breakers, the Railton Mobil Special itself. Not content with such successes, Railton also advised on the shape of bodywork for Goldie Gardner's MG EX135 and on the modification of just about every racing car to pass through T & T's shops (and in the 1930s that meant almost every racing car in the country).

Railton also found time to take on the redesign work needed to be done to the Hudson chassis before they could be given British bodies, be assembled at Noel Macklin's Cobham factory and be christened Railtons. Though there was no man who courted publicity less, his cars' exploits and the sheer technical bravery of some of them, made it inevitable that he should become well known. There was little that Railton could not apparently do and do well; his Railton record car was a masterpiece of miniaturised complexity (inspect it, with body removed, in the Birmingham Science museum, for proof) though the designer never doubted that it would work. What a pity for British motor racing prestige that this man was never asked to design a proper Grand Prix car, for even by Mercedes-Benz and Auto-Union standards he could probably have produced a winner.

In sport, there were very few famous British drivers and even fewer enthusiastic entrepreneurs. Of all the car makers, only MG made serious and long-term attempts to go motor racing. Their chief, Cecil Kimber, was extremely happy to be in racing, even though there are signs that he neglected his production cars to do this. The problem was that MG's financial backing came from Lord Nuffield, who most assuredly did not approve, even when it was helping to forge a fine reputation for these little cars. It was Kimber who had invented the famous MG 'octagon' in the 1920s and who fought so hard for the company to stay independent of the rest of the Nuffield Group. But just when MG were teetering on the brink of making proper second-generation single-seater racing cars, Lord Nuffield called a halt and capped this by deciding to sell his own private sports car company to the Group itself. Kimber was shattered and even though he stayed on as managing director at MG until the war years his fame slipped back; worse, the cars became less and less individual as the years slipped by. Kimber's influence on MG design decreased the more they became glorified Wolseleys and his influence on policy ceased when Miles Thomas (later Lord Thomas) became Nuffield's Vice-Chairman early in the 1940s. Thomas sacked Kimber in 1941, to the regret of every MG enthusiast and he died tragically in a railway accident near Kings Cross station early in 1945.

The public, of course, loved its record-breaking heroes and the few racing drivers who really made it to the top. But while Raymond Mays and 'B.Bira' were the darlings of the crowds at Brooklands, Crystal Palace and Donington, it was the glamorous and world-famous record-breakers like Sir Malcolm Campbell, Captain George Eyston, Major 'Goldie' Gardner and John Cobb who really caught the public eye. Never a season went by when one or the other of them was slipping off to France, to Italy, to Germany or to the United States with a car to attack yet another set of records.

Although Cobb, a wealthy fur-broker, was a brave and fine driver, he was no public personality, as the surviving newsreels and biographies confirm, whereas Sir Malcolm Campbell was the complete upper middle class extrovert. He was never backward in coming forward to publicise himself or his products. His speed successes were merely squeezed in between his varied business ventures. At one time he ran the British Bugatti concession, he was a member of a Lloyds insurance syndicate, he had at least one motoring column at any time and he sat on the boards of various public companies. He gained sponsorship from the most unlikely sources and gave his all to give that benefactor his money's worth. It was only necessary for Sir Malcolm to pronounce on the worth of a certain dog food and sales would leap.

Sport, and particularly record-breaking, was much more interesting to the public than the study of mundane cars and it is to this phenomenon of the 1930s that we must turn. It was a period when British sportsmen probably made as many headlines as they have since, without winning a single major race. It was a period, even now, which many of the industry's backers still regard with nostalgic pride.

# Chapter 8

# Motor sport – the big league

These days, of course, we are well used to the idea of British pre-eminence in many forms of motor sport. In Grand Prix racing or with production cars, on the race track or in a rally, British cars and drivers can be world-beaters. Unless you have the benefit of a very long memory, it would be easy to assume that this has always been so and some historical writers have chosen only to recall the great and successful occasions. But the sad fact is that, throughout the 1930s, our overall sporting record was very disappointing. Worse, at the time there seemed to be no way, technically or financially, that we could break out of such a gloomy situation.

I must start, therefore, by summarising the bad news. At no time could we British produce a race-winning single-seater to match the might of Alfa Romeo, Bugatti, Auto-Union or Mercedes-Benz and only a single Grand Prix driver was British. As far as outright wins were concerned, our sports racing reputation virtually died with the Bentleys. International rallies, though not then enjoying the importance they do today, were dominated by French and Italian cars and only two or three British drivers would today have been dubbed 'world class'. In one specialised field – that of record-breaking and high-speed endurance motoring – British cars and drivers were on top. The British press made much of

*Perhaps the strangest Grand Prix car of all time? This was Count Trossi's Monaco Trossi car, complete with radial air-cooled engine in the nose. It was never successful, but has been preserved in the Turin museum* (National Motor Museum).

our record cars and their dignified gentleman drivers – what did it matter, therefore, if we could not challenge the Italians and the Germans at Grand Prix racing?

In the big-time international motor racing, as the 1930s dawned, our morale was drastically in need of a boost. It was true that the Cricklewood-built Bentleys, which a jealous Ettore Bugatti had already described as the 'fastest lorries in the world', had virtually taken over the Le Mans 24 Hour race and had to be reckoned as potential winners of any other long-distance race they chose to enter. But Bentley were in trouble. Commercially they were already on their third set of capital and even with the wealthy Woolf Barnato as their chairman, there was no guarantee that he would allow them to stay financially afloat for long. Bentley made their very first operating profit in 1929 and were not to repeat it. Within months, after winning at Le Mans in 1930, they withdrew from motor racing completely and left the British without a champion.

They had no successes – real or imagined. In Grand Prix racing, for example, the British were complete non-starters. Not since the withdrawal of Louis Coatalen's S-T-D cars (variously called Sunbeams, Talbots or Talbot-Darracqs – it depended on the races entered and on who was paying!) had anything approaching a British Grand Prix car been built. Sir Henry Segrave was the only Briton to have won a major race in a British car and this had been as long ago as in 1924; Segrave had already turned his back on racing and record-breaking and was becoming obsessed with the Water Speed Record. His new boat, Miss England II, owned and financed by Castrol's Lord Wakefield, was fast enough to achieve the record for him, but crashed in an early and unsuccessful run and killed the gallant Segrave. From then on, Britain had neither a car nor a world-class driver.

There were many reasons, many problems and few obvious solutions. Most important, of course, was the question of money – or the conspicuous lack of it. Finance was the subject which influenced many of the happenings in this strange decade and another, undoubtedly, was the lack of the right sort of racing in Britain. There had, after all, been Grand Prix racing in the world since 1906, but only twice (at Brooklands in 1926 and 1927) were races to the current formula held in this country.

*A panorama of Brooklands in its Indian summer of 1939, when the outer circuit had become virtually disused and the Campbell Circuit (here in use by single seaters) was all the rage. On the right of the picture, starting from the gate near the advertising sign, is the Test Hill (Autocar).*

**Above** *Brooklands in its final form. This aerial shot, taken from the north east, shows the Members' Banking nearest the camera, the Finishing Straight across the scene and the Campbell 'road' circuit (which came into use in 1937) winding across the circuit infield. The Vickers aircraft factory is in the left foreground and the legendary Brooklands 'village' near the (far) Byfleet banking* (National Motor Museum).

**Below** *A busy paddock scene at Brooklands in the 1930s. This is the famous Paddock Clubhouse, which still stands to this day and which was later used by Sir Barnes Wallis for his war-time designing efforts* (National Motor Museum).

*All the bustle and atmosphere of Brooklands in high summer. This is an F. Gordon Crosby sketch of the scene looking out over the Finishing Straight to the Campbell Circuit and the start of the Members' Banking, from the new cocktail bar above the Paddock building* (Autocar).

Without the right sort of racing to be entered, there seemed to be little point in building suitable cars. Without the right sort of events to enter, the best of the continental opposition was not likely to be attracted to our own events. In those days the English channel appeared as a very formidable barrier. Without competition the stimulus was lost, without stimulus there was little technical progress and without such progress there was little prospect of commercial backing. British motor racing circles might have been worried about this, but rarely let it show. Racing centred around a tightly-knit circle of people whose activities were almost entirely centred on a single venue – Brooklands.

Anyone lucky enough to have attended the annual Brooklands Society re-unions must certainly have enjoyed the occasions, but must surely have come away with rather puzzling impressions of the place itself. Even though one must make allowances for the spread of modern buildings (the British Aerospace concern own much of the site and much of the track is now obliterated) one still gains the impression of a great empty 'white elephant' of a site. Could this really have been the home of British motor racing? If it was, is it at all surprising that we had drifted so far away from the mainstream of European motor racing?

To find out why, we must delve back even further into history, to the early 1900s when there was no motor racing at all in Great Britain. The law of the land forbade road closures, so racing could only take place in the Isle of Man or in Ireland. There was no specialised racing circuit of any nature. Into this vacuum stepped a great patriot, Hugh Locke-King, who decided to finance the construction of a vast new permanent circuit, one which could be used equally for racing, for record-breaking or for engineering test work by Britain's car makers. All of which was very laudable especially when we recall that this $2\frac{3}{4}$-mile concrete monster was to be built in Locke-King's own private estate at Weybridge! The neighbours were not as impressed.

Brooklands, so named after the house in the estate, was designed with high and steep bankings to accept 'hands-off' speeds of up to 120 mph and was expected to suffice for many years before cars' performance caught up with it. Brooklands had opened in 1907, but within seven years cars were already faster than that design speed – such had been the pace of progress which the track's designers could not have foreseen.

The bankings were rough and bumpy, requiring repair every winter, work which seemed to become more and more extensive as the years passed by. Because only three circuit variations were originally possible, one of which – the outer circuit – was virtually flat-out for all cars not specifically built as Brooklands monsters, there was little variety in the racing. But at least it *was* a British circuit; once the trade had become established and many small constructors had set up shop in the infield, there seemed to be little reason to look further afield. In 1930, therefore, as for some years past, the only other important competitive sport was to be found at Brighton (the speed trials) or at Shelsley Walsh (the hill climbs).

Brooklands, its confines and its layout, affected British racing car design considerably during the inter-war years. Thomson and Taylor Ltd were at the engineering centre of the Brooklands 'village' and showed on many occasions that they could build fine machinery, but many resident Brooklands cars were quite simply 'specials'. That, in fact, was the problem with Brooklands. Such was the nature of the track that in scratch racing the largest and fastest cars always won and such was the size of the vast kidney-shaped circuit that ordinary strung-out racing formations looked (and were) boring. To provide close racing, which would please the crowds, the Brooklands organisers had refined a system of handicap racing, which was, nevertheless, often difficult to understand. This, presided over by ace-handicapper A. V. Ebblewhite (by profession the owner of a music shop and looking like it!) purported to give cars of any pedigree and in any state of tune an equal chance. Theoretically all races should have terminated in a mass dead-heat.

It was a system which did not exactly encourage the building of beautifully engineered cars, for improved performance inevitably lead to more severe handicapping and made the *next* victory that much harder to achieve. The successful Brooklands cars were more likely to be much-modified Bentleys, MGs, Rileys, Aston Martins or Lagondas, whose preparation wizards tried to arrange minor, but significant, improvements in perform-

**Above left** *Crowd control was not considered important at the Northern Ireland Ards circuit (in the Tourist Trophy races), as this shot of the main street at Newtonards confirms. Dobson's 4½-litre Lagonda, which finished eighth, here leads Sammy Davis's ill-fated Singer Le Mans in 1935* (Autocar).

**Above** *Brooklands was a simple layout with many minor variations possible. Here a large field of single-seaters is coming off the Members' Banking into the Finishing Straight, really driving the 'wrong way' round the circuit. But where is the crowd?* (Autocar)

**Below** *'Ebby' – A.V. Ebblewhite – without whom Brooklands would probably have ground to a halt, carrying out his habitual time-keeping and starting duties in a sports car handicap race. The pipe and the hat always seemed to be present, even in a heat wave* (Autocar).

*The modern Formula One Constructors' Association would never have accepted this – the Donington racing circuit where at one point cars had to shoot through a brick arch* in single file. *An* Autocar *Gordon Crosby drawing depicts the duel between Arthur Dobson's white ERA and Raymond Mays' black ERA in the 1937 Nuffield Trophy event* (Autocar).

ance at successive meetings and thus tried to keep one step ahead of the attentions of the handicappers. Walter Hassan, who built several very successful Brooklands cars, deliberately set out to outwit the system with the Pacey-Hassan Special:

'The 4½-litre Bentley engine, after all, like all Bentley designs apart from the final 4-litre, had a fixed cylinder head, in one unit with the block, and the compression ratio was varied by differences in the depth of that block. So we specifically built the 4½-litre racing engine with a whole stack of compression plates under the block, on top of the crankcase, having already machined the base of the block considerably. This meant that we started the season with a very normal compression ratio of about 6.5 to 1. We won races at once, of course and were re-handicapped, but every time that happened I felt that we needed to rebuild the engine. Now I wasn't going to admit to being a forgetful mechanic, but somehow we always managed to complete the rebuild of the engine with fewer and fewer of those plates every time! It was really very careless of us, but of course the compression ratio kept going up, we kept changing the fuel mixture to suit, and the car kept on winning races. But that only lasted until we ran out of plates to 'forget', by which time the compression ratio had risen to about 12 to 1.'

Cars developed into Brooklands winners were rarely competitive anywhere else – indeed there were many famous Brooklands cars which never left the track until it closed down in 1939 – while all-purpose cars which won at other venues rarely shone at Brooklands. The number of single-seaters was very limited and none were ever built to the current Grand Prix formulae. Several pensioned-off Grand Prix cars (mainly Bugattis and Alfa Romeos) were imported, to begin the standard Brooklands process of being modified to battle with the handicappers. In view of the money spent, it is a miracle that no one ever offered violence to Ebblewhite, who was a mild old man with a quite unshakeable (and correct) view of his own abilities.

Cars could race elsewhere in the British Isles – at Pheonix Park in the Irish Free State, on the Ards road circuit near Belfast or on makeshift circuits 'round the houses' at Douglas, Isle of Man – but no other English circuit was available until Donington Park, near Derby, held its first meeting for cars in 1934. Donington, now happily re-born under the enthusiastic aegis of Tom Wheatcroft, was originally the grounds of the manorial Donington Hall, owned then by the Shields family and was developed from original estate roads. For spectators the circuit had everything to recommend it, being undulating, sinuous, narrow and very exciting, with its surround of matured trees and – at one point – a *single-file* passage under a very solid brick bridge!

Donington was road-racing at its best, with driver skills developing to suit, though few of the cars seen there were unfamiliar. Indeed, there were really very few purpose-built racing cars in existence and certainly not enough of any one size for many scratch races to be run. Donington, like Brooklands, leaned heavily on handicap racing to provide excitement for the spectators. For the public, however, Donington was a great advance. There was no question of the 'right crowd and no crowding' (as Brooklands used to advertise) and because spectators could park up close to the trackside they also got the correct impressions of speed, noise – and smell. Later in the decade, of course, Donington would achieve something Brooklands had wanted to do for ages – to organise a fully fledged Grand Prix, which attracted the fabulous German cars to show us just what modern racing *should* be all about.

*As a change from motor racing, what about a motor racing crowd? Donington, near Red Gate corner, on a fine day, with sports cars and tourers very much in evidence. The right crowd and no crowding? (Autocar).*

**Background photograph** *The Fiat 500 Topolino race at Brooklands in April 1938, won by S. Mond from C. B. Phillips (Autocar).*

**Inset** *That famous picture of Von Brauchitsch's W125 Mercedes Grand Prix car leaping over the brow of the hill at Donington on its way to second place in the 1937 Donington Grand Prix is none the less dramatic for being familiar! (Autocar).*

**Left** *A photomontage of the House of Lord's fastest peer – Lord Howe – who was still winning races and was among Britain's best, in his mid-50s! That is his well-known 3.3-litre Type 59 Bugatti completely airborne on the Brooklands banking* (Autocar).

**Below right** *The two occasions when German teams came to Donington Park (in 1937 and 1938) for the Grand Prix provided the most dramatic racing Britain ever saw. Here, in the fabulous 1937 event, Mercedes were at their most powerful, with Lang, Caracciola and Seaman all leading Rosemeyer's mid-engined Auto-Union at Red Gate corner. Rosemeyer was the eventual winner at 82.86 mph* (Autocar).

Among the hordes of Brooklands-orientated drivers there were a few heretics who longed for a more open and varied type of racing and for a few really competitive British racing cars. Raymond Mays, Lord Howe, George Eyston and Brian Lewis actually ventured abroad regularly to taste the continental scene, while the dashing Sir Henry Birkin even had the temerity to enter a four-seater 'blower' Bentley for the 1930 French Grand Prix (run to 'formula libre' that year) and finished a rousing second. Birkin and Mays were as brave and skilful as any continental driver, but a measure of the quality of British racing was that a noble Lord in his fifties could still appear competitive with the rest at Brooklands and a 1926 Delage could be updated in 1936 as a formidable 1½-litre car for Richard Seaman to drive with such success.

For a time, however, we had no Grand Prix cars with which to challenge the might of Alfa Romeo, Maserati and Bugatti and by the time the state-backed Auto-Union and Mercedes-Benz teams arrived on the scene in 1934 there seemed to be little point even in trying. Raymond Mays, then – as later – a persistent talker and negotiator, had made his name in Bugattis, Mercedes and a much-modified Riley and eventually persuaded Humphrey Cook to finance the construction of a new single-seater racing car – which would be the first such British machine for several years. This, the ERA, was still not a forward-looking design, as its layout was broadly based on the ageing Alfa Romeo P3 design and it had to use the bones of a six-cylinder Riley engine for its power plant.

The first car, with chassis and suspension designed by Reid Railton at Thomson and Taylor, was ready in 1934 and in 1½-litre form it became successful almost at once. Replicas were offered for sale the following year, in no fewer than three engine sizes. However, even at prices of £1,500 for the 1,100 cc version, £1,700 for the 1½-litre and £1,850 for the very rare 2-litre, it is a measure of the amount of racing money floating around in Britain in the mid-1930s that only 17 ERAs were built between 1934 and 1937.

Even so, before long the ERA had been developed into the best voiturette in the world. At a time when European motor racing was dominated by publicity about Grand Prix racing and the German cars which won nearly all of the races, it was easy to overlook voiturette (1½-litre) racing altogether, but there was no doubt that an ERA had the legs of almost every other 1½-litre machine – Bugatti, Maserati or whatever. Although their looks changed little over the years, their performance and specification improved regularly; independent front suspension, for instance, was introduced in 1937. Before Raymond Mays turned his attention to a new racing car, his 2-litre ERA was probably provided with more than 250 bhp and it held the outright record at several British venues. At Brooklands, for instance, where those regular improvements were needed Raymond Mays' famous 1½-litre car improved its Mountain Circuit record lap from 55.2 seconds to 49.96 seconds in just two years; surprisingly enough, his 2-litre record was somewhat slower than that.

Only MG, who early bankrupted themselves in the process, could build special racing cars on the same scale. More than 30 two-seater supercharged K3 Magnettes and a mere handful of single-seater R-Type models were made, but neither could match the performance of the ERAs.

These and other one-off racing cars found plenty to divert them towards the end of the 1930s. The Outer Circuit at Brooklands was being used less and less as the cost of attacking records rose and as the concrete surface began to break up, but to maintain the venue's appeal a new 'road' circuit, dubbed the Campbell circuit, was added for 1937. Donington Park was lengthened twice and finally attained a 3.1-mile lap length. London also gained another circuit when the Crystal Palace track was opened and to these were added a new and popular hillclimb venue at Prescott, near Cheltenham, which was owned by the Bugatti Owner's Club.

The building of a road circuit at Brooklands followed a very controversial period in 1936 when ownership of the famous 'Home of British motor racing' changed hands. Hugh Locke-King had died some years earlier and it was in the spring of 1936 that it was suggested that his widow, Dame Ethel Locke-King, was preparing to sell out. In June the track was sold to a shadowy syndicate known as Electrical and General Industrial Trusts Ltd, whose directors were Sir Malcolm Campbell and Percy Bradley (who was Clerk of the Course at the track). Unlike the sale which would follow in 1945, this was a very benevolent business, but S. C. H. Davis, *The Autocar's* respected sports editor told us much about the state of the circuit when he had this to say in his weekly column:

'From the track point of view, a completely new surface eliminating that awkward entry to the home banking and the almost equally awkward jump off that banking to the railway straight, to say nothing of many other famous bumps, is naturally greatly to be desired. So, as modern racing goes, would be bankings 10 feet higher.'

It was all, alas, wishful thinking. No improvements were carried out.

As far as the spectators of motor racing were concerned, the highlights of the 1930s were the two visits by the German Grand Prix teams to Donington in 1937 and 1938. In those days the race they contested was not called the British GP, which it undoubtedly was, but was known as the Donington GP. (The first official British GPs, incidentally, had been held at Brooklands in 1926 and 1927, but had not been a success and were not promoted again.)

Unless they had been used to reading about these exciting German racing cars, the majority of British race goers could have had no idea of their capabilities. Naturally there were no competitive British cars, which led to the rather ludicrous situation in 1937 where three Auto-Unions and four Mercedes-Benz models were faced with a motley collection of old Maseratis and ERAs. No one except the bookmakers expected the ERAs to win, so when the German cars crossed the line in the top five places it was hardly surprising that they all fled, leaving the German race mechanics to look vainly for their winnings.

As a race the 1937 Donington GP was purely a demonstration of German technical prowess. But in spite of the reputation that had preceded the cars in print, most of the crowd seemed to be completely unprepared for the drama of the start. In his *Autocar* report, S. C. H. Davis described it thus:

'Even lined up before the start, the silver German cars, four Mercedes, three Auto-Unions, looked extremely vicious and the dramatic effect was enhanced because all the German cars formed one group at the front, while the ERAs, Maseratis and the lone Riley were in another group behind, which group started its engines when one and a half minutes were yet to go before the flag fell. All those engines running together made a fine exultant noise, but meantime the silence of the silver cars was infinitely more ominous. And then, with thirty seconds to go, they started and at once every other noise was drowned. Nothing like this has been heard ever before in motor racing in this country. There was something about it which excited the spectators to the highest pitch of enthusiasm . . . When the noise of returning cars sounded, people stood up in the grandstand, climbed up on top of cars irrespective of their ownership and clung to every vantage point the better to see the machines. When Lang shot over the crest of the road into view with a cloud of dust behind, came shooting down the straight to Melbourne Corner at a terrific speed, followed by Caracciola, von Brauchitsch and Seaman, then all the Auto-Unions' inoffensive

*In the 1938 Donington Grand Prix there were many thrilling duels between the rival German teams. Here Muller's Auto Union leads Dick Seaman's Mercedes-Benz, both of which had supercharged 3-litre engines. Seaman was third at the finish and Muller fourth (Autocar).*

*Many forms of handicapping were tried at Brooklands, including this method, where the fastest cars had to wind their way through wicker fence channels to slow them down, while slower cars proceeded unchecked on the inside. The event was the International Trophy of May 1939, with 1½-litre cars streaming through the centre of three channels* (Autocar).

spectators clapped total strangers on the back beseeching them to observe an amazing spectacle.'

It was Rosemeyer's mid-engined 6-litre Auto-Union which won in 1937 and a year later it was Tazio Nuvolari's turn to take the flag with the new 3-litre Auto-Union. There was no race in 1939 because war had already started and even in 1938 the storm clouds of power politics caused chaos in race planning. The German teams arrived as the Munich crisis was brewing up, practised, left in a hurry, were recalled, then finally left as war began to look likely. The race had to be postponed for several weeks (what chance of that being possible in today's crowded calendar?) and run off at the second time of asking at the end of October.

In terms of sheer speed the Donington spectacle was surpassed by long-distance 'outer circuit' racing at Brooklands. Short-distance handicaps and gimmicky events which used (among other things) slowing-down chicanes all paled into insignificance beside the great high-speed thrashes of the year, notably the JCC's 200 Mile race and the BRDC's 500 Mile race.

The 500 was usually held at the end of the season, so that cars could be unleashed for long periods, then spend much of the winter repairing the damage and looking round for ways to pay for it. But endurance racing could be self-defeating, as the JCC found with their own 'Double Twelve' event. Run only three times, between 1929 and 1931, the 'Double Twelve' involved two sessions of twelve hour racing, with the cars locked away for the night between the two days. A straight 24-hour race would have been preferable, but local residents would have nothing to do with the concept of night racing in what was becoming a built-up suburb of London. A 500 mile race, occupying up to six hours of racing for small cars, and not much more than four hours for the heavy machinery, was a good compromise and produced exciting racing. One had to be knowledgeable to understand the handicapping (not even the 500 mile race was run off scratch) especially as the smallest cars had often been droning round the concrete bowl for up to two hours before the monsters even rumbled into action.

It was those monsters which really made a Brooklands spectacle. The Rileys, MGs and Singers were all very interesting and made nice noises, but it was the big-engined cars which

**Above left** *All sideways, with four litres of ferocious power is Sir Malcolm Campbell in the famous Sunbeam Tiger, at Shelsley Walsh* (Autocar).

**Below left** *Too late, and unsuccessful when it was eventually completed, was the E-Type ERA, which had originally been intended for use in the revised Grand Prix formula. It was not, however, good enough even to supplant the successful 'conventional' ERAs which dominated British racing from 1934 to 1939* (Autocar).

**Above** *Freddie Dixon replenishing his famous 2-litre Riley at Brooklands – with petrol, water and a set of new tyres. He and Charles Martin were on their way to winning the 1936 BRDC '500' race. Isn't that Dick Seaman officiating in the background?* (Autocar).

really stirred the senses. At the start of the decade, Kaye Don's 4-litre Sunbeam 'Tiger' held the outright lap record at 134.24 mph, but by 1935 John Cobb's 24-litre Napier-Railton had carved 4.7 seconds off the record, pushing it up to 143.44 mph, where it now stands for all time. Without recourse to dramatically streamlined shapes (and that science was still not completely understood) higher performance could only be gained by increases in engine size and power. The Tiger had had 4-litres, Birkin's supercharged Bentley 4½-litres, Bertram's Barnato-Hassan Special an 8-litre, but the Napier-Railton put it out of anyone's else's reach and was not even fully extended! In the endurance races which favoured these big strong cars, even the vast concrete areas of Brooklands could not hide the pace of the Napier-Railton and the Barnato-Hassan lapping continuously at more than 130 mph, while the stirring sight of Freddie Dixon's remarkable 2-litre Riley Special nearly keeping up with them was something not to be missed.

But by the end of the 1930s the glory of Brooklands was fading away. Even the rich men who sponsored the monsters – Woolf Barnato and John Cobb among them – were no longer willing to stand the cost of the special track tyres which wore out so quickly, nor the big rebuilding bills which followed a season's rough riding on the outer circuit, nor especially the frustration of having to beat the handicappers before they could beat the opposition. Speeds had now far outstripped the track's potential – the fastest cars were even having to brake before going into the banked turns – and the often-repaired concrete surface was prone to break up under the strain. Along with all the other hazards, this made the track a forbidding place to race in close company; one of the additional obstacles to John Cobb and Oliver Bertram fighting each other in the 1937 '500' was that plate-sized lumps of concrete were dislodged and thrown around like shells. Perhaps the war came as a merciful release for the owners; the last race was held on August 7 1939, though the last speed records (by Forrest Lycett's 8-litre Bentley) were marked up on August 29.

In spite of the undoubted advantage of having Brooklands for testing, along with all the assembled engineering know-how of the 'village', British motor sport was no closer to having its own Grand Prix contender in 1939 than it had been in 1930. Although the ERAs had done magnificently well in their own category, no one seemed anxious to match their brains (nor could they raise enough money) against the might of Germany. It was true that ERA produced a brand new machine in 1939 – the E-Type, which was a look-alike with the latest Mercedes model – but it still retained the Riley-based 1½-litre engine and was intended for voiturette racing.

In the sports car racing sector, patriots tried to drum up support for a new design from time to time, to take on Alfa Romeo, Bugatti or Delehaye, but always had more enthusiasm than resources to convert their ideas into the metal. Lord Howe, for instance, took his proposal for a new car to out-Alfa the 8C2300 all round the motor industry, but got no encouragement from the tycoons. Triumph, and Donald Healey, eventually produced the beautiful supercharged straight-eight Dolomite as a near-copy of the Alfa, but also ran out of money and it was never raced. MG collected hundreds of trophies with their K3s, Qs and R-Types, but the surprise of the decade was certainly the Lagonda win at Le Mans in 1935 (driven by Fontes and Hindmarsh), even if that car was no quicker than the Bentleys had been in 1930.

Bentley, who had waved the Union Jack so successfully in the 1920s, withdrew from racing with a flourish in 1930. Their swansong was a runaway victory at Le Mans that year, their team tactics having demolished a challenge by Mercedes (with a 7-litre super-charged car) on the way. But Bentley's wins at Le Mans had become so regular and their control of this prestigious 24-hour race so complete, that in 1930 only 12 other cars had bothered to start. W. O. Bentley himself then disappeared from the racing scene until the end of the decade. Under his control, though apparently against his wishes (because the

*The last of Bentley's five splendid wins at Le Mans came in 1930, after which the firm withdrew completely from motor racing. The winning drivers, at 75.87 mph were Glen Kidston and Woolf Barnato* (Autocar).

project was conceived in a great rush), two splendid V12 Lagondas were entered for the 1939 Le Mans race, where they might even have won if his orders as to driving speeds had not been rigorously applied.

The other British marque which won sports car events, almost in spite of its manufacture, was Talbot. George Roesch himself was keen enough on motor racing and knew that the engines he had so painstakingly developed were as good as any others, but his company could spare very little time and money, so the works cars had to be run and prepared by Fox & Nicholl in Kingston. After Talbot had been taken over by Rootes, privately-owned examples went on to perform even better than before.

However, if Britain was weak in producing real racing cars and perenially short of money with which to run them, there was certainly no shortage of hopeful drivers. However Raymond Mays, who was already past the first flush of youth, was the outstanding driver in British events, although he was not a 'big car' man and could not be expected to graduate to a real Grand Prix car. The young man who really made his name and became the country's outstanding driver, was Dick Seaman. Seaman was a well-to-do middle class Englishman who had survived a comfortable upbringing and a public school education to race ERAs and that fantastic ten-year-old GP Delage, before being invited to join the all-conquering Mercedes-Benz team for 1937.

Even at the end of 1936, when this invitation materialised, there was quite a lot of anti-Nazi feeling around and Seaman's move to Mercedes-Benz was not universally popular. By taking a nationalistic line Dick Seaman would merely have remained as Britain's best driver and never sat in a competitive GP car at all; but he was not politically-minded and with Mercedes his opportunities were limitless. Stirling Moss faced a similar dilemma in the 1950s and resolved it in the same practical – and successful – manner. Incidentally, Seaman blotted his copybook even before he raced a Mercedes – by crashing one in practice at Monza, in pre-season trials!

In his first GP season the young Briton finished in six races, with a best performance of second over all in the American Vanderbilt Cup event. In 1938 he at last emulated Sir

*The war put a stop to one of Britain's most promising projects – the racing V12 Lagondas which W. O. Bentley had built for the 1939 Le Mans race. They finished third and fourth, running at closely controlled speeds and could have speeded up considerably. This was the Dobson-Brackenbury machine which took third place (Autocar).*

*Britain's best driver was undoubtedly Dick Seaman and the car which he used to great effect in 1936 was this 10-year-old Delage Grand Prix car, seen at Donington on its way to yet another win* (Autocar).

Henry Segrave, by winning a Grand Prix. Not that this pleased everyone, particularly Mercedes themselves, for the event he won was none other than the German GP. With nationalistic fervour in the country rising to new heights, it had been hoped that Lang or Caracciola would win. Perhaps the Germans had their own whimsical revenge, however. Seaman's biographer, Prince Chula, later wrote that: '. . . the most notable feature of the whole affair was the uncomfortable expression on Dick's face as he had to perform the Nazi salute at the close of the race.' Later in the season, Seaman also took second place in Switzerland and third in his 'home' event, the Donington GP.

Tragically, Seaman's brilliant driving career was cut off abruptly by a crash. In 1939, with political complications overhanging the world and with Seaman's place in the team in question (even though he had lately married a German girl), his Mercedes crashed at Spa while he was leading the Belgian GP. It was not a critical accident, nor was Seaman badly injured by it, but before helpers could unfasten the large steering wheel and drag him clear there was a fire; the gallant Seaman died later in hospital.

But if Seaman was Britain's only internationally known racing driver in the 1930s, we were not short of heroes in the record breaking business. Our motor sport at this time posed something of a paradox. Apart from the ERAs, we seemed to be incapable or uninterested in building proper racing cars, but we were very adept and most enthusiastic, in building special cars to squeeze the last ounce of straight-line speed from a particular machine. Record-breaking in the 1930s was almost entirely a British preserve – if it had not been for the annual flag-waving record attempts by Auto-Union and Mercedes-Benz *autobahnen* there would have been no other nation in the hunt.

In record-breaking, MG was most active (with cars which were, theoretically at least, privately owned) – attempting and achieving records with anything from a 750 cc to a 1,500 cc engine over distances as brief as one kilometre and times as long as 24 hours. MG's greatest achievements, in sprints along the German's special straight and wide new autobahn, were achieved with very little support from the factory; before 1935, when Lord

Nuffield sold his own personal company to his industrial combine, MG were far closer to 'official' sponsorship of such attempts.

Although the first MG Midgets were nothing more nor less than re-bodied Morris Minors, Cecil Kimber's mechanics soon developed the little M-Type into a nice taut little sports car and it was not long before faster and more super-tuned versions were being built. Cars developed from M-Types dominated the 1931 'Double-Twelve' Brooklands race (on handicap, of course) and by this time the tiny 847 cc engine had been developed to phenomenal levels with the aid of super-charging. It was burly George Eyston (soon to become known as 'Le Recordman' by the sporting French) who started MG on their road to success in record-breaking. MG built the stubby little single-seater, coded EX120, which was good enough for Eyston to record 87.3 mph over 100 kilometres, in December 1930 with an unsupercharged 750 cc engine. Even today that would be creditable enough for any car with a 750 cc engine, but by the standards of 1930 it was quite remarkable. Nothing daunted, and by no means complacent, MG then carried out a crash development programme to supercharge the engine (it was no coincidence that Eyston had business connections with the Powerplus supercharger concern, whose equipment was chosen) and within six weeks had pushed up their own record to 103 mph.

From then until June 1939 there was never a time when some new MG attempt was not brewing. With a further-developed engine, EX127 pushed speeds up to 140.6 mph by 1936, but bigger-engined MG made even bigger headlines. All MG's later cars were supercharged and the power they eventually extracted from the 1,100 cc engines, modified from K3 power units, was quite startling. By the time Major Gardner persuaded MG to build a special streamlined car based on the K3 chassis, speeds were quite extraordinary. The man in the street, whose Austin Ten or Standard Flying Nine with similar-sized engines could perhaps reach 60 mph on the open road, was quite out of his depth and thought it was done by magic.

The key to Gardner's final achievements lay in the all-enveloping body shape, lovingly and so scientifically evolved by Reid Railton at Brooklands. When Gardner took EX135 to a German autobahn in 1938 and recorded 187.6 mph with the aid of a supercharged 1,100 cc engine, the press in London were not willing to believe the first despatches they received! Months later the car returned to Germany and with an even more powerful version of the engine proceeded to record 203.5 mph. Even in post-war years a re-engined EX135 never went so quickly again.

George Eyston was completely committed to the idea of setting more and yet more records and – backed by generous sponsors like Castrol – continually searched around for new classes to conquer. With the indefatigable help of Ernest Eldridge, himself an ex-Land Speed Record holder of the 1920s, Eyston produced bigger and ever more bizarre vehicles. A robust but crude machine fitted with nothing more exciting than an AEC diesel engine of the type used by London Transport was good enough to give him various 'compression ignition' records, but he then capped this by acquiring an ugly but effective front-wheel-drive endurance monster into which he squeezed a Rolls-Royce Kestrel aero-engine. 'Speed of the Wind', thus equipped, gave him many endurance records and was eventually transmuted into 'Flying Spray' with a vast, specially designed Ricardo V12 diesel, for more and more long distance work at Utah's salt flats.

But even then, in the mid-1930s, Eyston was not content. Always a man with healthy ambition, he would not be satisfied until he had had a crack at the Big One – the outright Land Speed Record. This, above all, was the record the British thought they owned and one that was ripe for improvement. But by the time Captain Eyston had turned his pebble-glassed gaze on the 'Blue Riband' of speed, much had already been done.

When the Great War ended in 1918, the fastest speeds achieved by a car were no higher

**Above** *George Eyston on his way to yet another set of records, this time in the strange AEC diesel-engined car which also had a truck chassis. This car achieved almost 100 mph at Monthléry in 1936* (Autocar).

**Above right** *Dignity and streamlining side by side. 'Goldie' Gardner's sensationally fast 1.1-litre super-charged MG record car, EX135, parked at the side of a German autobahn after its 203 mph runs in June 1939. The V12 Lagonda was in use as a high-speed chase car* (Autocar).

**Below right** *Captain George Eyston seemed to spend the entire decade setting and breaking speed records. 'Speed of the Wind' was the first of his Rolls-Royce aero-engined monsters which took endurance records in 1935 and 1936.* (Associated Press).

than 124 mph, by a massive Benz, officially timed on the Brooklands track. Before the next world war put a stop to all motor sport, that record had been raised to a shatteringly impressive 369 mph. In 20 years the speed had risen, therefore, by 245 mph – or by an astonishing 300 per cent – but the power needed to ensure this had rocketed from 200 to 4,700 bhp! Further, the space needed to demonstrate such speeds in comparative safety had increased to at least 15 miles, a stretch which could only be found on the eerily flat and barren salt flats at Utah, in the United States. The uncheatable laws of aerodynamics dictated that if cars were to go that much faster they would either have to be almost perfectly streamlined or would have to use enormously powerful aero-engines. It was British drivers, British engineers and British backers who solved these requirements in the 1920s and by the time 1930 arrived, no other nation was even in the hunt.

At the time, too, it would be reasonable to point out that no other driver apart from Captain Malcolm Campbell was actively involved. In recent years his main rivals had been Parry Thomas, Ray Keech (who was American) and Sir Henry Segrave – Segrave having raised the record, in 1929, to 231 mph with Golden Arrow. Now, however, Thomas was dead, as was Keech, and Segrave had turned to record attempts on water.

Campbell was one of the rare (and fast-disappearing) breed of men who was intensely patriotic and wanted to keep the reputation of Great Britain at the top of the prestige table. His very first record attempts, with more simple machines, had been largely self-financed, but by 1930 his trade connections and actual cash contributions from tycoons like Lord Wakefield, were helping to make more ambitious machinery possible. When Campbell

had built his first Bluebird car his target had been 180 mph, and the engine chosen produced a mere 500 bhp, but by 1930 the car had already undergone two major rebuilds and engine change. His best speed, to that time, had been 207 mph in 1928, but with Segrave now out of the hunt and his own burning ambitions unsatisfied, he was on the look out for even greater speeds.

At this point the illustrious name and reputation of Reid Railton appears on the scene. When Campbell managed to cajole the Air Ministry into releasing a Schneider Trophy Napier Lion engine of 1,450 bhp, he then commissioned Railton, along with Thomson & Taylor, to redesign the car. By the beginning of 1931 the latest car, much longer, sleeker and more purposeful-looking than before, was ready to roll. Campbell took it to Daytona Beach in Florida (there was no suitable raceway in Britain for the high speeds he was attaining) and with little trouble pushed the Land Speed Record up to 246 mph.

By present-day standards this is not particularly high – in 1970, for instance, the Le Mans Porsche 917s were reputedly capable of 240 mph and only needed 5-litre engines to achieve this – nor was it even approaching the fastest aeroplane speeds of the day (the Supermarine S6B seaplane was to set a new air record at 407 mph later in 1931) but it was

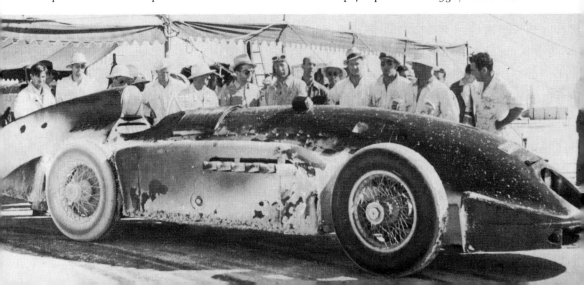

enough to discourage the opposition. 'Wizard' Smith made an abortive attempt in New Zealand and Kaye Don's spectacular 24-cylinder twin-engined Silver Bullet had already failed dismally to set competitive speeds.

From 1931 onwards, Sir Malcolm (he was knighted in 1931 for his exploits) was racing against himself. In 1932 a slightly improved Bluebird was back at Daytona to add 8 mph to its own speeds, but for 1933 another big rebuild was needed. This time the persuasive Campbell had winkled a Rolls-Royce R-Type V12 aero-engine out of the Ministry and with 2,350 bhp at his disposal he could hope for better things. He set the record at 272.46 mph in 1933, and after taking a full year off for a full-width bodyshell to be evolved, was back early in 1935, looking for 300 mph.

Conditions on the beach in March that year were poor and it was a very frustrated Campbell who could only raise the record to 276.8 mph. No amount of persuasion, or even financial inducement, could make Sir Malcolm race over that bumpy, tide-swept beach again and later in the year he returned with an unchanged car to the salt flats at Utah. After surviving a terrifying tyre blow-out at very high speed on his first run, the gallant knight finally notched up 301 mph for the two-way run through a kilometre – and promptly retired from the car record-breaking business.

After Sir Malcolm had let it be known that he was now turning his attentions to the Water Speed record, both George Eyston and Cobb decided to attack his Bluebird mark. Eyston, a doer rather than a philosophical engineering thinker, conceived a massive but brutally effective design – a real monster with no fewer than eight wheels, two Rolls-Royce R-Type engines and 4,700 bhp, which weighed seven tons! Beans Industries of Tipton in Staffordshire built the beast – dubbed 'Thunderbolt' – in a mere six weeks and by the end of 1937 Eyston had managed to nudge the record up to 312 mph. His huge car was so heavy that it needed two front axles and four steerable wheels, but under its bluff-nosed shape there was a great deal of technical bravery to be studied. It might have been brute force, but it certainly was not ignorance; incidentally, Thunderbolt is certainly *the* most powerful wheel-driven record car ever to be built.

While Eyston's car was being built, John Cobb was commissioning Reid Railton (now released from his Campbell activities) to build him a record car. As could have been expected from the inventive Railton, the new car was a very advanced design. Like Eyston's monster it had twin engines, but these were 1,250 bhp supercharged Napier Lions, slung at each side of a tubular backbone frame. Logically enough, the new car was simply called a 'Railton Special'. All four wheels were driven (the front wheels by one engine, the rear wheels by the other) and all up weight was not more than 3½-tons. Topping it all was the most beautifully streamlined shape one could imagine, one which Railton thought would make up for the 2,200 bhp power deficiency compared with Thunderbolt.

Both cars were at Utah together in the summer of 1938 and their duel is something which will perhaps never be forgotten. There was intense rivalry, but there was also friendly co-operation between the two drivers, who had base camps adjacent to each other. Conditions took time to become ideal, as did the weather itself and it was Eyston (with Thunderbolt) who first set a new record at 345.5 mph. A few days later, the Railton, looking tiny and beetle-like by comparison, scudded over the same salt to reach 350.2 mph, but the very next day, almost before Cobb had had time to enjoy the celebratory champagne, Eyston took out a specially-modified Thunderbolt to beat him at 357.5 mph.

Eyston's approach, incidentally, was certainly that of a mechanic rather than a designer or even a businessman. When he was faced with the urgent need for more speed and little time to achieve this, his 'instant' solution was to throw away the carefully designed water

**Top left** *Sir Malcolm Campbell facing the press at a conference before setting out for Daytona Beach (and another successful record attempt) in January 1935. This car eventually achieved 301 mph at Utah later in the year (Autocar).*

**Above left** *Side view of the final Bluebird which Sir Malcolm Campbell used to leave the Land Speed Record at 301 mph in 1935. Note that in this final form it had twin rear wheels to aid the traction (Autocar).*

**Below** *A contrast in record breakers in this photomontage. Lord Nuffield stands by the side of the sleek and low Gardner-special MG record car (which eventually achieved more than 200 mph on a German autobahn), and workmen push out the completed Thunderbolt Land Speed Record contender from its workshops at Beans Industries at Tipton in 1937 (Autocar).*

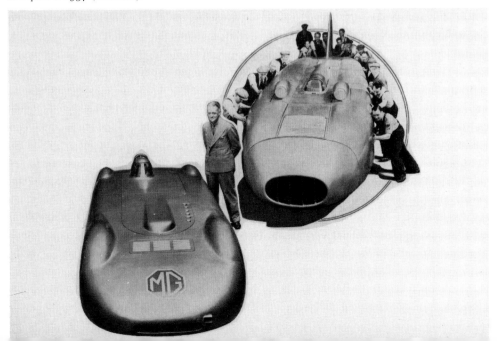

**Above left** *Captain George Eyston, who so kindly provided the Foreword to this book, was one of our leading racing motorist/record breaking personalities of the period. At one time he held the World's Land Speed Record in the gargantuan Thunderbolt* (National Motor Museum).

**Above right** *The huge (7 ton) Thunderbolt car which George Eyston used to break the World's Land Speed Record on three occasions in 1937 and 1938. Its highest speed was 357.5 mph. It used two 36.5-litre Rolls-Royce V12 engines (each of 2,350 bhp), had six wheels, but drove only the rear pair. It was destroyed by fire in New Zealand a short time later* (Autocar).

cooling system, close in the vast nose with a light cone and rely on ice cooling for the short record runs! Modern drag-racing fans will recognise the technique.

With the Munich crisis in the air both protagonists returned to Britain, Eyston to think about a drastic lightening programme for his car and Cobb merely to refine the complicated little machine he already had. A year later, the Railton re-appeared at Utah, raising the record to a splendid 369.74 mph (even though Reid Railton was convinced that it could eventually exceed 400 mph) but did this so late in August 1939 that when war broke out Cobb himself was still on his way home, by sea, and the car had to stay in North America for a time.

The Railton, incidentally, re-appeared again in 1947, after the war and raised the record to 394 mph (with a one-way best of 403 mph, thus vindicating Railton's theories), while Thunderbolt was finally destroyed accidentally in a fire in New Zealand, where the car was being stored in the war years. The record-breaking fever of the 1930s was not revived again until the 1960s, when Sir Malcolm Campbell's son, Donald, persuaded the British motor industry to build him an expensive and (finally) successful turbine-powered Bluebird.

Without the record cars and their brave drivers, there would have been little British success to boast about in the 1930s. It is easy enough, and true enough, to point this out now, but at the time not many enthusiasts would have agreed. For in politics and in the design of family cars, the British were then quite depressingly insular. It did not seem to

*Personalities all – (left to right) Cecil Kimber of MG, A. C. R. Waite of Austin, Sir Malcolm Campbell and Captain George Eyston, inspecting the chassis of the all-independent suspension R-Type single seater racing MG* (Autocar).

matter what was going on in the world outside, as long as we inward-looking British were self-satisfied. That notorious *Times* headline: 'Storms in English Channel. Continent cut off', might have belonged to another age and other occasions, but it still summed up our attitudes very well.

In motor sport, what happened at Brooklands, and occasionally at Donington, was thought to be exciting enough and few questioned it. But drivers who ventured abroad were not so easily fooled. Sir Henry Birkin, in the 'ghosted' autobiography published in 1932, said:

'I think that (Brooklands) is, without exception, the most out-of-date, inadequate and dangerous track in the world . . . it has only kept its importance so long because it has never had a rival in England since its creation . . . A system of handicapping has been made essential . . . and had the handicaps not been so brilliantly proportioned by Mr Ebblewhite, the official starter, all public curiosity would have vanished years ago.'

In his foreword to the same book, Earl Howe wrote that:

'Few of us in England realise the enormous importance attached to motor racing on the Continent . . . Success in the big Continental events carries great international prestige and is looked upon as being a great advertisement for the industries of the countries concerned; so much so that it is common knowledge that in some countries the governments concerned have considered it worth while to render assistance to the competing firms, either directly or indirectly. This being so, one cannot help feeling that it is a very great pity that some of the English firms cannot make greater efforts to compete either individually or collectively . . ..'

Elsewhere in this book, Birkin pleads:

'It is so little to ask, either a team of three cars, or a road circuit that will allow us to hold up our heads once more among foreigners. One would follow the other; and lest any person, horrified by my mention of the Schneider Trophy and £100,000, be inclined to exaggerate the cost, I give my word that £20,000 would cover all experimental and incidental expense and build a team of three cars good enough to lead the world . . ..'

How times have changed. Birkin's £20,000 would not buy a single 'identikit' Formula One car, let alone race it, rebuild it, test and develop it or pay its second-rate prima donna of a driver. Today sponsorship is sought in public, assiduously courted and performed for. Although motor racing in the 1930s was much too dignified a pastime to descend to this level, there was still a great deal of covert sponsorship about. But however much we plead that more and more of the middle classes were happy and able to go motoring, it was also true that not many of the car makers were prosperous enough to consider throwing their money around in motor sport. Nuffield might have tolerated the appearance of MGs in international events and 'Pa' Austin the building and racing of three very special little twin-cam Austins, neither was the slightest bit interested in sponsoring a Grand Prix team. In that respect, at least, times have not changed a lot!

# Chapter 9

# Motor sport for us – the clubmen

Getting started in motor sport now is easy. Once armed with a competition licence and with almost any sort of car, there is no problem in finding somewhere to use it; the biggest problem is one of choice. Whether we choose autocross or rallies, driving tests or hill-climbs, sprints or club races, production car trials, sporting trials or drag racing . . . there is something for everyone. There is also a vast 'bolt-on' tuning business to service the demand for car improvements and book shops full of specialist magazines catering for every quirk. As with almost every other aspect of the leisure business, facilities have mushroomed and interest has expanded to match. Big business, marketing, promotion, publicity and sponsorship have all arrived on the scene, even at local motor club level. The whole scene is multi-coloured, brash and actively exciting.

Forty or fifty years ago it was all very different. Motoring, especially for sport and pleasure, was still developing its ideas. There was very little commercial involvement and we British lacked almost every sort of circuit, organisation or facility. Just look back and consider: fast road-rallying, autocross, drag racing and sporting trials for outright 'specials' had not even been invented. We could choose between only two racing circuits, very few hillclimb courses and had only one noted sprint venue. Sporting enthusiasts could read only two important weekly motoring magazines (*The Autocar* and *The Motor*, although *The Light Car* was still struggling on) and two sporting monthlies (*Motor Sport*, which included *The Brooklands Gazette*, and *Speed*). The weeklies were very middle class and upright (one nearly wrote 'uptight' – with some reason) while the monthlies were obsessed with Brooklands and Donington to the exclusion of much club interest.

There were few active motor clubs, particularly by comparison with today and the sporting calendar was decidedly thin. Nothing of any note took place before Easter and the year's racing was all over by October; apart from sporting trials and the annual pilgrimage to Monte Carlo in January, the winter was a sporting wilderness. This, of course, helps to explain why the press should make so much of the Brighton Speed Trials, of the Shelsley Walsh hill climb or of long-distance trials like the 'Lands End' and 'Exeter' classics. It was not that these had been singled out for special reporting, but that they were pre-eminent events in the non-racing calendar.

As far as motor racing itself was concerned, the clubman (which tended to mean anyone who was not rather wealthy) was faced with two major snags. The almost complete lack of circuits or other venues has already become obvious, but there was another – no British company made racing cars at the right price. Almost throughout the 1930s, the racing car 'industry' was non-existent. The exceptions were ERA (who built 17 voiturette single-seaters between 1934 and 1937) and MG (whose 10 R-Type single-seaters sold for no less than £750 each) and Geoffrey Taylor's Alta concern.

How on earth did we manage? With enough money available today, we can go out and choose from dozens of single-seaters in a totally confusing number of classes; they can have alternative engines, bodywork, wheels, transmissions . . . we are almost embarrassed by the choice. In the 1930s, as far as single-seater racing cars were concerned, the only alternative to the rare ERAs or MGs was to build a special for oneself, or to look at the very expensive offerings from Europe. It was all very well for the wealthy young Whitney Straight to go off to Italy in 1933, buy a trio of new Maseratis, commission Reid Rilton to install British pre-selector gearboxes, then race them in Britain and in Europe, but few could afford to emulate him. Lord Howe might be able to afford to buy a fearsomely fast Bugatti or two, while other wealthy patrons could run to 8-cylinder Alfa Romeos, but they were in the tiny minority.

Even on the mainland of Europe, the racing-car industry was tiny. Mercedes-Benz and Auto-Union were only interested in building the world's best Grand Prix cars to race against each other and they *never* sold off last year's models. On the contrary, Mercedes-Benz, having finished with *any* racing car, liked to lay it down in storage, like a good vintage wine, to be sampled again in later years. Only Alfa-Romeo, Bugatti and Maserati were equipped to race their own factory cars and also to sell new racing cars, though they made sure that the cars they sold were never quite as fast nor as up-to-the-minute as the ones they kept to race! But there is nothing new in that: Ferrari, Maserati and several British companies operated in the same way in the 1950s and 1960s.

Grand Prix racing rapidly became so expensive and so prestigious, as the two German teams tightened their grip on proceedings, that the French and Italian teams virtually gave up trying to compete. At least, as a by-product, this made it a little easier for the well-heeled amateur to enjoy racing in a thoroughbred racing car at other levels of the sport, for the out-dated Alfas, Bugattis and Maseratis were still useful away from the Grand Prix circuits and could often be up-dated and modified by their new owners.

But if one was unwilling to buy foreign, the only alternative was to build a racing car oneself. More than any other time, probably, the 1930s was the era of the 'special', which in all probability meant that it was a 'Brooklands special'. The basis was usually that of a British sports car, though the crashed remains of suitably glamorous imported racing machines were often rifled for likely bits and pieces. A really big car, however, would often have a Bentley engine – sometimes a supercharged $4\frac{1}{2}$-litre, but occasionally one of the rare race-tuned 8-litre versions – but in most cases an MG or Riley unit would be chosen, of between 1,100 cc and 2,000 cc. Razor-edge tuning was developed into a fine art and usually pin-pointed time and time again the lack of knowledge about high risk items like cylinder head gaskets, pistons and crankshaft bearings.

Although the art and science of cylinder head gas-flowing was not yet fully understood, an obvious and superfically easy way to boost any engine's performance was to resort to supercharging. The laws of aerodynamics were not known to many, which explains the bluff and gangling shape of some cars which appeared at Brooklands. Reducing friction, by taking infinite pains, was a good way of helping things along. Legend had it that mechanic-tuner-drivers like Freddie Dixon could raise any car's maximum speed merely by stripping out the gearbox or back axle, then re-assembling them properly. Time was considered as valuable in engine preparation as was the use of special parts. In his monumental history of MG, Wilson McComb recalls the belief that MG's own racing engines differed fundamentally from the normal overhead-camshaft units supplied to customers: 'They were not [although certain special components were used], but they *were* properly assembled. Phillips commonly devoted at least a week to preparing the top end of a racing engine and no one considered that he was wasting his time.'

Consider, now, the difficulties facing the builder of his own 'special'. Where was he to race it? At Brooklands, certainly, which was a unique track placing absolute emphasis on speed and stability and precious little on road-holding. How, then, was he to reconcile this with the requirements of Donington Park (a splendid artificial road circuit, in much the same vein as was Oulton Park in the 1950s and 1960s) and, latterly, with the serpentine twists of Crystal Palace? What engine size should he choose? 750 cc – and be faced with hordes of Austin Seven or MG specials? 1,100 cc – a Riley or MG engine would suffice? An unfashionable engine, perhaps – a Lagonda, a Singer, an Anzani? How tuneable or how reliable were these units? Should he build a single-seater, which would probably mean that a special chassis was needed too? Or a two-seater, with more frontal area, which would be slower on the long straights at Brooklands and Donington?

Yet many built their own cars and several became rightly famous. A real 'Dixon' Riley (140 mph from only 2-litres) or a white-hot supercharged Austin Seven (more than 100 mph from 750 cc) would be notable in any age. Tyres were a problem, particularly at Brooklands and especially on heavy cars, where the combined effect of cornering and banking forces gave the rubber a very hard time. Classes were not so rigid as they are today and even though entrants were just as adept at preparing their cars to the very edge of a regulation or limit, there was no use for things like scrutineers' bibles or homologation forms.

At first sight, there was no rhyme nor reason in some people's choice of cars with which to race. How could anyone with an older 3.3-litre Bugatti compete on equal terms with an Austin Seven Ulster? How could an 1,100 cc Brooklands Riley expect to compete with a chopped-and-channelled 6½-litre Speed Six Bentley. Would you expect to race a pure-bred 2.3-litre Monza Alfa Romeo against a much-modified 3½-litre Rolls-Bentley? This was the problem with which the administrators of national motor sport had to grapple and, as I have already pointed out in an earlier chapter, this was solved with recourse to handicap racing. In this the British were isolated from the rest of Europe, where there were enough pure-bred racing cars to make class racing possible and competitive.

Handicap racing was exciting enough if officials had done their sums properly, but was only really appropriate to short events (a five lap race, say, at Brooklands) where all competing cars would always be on the same lap, and where the fastest 'scratch' runners could be seen visibly to be catching up with the limit men. There was, naturally, a temptation for a driver to 'pull' his car in minor races, so as to save it for bigger (and more lucrative) events *and* to gain a better handicap; in the small circle that was British motor racing this rarely happened, and when it did it was swiftly discovered.

Brooklands, Donington and Crystal Palace were our principal circuits, but for a time there was one very popular racing week in the Isle of Man, when the Mannin Moar and Mannin Beg races saw racing cars snarling around the streets of Douglas. But how times have changed. Silverstone, Goodwood, Brands Hatch, Snetterton and Oulton Park literally did not exist.

In a full season, there might be one race meeting every weekend between April and October, with only a few gaps, but never with any clashes. A racing car might be limited to not more than 15 appearances in a season, even if it was perfectly reliable and was not crashed. At the end of the year it was most certainly not obsolete and would disappear into the owner's little garage for a six-month modification session which might result in minor performance gains for the next season. Ultimate tuning sessions often resulted in 'expensive noises' (this was an 'in' phrase of the 1930s) and sometimes required startling engineering innovations to suit. Murray Jamieson, before producing those exciting little twin-cam Austin racing cars at Longbridge, concentrated on the supercharging of side-valve Austin Seven engines – with such success and such high combustion pressures that their cylinder heads had to be held down by no fewer than 32 studs and nuts! Bronze cylinder head castings (which were even better than aluminium for dispersing heat) were fashionable and alcohol-based fuel 'brews' were essential. The Brooklands 'village', replete with tiny

**Above** *Massed-start racing was comparatively rare in Britain due to the preponderance of handicap events. This is the scramble to gain advantage at the beginning of the 1937 JCC Donington 200-Mile race, with 'Bira's' Maserati (No 4) marginally ahead of Mays' ERA (No 8) and Dobson's similar ERA (No 9). Dobson was the eventual winner* (Autocar).

**Below** *Racing in the streets! The promenade at Douglas, in the Isle of Man, welcomed the British motor racing circus several times for the Mannin Beg and Mannin Moar races. Bugattis, Alfas and ERAs completely dominate this start line scene* (Autocar).

engineering firms which could produce special pistons in a week, or machined castings overnight, was the centre of the business and tiny firms like Vic Derrington's were already famous. In those cash-short days no one had masses of spare parts. To change one blown Grand Prix engine for another is strictly a post-war phenomenon – in the 1930s a major break-down was a disaster.

New circuits were proposed from time to time, but were little more than pipe-dreams. Facilities on Brighton Downs, in the Chiltern Hills near Ivinghoe, in Scotland near Edinburgh and close to Scarborough, were all canvassed, but progressed no further than paper dreams. One very grandoise scheme actually got as far as a few stakes in the sand, a set of offices in Boston, Lincolnshire and a flood of well-intentioned press releases. This exception was the so-called 'Wash Speedway' – which was more of a records *piste* than a motor racing circuit and which relied more on faith and big ideas than on practicality.

First announcements came in 1929, but a start was not made until two years later. The Speedway, it was said, would have a 15-mile straight strip of concrete 100 ft wide, with no less than four *miles* of grandstand along the middle stretch and would be built on the foreshore of the Wash, roughly between Boston and Skegness. There would also be a road racing circuit and a large speed-boat racing area; in the interests of safety the track and grandstands would be separated by the lake itself. It was all supposed to be built for £300,000, so that our heroes could go on to break their records without leaving Britain.

At first, well-respected figures like Earl Howe and Woolf Barnato joined the board of

*During the 1930s Lord Austin authorised the construction of a team of very special Austin Seven single-seaters. Three twin-cam 750 cc machines were built, of which one was written off in a crash and the other two became very successful in British handicap events. In this group picture, the two twin-cams are on the right, while Kay Petre is in a supercharged side-valve machine (whose engine was broadly based on the existing Austin Seven engine). The other drivers are Charles Goodacre (centre) and Bert Hadley (right) (Autocar).*

**Background photograph** *The well-known MG 'Cream Cracker' trials team of much-modified TA models, on their way to yet another prize-winning performance in a British sporting trial. Note the 'knobbly' tyres which were outlawed in 1938* (National Motor Museum).

**Inset** *Raymond Mays and an ERA seemed inseparable in the later 1930s. Here he is, with only a linen helmet for head protection, on his way to yet another record-breaking climb of Shelsley Walsh. The year is 1939 and his time was 37.37 seconds* (Autocar).

directors, but within months they had smelt a rat and resigned. The offices on Boston were only 'window-dressing', as by the time the receiver got his hands on the scheme it was found to be fraudulent. He reported debts of more than £8,000, but assets of only £72. All that remained then was that line of stakes.

But even if the scheme had come to anything, it would not have been valuable for long. A 100 feet might have sounded wide enough, but at the speeds Cobb and Eyston were to reach before 1939, that width would have been dangerously narrow.

On the fringe of circuit racing were the hillclimb and sprint courses, along with a modicum of events like sand-racing at Southport or the occasional light-hearted hillclimb on private estate roads in the West Country. When the Bugatti Owners' Club bought the Prescott estate near Cheltenham and produced a short but demanding hill-climb course, this was a major advance in facilities.

Special cars for sprints and hill climbs were often even more spidery and improbable-looking than their circuit equivalents and in many cases things like bodywork and front brakes were discarded in the interests of weight reduction. If one engine could not be persuaded to produce enough power a second engine was added; the ultimate in this respect must surely have been John Bolster's 'Bloody Mary' and the *four*-engined car which evolved from it.

Brighton, with its one kilometre-long sprint course laid out along the sea front at Madeira Drive, was a very good place for the boaster to prove the claims of his latest machine, for all that was needed was traction, stability and straight-line performance. It was at Shelsley Walsh, a short and twisty little hill climb on private ground, not far from Worcester, where every possible demand could be made of a car in a short space of time and it was a mecca for the clubman. A big car, even a big-engined small car, was not necessarily the best suited to its serpentine slopes; Raymond Mays usually proved this each year in his Bugattis, his White Riley or with faster and ever faster ERAs. We all became thoroughly used to hearing that Mays had won at Shelsley Walsh, so when A. F. P. Fane's single-seater Frazer Nash beat him one year it caused something of a sensation in the motoring press. But Shelsley Walsh, like our own motor racing circuits, bred a particularly British type of sport. There was little interest shown from continental drivers, who were more accustomed to tackling ten-mile climbs on fast public roads closed for the occasion. Sheer power was not enough, in any case, at Shelsley, as was proved in 1936 when Hans Stuck turned up with a mid-engined GP Auto-Union to try his hand. It was a talking point for weeks before and afterwards, but his performance was hampered by wet roads and by a lack of local expertise.

Shelsley Walsh might have drawn big crowds, but the branch of motor sport which drew the biggest entries at the start of the 1930s was the rather masochistic business of sporting trials. Even today there are dozens of people willing to hurl perfectly good sports and touring cars up the worst of gradients and on the mud and rocks of tracks laughably called 'Observed Sections', but their heyday was the 1930s.

The tradition had probably developed from the original Thousand Miles Trial and had become most famous in the terrible trio of events, the Exeter, Lands End and Edinburgh Trials, which were all organised by the Motor Cycling Club (MCC – not to be confused with the administrators of world cricket). By the end of the vintage years this peculiarly British type of motor sport had developed its band of fanatics, whose special kinds of skill had to be matched to a special sort of car.

In the beginning British trials had been reliability trials, where reasonably uncouth roads had been slotted into a road course in some profusion to encourage the early motor car to break down. Timing and reliability was thought to be as important as hill-climbing ability at first and many competitors were quite unable to reach the finish of events because of mechanical disasters. As cars developed, so trials had to change their ways to keep up their standards of difficulty. It was no longer enough to place a steep hill in their way. Now it had to be a loose-surfaced steep hill, or – better still – a rough, boulder-strewn, muddy, steep hill, with hairpins and a stop-restart test thrown in as well!

Surprisingly, this had not then led to the development of special 'trials cars' of the type now essential in British sporting trials, though the Allard Special was developed towards the end of the decade with this in mind. In the main, however, a typical long-distance trial at the start of the 1930s attracted a huge entry mainly consisting of outwardly standard-looking sports and touring cars, which nevertheless seemed able to climb the most alarming looking declivities.

Certain geographical areas were very popular, because all manner of difficult sections could be found. Either these were over thoroughly neglected public rights of way, or were on private tracks, lanes or hillsides where the land-owners were friendly and did not mind the invasion of spectators, who often turned up in their thousands. The really famous hills – like Bluehills Mine and Beggars Roost in the West Country, Piccadilly or Juniper in the Cotswolds, or Jenkins Chapel in Derbyshire – would be lined by an army of lookers-on. Local police would often have a difficult job regarding parking, localised traffic jams and congestion in general.

Standards of driving and of car preparation, improved rapidly, so that many of the old favourites became 'easy'. Beggars Roost might have been famous and difficult once, but it rather lost its reputation when the fans realised that the local post van was quite accustomed to drive up it every morning.

Locals were often aghast, or more often openly amused, by the hills chosen for attack by

*Sporting trials were extraordinarily popular in the 1930s. Here is a large crowd watching an MG Midget climb Beggar's Roost in a West Country event* (Autocar).

the trials fraternity. Many of the later sections, which were difficult enough to stop most of the runners, led nowhere and were certainly never intended to be normally used by any form of car; after an unexpected successful climb a car had to return the way it had come! The whole atmosphere and friendly spirit of pre-war trials is beautifully caught in C. A. N. May's book *Wheelspin*, which covers his years in the sport. May was a private owner living in the Midlands, who stayed loyal to MG sports cars throughout the decade, in spite of various mechanical disasters, had a fair amount of success and stayed with the trials scene until it closed down in 1939.

His book draws freely on contemporary magazine reports to illustrate his own experiences in these events. This quote, regarding one horror near Cheltenham, tells us much about the way the hills were rapidly turning into freaks which no motorist would normally visit:

'Frightful rumours had been current all day concerning the severity of the last hill, called Leckhampton in the programme and known locally as the Jinny. This hill turned out to be like at least four Simms Hills rolled into one, slippery surface, 1 in 2½ gradient and tractor were all there.' (Note: The tractor, actuating a wire cable, was stationed at the summit for the purpose of hauling up cars which could not climb unaided, as it was quite impossible even for a mass of spectators to manhandle a car to the top.) 'Special permission had been obtained for the use of the hill, which is common land and reserved as a rule for walkers only.' In fact it formed the base of a now-dismantled wire-rope railway to the quarry at its summit. I have inspected this 'road' in recent years and been quite unable to see how any car could ever have climbed it, but climb it they did.

Again, he also quotes comment on one unbelievably nasty hill called Colly, near Luxborough on Exmoor, which was only ever used twice to defeat the dedicated experts:

'Colly starts as little more than a V-bottomed ditch, between very high banks, with foliage meeting overhead and giving a tunnel effect. It emerges into the light of day at a right-handed, right-angle corner, at which point the gradient stiffens sharply and there are some fierce rock steps. As it continues, still between hedges and very narrow, there is mud, rocks, mud, rock outcrop and ledges like a flight of stairs. It is the ditch at the beginning that is the most alarming part. The shelving sides go down to meet in a sharp deep V, so that cars have to be forced to straddle the ditch – a precarious performance.'

It was here, indeed, in 1937, that Sidney Allard overturned the Allard Special, jamming it across the track and slightly injuring himself and his wife in the process. His car had, quite literally, slid down into the V and overbalanced.

The Exeter, the Lands End and the Edinburgh were the long-distance 'classics' and there was a special 'Triple' trophy for gaining a Gold Medal (for an unpenalised run) in each event of one year. Other favourites were the Colmore, the Gloucester, the Abingdon and the Brighton-Beer. Tradition, it seems, dies hard. By mid-1930s that last-named event had not started anywhere near Brighton for some time and it often did not finish anywhere near the Devon township of Beer!

It was a good-natured, friendly and social type of motoring, in which breakdowns were expected as a matter of course and were tackled cheerfully at the road side. Modern rally enthusiasts who talk about half shaft and differential changes at service points may like to know that the trials fraternity tackled their own re-builds without the assistance of mechanics and carried their own spare ring-and-pinion sets behind the seats, the better to aid traction as well as being good insurance.

**Opposite** *One of the public relations problems which eventually brought sporting trials into disrepute in the 1930s. Queues of cars often had to wait to tackle difficult sections (while failed cars were manhandled clear). This was a Colmore Trial, near Cheltenham, in the mid 1930s (Autocar).*

The start of a long-distance event would often be many miles away from the action –
one of the popular road-houses was ideal for this sort of thing – and the finish would be at
some welcoming and understanding hostelry where blazing fires and a multitude of hot
baths were almost mandatory. Almost by definition, the really popular trials were held in
the autumn and winter months and always seemed to attract rain, fog and mud. Since
many competitors used open cars and it was very *infra-dig* to erect the hood, their state at
the end of a day's bouncing and mud-slinging can be imagined.

But even this branch of motor sport could not be expected to survive forever on the basis
of friendship and good competition. Professionalism and the support of some teams by
factories, was quick to spread, particularly when interest in the support of expensive sports
car racing begane to wane. MG, Austin and Singer were most active. All sponsored semi-
professional teams – Austin with their Grasshoppers, MG with the Cream Crackers and
Musketeers and Singer with the Candidi Provocatores – which brought a very smart new
approach to this essentially scruffy sport. The cars themselves were by no means standard;
supercharging and super-tuning was a matter of course and – when it was still allowed –
locked back axles were fitted in place of normal differentials. Special low gears were usually
fitted, as well as abbreviated wings, skimpy bodywork, wooden or even canvas body panels
and much lightening of the vehicles where wheel loadings were not important. On the
other hand, there was rarely any attempt to shield sumps and transmissions; cracked sump
pans and axle casings were common problems. But this sort of enterprise soon led to ext-
treme modifications; for 1938 the Musketeers' MG TAs had Marshall-supercharged
engines, while the Cream Cracker TAs had much-modified VA engines which were
eventually enlarged to 1,700 cc. It was enough to ensure their continued success, but it was
also enough to discourage the private owners.

The popularity of sporting trials in the mid-1930s began to produce its own probelms.
As the competing cars, particularly those crewed by sponsored drivers, became more and
more effective, organisers had to abandon their traditional hills and find more and more
lurid challenges. Special 'knobbly' competition tyres were developed to meet this challenge. The result was that seemingly impossible quagmires could be conquered. In
time the residents of peaceful little country villages, through which the routes often led,
began to protest strenuously, and with justification, about their weekends being disturbed,
their roads being blocked and their surroundings being strewn with mud. To those suffering from the tyranny of night rallies in modern times, the cause and effect is all very
familiar.

By the beginning of 1938 government departments had already noted a possible nuisance and were casting around for ways to minimise it. They had already asked the RAC
to find ways of solving the problem. By mid-year it had been decided to ban competition
tyres, which – in theory – meant that a return would have to be made to more hills, where
gradient rather than knee-deep mud would provide the challenge and would render some
sections quite unattainable.

The ban came into effect in January 1939, but the Gloucester Trial of December 1938
applied the ban as an experiment to assess the effects. The result was predictable – there
were wholesale failures to climb most of the hills and huge delays, plus even more road
blocking and traffic jamming. Another result, quite unexpected, was that the semi-
professionals were better-placed even than before. As R. A. MacDermid (himself a
successful trials driver) pointed out in a magazine article:

'With a reversion to plain treads the advantages of the car built for trials and trials alone
are increased instead of decreased and my reason for saying this is weight. Total weight,
not merely power-weight ratio, has always been a factor of major importance; plain tyres
make it doubly so. Power is useless if you cannot transmit it and when you come to a slip-

*This was Red Roads – a very steep freak climb much loved by trials enthusiasts in the Home Counties. There was a lot of grip, but the gradient was more severe than 1-in-2 in places* (Autocar).

pery hill, the man with the least amount of motor car to carry up with him will get the highest.'

By now, however, entries in sporting trials were consistently on the wane. The peak had been recorded in 1935, but the combination of 'factory entries' (which they were, in all but name) and the use of more damaging and more difficult sections had seriously weakened the interest of the true amateur. The banning of competition tyres, which made the whole business farcical at times, was another severe blow. Even before the end of 1938, however, entries had often dropped by half and it was clear that a new vogue was developing; this, of course, was the sport of rallying.

To rally is an activity defined one way in the dictionaries and another way by motoring enthusiasts. *The Concise Oxford Dictionary* might define it as 'to reassemble, get together again' or even 'to revive by effort of will', but surely this does not define the steady stream of cars making for obscure control points at exact times? In any case, even the sport of motor rallying has changed so much over the years that we cannot compare the 1930s with the present day.

In the 1930s there was no question of highly-specialised 250 bhp projectiles being involved. There was no question of cars hurtling through forests and over military ranges, nor was the special navigational technique of directing a car along obscure country lanes yet developed. Apart from the very few European marathons which pointed the way to post-war rallying standards, most events were seldom more than gentle long-distance

*A ceremonial parade of competing cars in the RAC Rally of 1936, on its way towards Torquay's promenade. The RAC Rally always finished at a popular seaside resort and was usually held in the spring of the year* (Autocar).

trundles over good roads to a final collecting point, where a few simple driving tests, an elegant *Concours d'Elegance* and a riotous prize-giving rounded it all off.

It was all so much more civilised (and potentially enjoyable) than the grubby business of trials. Finishing points were often comfortable and placid seaside resort and the wear and tear on one's own car was much less serious. At first, in the 1920s, it had been different classes of persons who competed and the 'social atmosphere' was considered to be very important. The Monte Carlo Rally and the Alpine Trial, on the other hand, were entirely different propositions and were not tackled in the same spirit. In Britain, however, the gentle sport of rallying took in more and more followers. A 'good rally car' was not necessarily the fastest, nor the strongest, but it certainly had to be a useful proposition in and with the *Concours d'Elegance* as an added attraction it also had to be smartly finished.

At the beginning of the 1930s, surprisingly, there was no major national event, although something of the sort had been organised in 1928, when the rallying point had been Bournemouth and when Donald Healey had elected to start from John O'Groats in a Triumph Super Seven and won outright. Phil Drackett, in his history of the RAC Rally, sums up developments at the beginning of the decade as follows:

'The idea of the RAC Rally was born in the stately portals of Pall Mall, home of the Royal Automobile Club, energetically fostered by Captain A. W. Phillips with the formidably efficient approval of the then secretary Commander F. P. Armstrong and actively nurtured by *The Autocar* magazine. Plans were laid in 1932 for the first of what it was hoped would become a series of annual events . . . .'

The most difficult aspect about the pre-war RAC Rallies was not the terrain used, nor the high speeds required, but that of keeping awake in the cars over the long and often boring runs to the rallying points. That first event had been advertised to would-be competitors by the slogan 'Enter the Rally and see Britain'. Since the object of the exercise was to reach Torquay on 5 March in good order and there was a choice of starting points at

*Rallying in style, and in glorious scenery – the downhill passage of the Inverfarigaig 'corkscrew' during a Scottish Rally* (Autocar).

London, Bath, Norwich, Leamington, Buxton, Harrogate, Liverpool, Newcastle-upon-Tyne and Edinburgh, that claim looked assured. There was no competitive motoring of any sort on the long run to Torquay, where the whole thing was to be sorted out by a 'flexibility and braking' test. Naturally the coachwork competition would provide an important finale.

The first event attracted a huge entry. In all, 341 cars started and no fewer than 259 got through to Torquay without losing time on the road. One might well ask how the other 82 came to lose time or to retire, but as it was March and there was a bit of snow in the north, perhaps they had an excuse. The average speed required for the 1,000 miles was only 22 mph – which meant 45 hours of motoring. It would all have been much easier if cars were consistently making towards Torquay, but anyone starting from London found himself having to visit Preston and then Cambridge, before turning south-west.

The 'flexibility test', if only the organisers had thought about it in advance, was a real gift to cars having fluid flywheels. The tests required 100 yards to be covered in top gear as slowly as possible, after which the next 100 yards had to be covered as fast as possible (with gear changing allowed), followed by crash braking into a 'box' marked on the road. Going fast and braking hard was easy enough, but going really slowly was extremely difficult. It was little wonder that Colonel A. H. Loughborough, in a specially prepared Lanchester 15/18, dominated the event – after all, his car took no less than 5 min 7 sec to complete the 100 yards. At times the car barely seemed to be moving, which is hardly surprising as its average speed worked out at 0.67 mph!

Those people running cars with conventional transmission were supposed to run that test without help from the clutch pedal. There were observers in each car to see fair play, but even they could not guard against the cheats who had installed a concealed clutch mechanism in the rear seats, under the floorboards and employed a passenger to operate it. Cheating, it seems, was not invented recently!

**Background photograph** *Where else but the Monte Carlo Rally, in the hills behind the Principality, with a Ford V8 followed by a Hotchkiss on the way to the finish of the 1938 event? (Autocar).*

**Inset** *A really splendid effort by Donald Healey (at the wheel) who won the 1931 Monte Carlo Rally in a 4½-litre 'flat-iron' Invicta. It was to be Britain's only Monte win of the decade (Autocar).*

After the first event there were complaints that it had all been too easy (driving tests on the moors, hill climb tests on Bwlch-y-Groes, Porlock and other 'killer' hills, were all suggested) yet by 1934 there were no fewer than 384 starters. Hastings, Eastbourne, Brighton and Blackpool all had their turn to entertain the event before the end of the decade. As trials declined, so rallying boomed and the Scottish and Welsh national clubs built up their events on the back of this trend. The MCC started their own international rally (which finally disappeared at the end of the 1950s, still running to the same basic format) and when the Scots promoted a major trade exhibition in 1938 it seemed to be a good excuse for yet another rally to be organised.

The best I can say about pre-war rallying of this type is that it was harmless and did not cause much public nuisance. Several features which improved driving comfort (seating, heating and de-frosting schemes) were all inspired by these events, but these was really no worthwhile spin-off from some of the lavishly-equipped 'Concours' cars which appeared. Was fitted accommodation for golf clubs an advance? Or the provision of hot and cold water? A fold-away wash basin? Special lighting and curtains around the rear seats? All these appeared but, on the other hand, no one appears to have pioneered safety belts or other really useful items of equipment.

The more severe events in Europe, which had such a fine reputation, found no imitators here in Britain. It is true that there was always a starting point for the Monte Carlo Rally in this country – usually at John O'Groats to make the itinerary as difficult as possible and there was always a strong contingent of British entries, but the civil authorities treated it as an exceptional occasion. Such harum-scarum activity, in general, was discouraged and the habit did not spread.

Because the winters in the 1930s seem to have been more severe than they are today and because special tyres had not been developed, the Monte Carlo Rally was as tough and demanding as could ever be desired. The organisers could almost guarantee their entrants really copious quantities of snow and ice on the way to the Riviera. Like the RAC Rally, the Monte also had its 'formula', which included long runs to the Principality from far-flung starting points and one or two simple tests to sort out all the unpenalised arrivals. Naturally, the Concours was important. Naturally.

The tests were assiduously practised – the Brooklands Club usually laid out a close copy of them on the finishing straight for British entrants to try – and a good performance was critical to success or failure. One missed gear-change could make all the difference and an engine prone to stall under heavy braking could ruin one's performance. Because of the weather, road sections tended to be difficult. In some years there were declared bonuses for those people electing to start from the least accessible points – which were sometimes so inaccessible that competitors could not even reach the starts.

Our most famous Monte driver was undoubtedly Donald Healey, who won the event outright in 1931 in his $4\frac{1}{2}$-litre Invicta. His experiences in 1929 were, however, typical of many private owner's fortunes. Entering a little Triumph Super Seven saloon, Healey chose to start from Riga, in Russia. The snow was so deep and the forecasts so appalling, that he could not even get to Riga, so he decided to start from the nearest alternative point, which happened to be Berlin.

No British car won the event again in the 1930s, although the great man came close on two later occasions – second in 1932, also Invicta-mounted and third in 1934 in a Triumph Gloria. In 1935 he took the exciting straight-eight supercharged Dolomite on its first event, started from Umea in northern Sweden, but wrote off his car under a train at a level crossing in Denmark!

In 1936, in an unsupercharged version, he took eighth place. In those days there was no question of steep and narrow little passes being needed to increase the difficulties of the

route in the Alpes Maritimes. The main *Routes Nationales* were quite awful enough, especially if we recall that there were no studded tyres, very skimpy heaters for the cars and just
about no foolproof way of keeping the windows clear of ice. As to headlamps, ice-proof
ignition systems and engine oils for ultra-cold weather . . . their standards can be imagined.
In post-war years even into the late 1950s, the BBC kept up the legend that the Monte was
the world's most difficult event; in the 1930s there was no doubt about it. There *was* no
more difficult or unpleasant way of spending a week on the roads in January. With those
cars? With tyres like that? In those winters? From Norway, Sweden or darkest Serbia?
They were brave men.

If we take 1935 merely as an example, the most popular starting points were from
Palermo, Stavanger and Umea. There were 165 entrants, many of them British. Donald
Healey, Rupert Riley, Tom Wisdom, Humfrey Symons, Jack Ridley, Stanley Barnes,
'Sammy' Davis, Miss Margaret Allan, the Hon Brian Lewis, and two members of the
nobility (Lord Crichton-Stuart and Lord de Clifford) were among the drivers and they
chose to run Rileys, Triumphs, MGs, SSs, Lagondas, Bentleys, ACs, Alvises and Singers –

*The famous Arrival arch on the quayside at Monaco, used for all the Monte Carlo Rallies of the 1930s. The*
*winters seemed to be colder and more perilous than they are today and even a 2½-litre SS Jaguar had to work very*
*hard to keep up with the schedule. This is A. J. E. Cowey's car in the 1937 event (Autocar).*

**Above** *Colonel Berlescu's extraordinary Ford, as prepared for the 1936 Monte Carlo Rally, complete with four rear wheels, two driven axles and tracks which could be fitted at will. It so nearly won (coming 21st overall after one mistake), but such devices were banned the following year (Autocar).*

**Below** *Clarke's Aston Martin at the top of the Stelvio Pass hill climb in one of the gruelling Alpine Trials (Autocar).*

'Sammy' Davis even chose a Railton. There was no nonsense about running standard cars either – it was Donald Healey who started the trend by using massive 'balloon' tyres, while one particular Ford-based 'special' from Eastern Europe (which so nearly won the event in 1936) looked more like a desert-specification vehicle with half-tracks, than a private car.

The summer counterpart of the Monte, which was equally as feared because of the challenge of the terrain chosen, was the Alpine Trial. It was a 'trial' in every sense, because it bore little resemblance to any of the other current rallies. The Alpine, more than any other event, was the prototype of fast post-war events, with high average speed targets set over mountain roads, hill-climbs and driving tests, with a gruelling work-load on driver *and* co-driver throughout the week. All the high passes used in recent years – Allos, Cayolle, Galibier, Iseran and Stelvio – were in any 1930s itinerary and all were very fierce. Their gradients were severe and their surfaces often loose, with inches of choking dust. Cooling systems were not as efficient then, tyres certainly did not last very long (radial ply construction had not been invented) and the performance of heavily-shrouded drum brakes was a constant source of worry. On top of all this was the heat, the dust – and the endurance.

Although British manufacturers were happy to advertise their successes, if any, in the Monte Carlo Rally, it was the Alpines which taught them the most. Even William Lyons, who was not very interested in motor sport at the time, approved of teams of SS cars being entered – and they usually rewarded him with splendid individual performances; Tom Wisdom put up the best overall performance in 1936 in a 2½-litre SS 100 lent to him by the factory. After the finish, of course, there was always the prospect of a monumental party at some swank hotel on the French Riviera – the British were really keen on that sort of thing – but the problem of the long drag back to reality remained, for there were no French *autoroutes* then.

The essence of the sort of motor sport in which we all could have indulged in the 1930s was that it was great fun. Today, of course, even British rallies have become very professional and the cars have become ultra-specialised. No serious rally driver ever uses his car for normal transport and it is often transported by trailer to and from the venues of the events. In the 1930s this simply was not necessary and – somehow – it would not even have been thought to be acceptable. This was true sport and sportsmanship which still survives with events dating from this period. The best way to savour these events is to be a spectator at, or even compete in, one of the current MCC long-distance trials. Even the smells are different and there isn't a sponsor's badge in sight.

# Chapter 10

# Making and selling the product

As I have already pointed out, by the end of the 1920s the British motor car industry – production, sales and service – was in a state of transition. By the end of the 1930s that process of change was complete. If the motoring business of the late 1920s still looked recognisably like that of the Edwardian and early vintage era, that of the late 1930s had taken on the appearance of a thoroughly modern industry.

Lovers of vintage cars say that one attraction is that they had been built by craftsmen, individually and with some care. Cars of the 1930s, they say, were turned out in greater numbers, were not as distinctive and did not have as much built-in quality. This is an over-simplified verdict which ignores two other important factors – that cars of the 1930s were much cheaper to buy than those of the 1920s and that, as a consequence, many more of them were sold. Not only were more cars assembled in a reasonably efficient manner, but they were advertised and sold with every trick known to the fast-developing trade.

In the Appendices which follow this chapter, a few statistics are, I hope, enough to show how radically the pattern of the industry changed over the ten years leading up to the outbreak of war. Although only one brand-new, major, car-assembling complex was opened in the 1930s (at Dagenham in Essex, where all Ford cars would henceforth be assembled) the industry could build up to 400,000 cars a year in 1939, whereas ten years earlier 200,000 would have been the top limit. Re-building, re-thinking modern production engineering and some concentration of resources, all helped; the dramatic swing to 'mass-production', as opposed to individual assembly, was the most important factor.

Before going on to consider the individual fortunes of some companies in the industry, it is time to point out the *status quo* at the beginning of the 1930s. Although between 40 and 50 different marques were on sale, two of them – Austin and Morris – accounted for nearly 60 per cent of all sales. In 1930 there was, quite simply, no such thing as the 'Big Six' which had developed by the end of the decade. Austin and Morris completely dominated the sales scene, with Ford, Humber-Hillman, Singer, Standard and Vauxhall trailing far behind. The feature of the 1930s, however, was the way in which these four concerns made strenuous – and successful – efforts to close the gap. Although Austin and Morris could build and sell twice as many cars in the 1930s as they had in 1929 or 1930, the other firms boosted their sales by up to 900 per cent.

Major technological changes ushered in throughout the period were often made with an eye to simplifying production methods, making it possible to assemble thousands of cars a month where hundreds had previously been assembled and yet to retain the option to make frequent changes. That most obvious of aids to mass production, the moving production line, was not installed at the Morris factory at Cowley until 1934, for instance, and production (urged on by attractive new ranges) jumped by more than 60 per cent in 1935. The growing popularity of pressed-steel body shells (and the ability of firms like the

Pressed Steel Co, Fisher & Ludlow and Briggs Motor Bodies to supply them) made a startling contrast with the hand-building methods normal in the 1920s. *All* the major concerns, too, reaped the harvest of careful planning of new engine ranges, where a simple cylinder bore change could provide another capacity (and RAC horsepower rating) for yet another new model variant.

Such changes, I must admit, were often made with little thought to the workers themselves. They were not then organised into 'powerful' industrial groups (in the unionised 1970s sense) and for the most part were relatively resigned to their lot. At least they were in work for most of the year and probably earned rather more than most other manual workers in Britain – by comparison with unemployed workers in the north-east, in Wales or in Scotland, their industrial status must have seemed Utopian.

Although building methods changed considerably in a few years, the factories themselves did not. The industrial companies which became the 'Big Six' each had their traditional homes, once, that is, Ford had made their big move from Manchester to Thameside. From 1932 Dagenham was the British centre of Ford's operations. Morris had Cowley, near Oxford (plus Wolseley at Ward End in Birmingham and MG at Abingdon) and Austin built all their cars at Longbridge, on the southern outskirts of Birmingham. Humber-Hillman became the Rootes Group and retained all their factories in Humber Road, Coventry, Standard settled their headquarters at Canley in Coventry, while Vauxhall built more and more cars at Luton.

Coventry was the single most important British 'motor city'. In the 1930s Alvis, Armstrong Siddeley, BSA, Daimler, Hillman, Humber, Lanchester, Lea-Francis, Riley, Rover, SS and SS Jaguar, Singer (some models), Sunbeam-Talbot, Swift and Triumph were all built in Coventry, along with Coventry Climax Engines. The vast Morris Engines Branch plants and several important coachbuilding concerns were located there too. In spite of what Austin and Morris might have hoped, the centre of the motor industry was most definitely in Coventry.

Apart from Ford's new Dagenham factory, no other concern built new plants. Most – especially Longbridge and Cowley – were expanded from time to time, but no tycoon had the capital, the courage or even the need to look elsewhere for his output. This meant that the buildings were often not at all as up-to-date as the products they housed. Even as recently as the late 1960s, when Leyland first took control of Cowley, finance director, John Barber, is reputed to have called it 'one of the original dark satanic mills'. SS and Triumph moved into adjacent empty ex-Great War shell-filling factories, but these were exceptions.

It was only the Government's 'shadow factory' scheme, launched in 1936 by Lord Swinton, which brought new buildings within the industry's grasp and even then it was necessary to wait for ten years before cars could be built in them. This scheme, set up to expand production of aeroplanes and aero-engines, envisaged new factories, fully-equipped and staffed with a new workforce; firms in the motor industry would be given administrative control of these plants and a few for doing the job. It was one of the National government's few decisive moves and it worked out well. Lord Nuffield, as perversely-inclined as usual, would have nothing to do with it at first (he was in dispute with the War Ministry over a Wolseley aero-engine project), but the rest of the industry joined in with a will. No doubt they could all see the long-term possibilities – foresight was something for which Lord Nuffield was noted. By 1938 the Midlands was dotted with vast new factories – which were certainly not 'shadows' to those who drove past them – which are all still in active use by the motor industry. Austin built their factory at Longbridge and expanded into it in the 1940s, Standard built theirs at Fletchamstead and took it over later, Rootes (Chrysler now) assembled cars at Ryton-on-Dunsmore in post-war years and Jaguar took over an unwanted Daimler 'shadow' factory at Allesley in the 1950s. The 'Standard No 2'

A line-up of completed Ford 8 and Ford 10 bodies (the 1937-1939 models, of which a total of 107,000 were sold) on the final inspection line at Briggs Motor Bodies. These designs carried on into the 1940s and 1950s as Anglias and Prefects (Ford Motor Co).

factory at Banner Lane, Coventry now makes Massey-Ferguson tractors and Rover's Solihull plant was originally an aero-engine factory in 1939/40.

Because the cars, in general, were simply engineered and could be assembled easily, it was a great temptation for management to make frequent changes. Most prominent firms, in the early 1930s, made annual announcements about their new season's programme – usually concentrating these sweeping announcements in the weeks between mid-summer and the opening of the Motor Show. Most companies – Armstrong Siddeley and Daimler for the 'county' set as much as Austin and Standard for the lower middle classes – had complex and interlocking ranges of cars; it was easy for them to shuffle things around to give an impression of energetic improvement, even if the capital outlay needed was relatively small.

The habit of making an annual change was traditional – so traditional that it created its own special problems. Most people seemed to have formed the habit of buying their new cars between March and August. There was then a lull as everyone drew back and waited for the announcements of 'next year's models'. Car makers brought in their new cars between August and October to stimulate sales in the autumn and the winter, but found that most people had already committed themselves for that year and would not actually buy the new cars until the start of the next year.

It was a vicious circle which the makers themselves had worsened. The public came to expect new models in the autumn and the car makers eventually came to expect sales of old ones to die back at the end of the summer. Annual changes, therefore, might be good for an advertising spree and were encouraging to a sales force, but they could also be absolute murder for a factory's production planner. Even in those days of simple cars, production quantities were enough to make substantial tooling essential. Specification changes meant tooling changes, tooling changes meant production line changes – and with production lines torn apart you could not make next year's *or* this year's models.

One solution to this was to stop everything, close down for a time, make the changes in a silent factory and start up again when ready – which was convenient for a planner, but brutally unfair to the workers. Things began to improve after a while, but for years it was almost a motor industry tradition that the track workers should be laid off for a time during the autumn while the facilities were being rebuilt. For a hard-nosed businessman or an accountant, the logic was that one should make changes while sales were low. For the unfortunate workers, however, the end of the summer was a time of dread – their lay-offs would depend on the scope and nature of the 'annual change'.

There were two obvious ways to solve the problem. One was to put a prototype of a new model on show at Olympia or Earls Court, knowing that one could not possibly hope to deliver before the following spring. Equipping the factory for that major new model could then take place later, after the more straightforward changes had been completed, thus ensuring that most of the workforce would be at work most of the time. This practice was widespread in the 1930s, but usually only when a car was new in every way and therefore did not have to replace a previous model. In some cases firms had not made any production plans, but wanted to gauge public reaction before committing themselves. MG with the first SA '2-litre' model, Hillman with the Minx, Lagonda with the V12 and Riley with the first of the Nuffield-sponsored cars were all good examples.

The other more civilised and businesslike way was to get away from the ritual of autumn releases and only show a new car when production had begun and examples were already in dealers' hands. But in the complacent atmosphere of fixed ideas which enveloped our motor industry at the time, it needed a powerful concern to make the first moves. Only Austin or Nuffield were big enough and it was Nuffield which took the plunge first. In May 1935, having done very little indeed in the autumn of 1934, Nuffield announced

*Labour was much cheaper than machinery during the Depression years. Even at Austin's high volumes, it was still worth having the bodies coachbuilt by traditional methods* (Autocar).

their 'Series II' Tens and Twelves, which had all-new bodies and frames. At the same time, they stated that: 'No longer will seasonal changes in design be made and no longer will models be referred to as 1934, 1935 and so on. Instead, "Series" will be used and a series will be continued until such time as major improvements become possible or desirable.'

This worked very well for them, even though they continued to rely on autumn new-model launches for the Ten Series M and the new Eight Series E. Wolseley, being firmly linked to Morris in engineering terms, usually followed suit, though their Series II Super Sixes were held back for the 1935 Motor Show, as were the Series III Sixes in 1937. Austin took time to take up this new philosophy, but launched new Eights and Tens in the first half of 1939, to break with their own traditions.

The result of such logical industrial planning was that more variety was made available without any increase in costs. By the mid-1930s, indeed, a typical mass-production small car cost little more than half its equivalent had cost ten years earlier.

It was a situation which suited Sir William Morris (who became Lord Nuffield in 1934), though at times – as in the aftermath of the Depression – his company was caught flat-footed by changing trends and Morris lost sales when others were forging ahead. Morris,

*Profile of one of Nuffield's Series II cars – this was a Morris 12, which was almost identical except in engine size with the 10. There was no separate boot lid and luggage had to be stowed through the rear compartment* (Autocar).

like Austin, was never keen on producing the minimum number of models and the confusion at the planning stage must have been considerable. This short table tells its own story:

| Year | Number of Morris ranges (and styles) | MG ranges | Wolseley ranges |
|------|-------------------------------------|-----------|-----------------|
| 1930 | 7 (22) | 2 | 3 |
| 1933 | 9 (26) | 3 | 3 |
| 1936 | 7 (18) | 3 | 6 |
| 1939 | 5 (13) | 3 | 6 |

The big and sprawling factory at Cowley had – like Topsy – 'just growed' from year to year. Starting from the Oxford end of the complex we see today, and having only modest premises on the north side of the site, it spread gradually and in a haphazard way eastwards along the Horspath road and by 1933 it was well overdue for renovation. Sir William therefore turned to Leonard Lord, that production engineering specialist who had already made sense of the ex-Hotchkiss engines factory at Coventry and was just completing a similar job at Wolseley in Birmingham, to lead the transformation of Cowley.

The re-organisation process lasted well over a year and more than £300,000 was spent in 1934 alone. Not many people realise that before then there had been no moving assembly line at Cowley. Until this time the chassis had been pushed along the line as each stage of work was completed and parts necessary to complete the job had been stacked on the floor alongside. Now, starting with the new Morris Eight of late 1934 and gathering momentum with the Series II machines announced the following year, moving lines were installed and a complex of overhead delivery conveyors was installed. The total workforce at Cowley – between 5,000 and 6,000 – was actually down on 1931/32, but because of the rapidly expanding Pressed Steel Co concern further eastwards the job opportunities in Cowley itself were continuing to increase. The Morris factory itself covered more than 80 acres. The Coventry Engines Branch was a vital components supply division and had a workforce of nearly 3,000. Exports were becoming so important that a separate concern – Morris Industries Exports Ltd – was formed to look after this and in time this took over responsibility for all Nuffield Group exports.

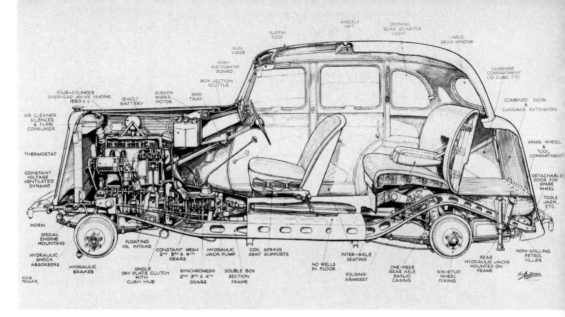

**Above** *Morris's new Series III Twelve of 1937 – with an absolutely typical 1930s family car layout. Compare this drawing with the layout of the Series II model (page 194). The major technical advance of the Series III model was that it had the steel body shell welded to the chassis frame, which was a good first step towards integral construction. The price for this very well-equipped model was only £177 10s* (Autocar).

**Below** *The Morris works at Cowley, in the 1930s, was one of the biggest in Britain, but has now expanded to an enormous size in recent years. This aerial view is from the west, or Oxford city end. The original Military Academy building is in the foreground and buildings erected in the 1920s and 1930s stretch away along the Horespath road. The separate factory in the distance is the Pressed Steel Co Ltd's works, set up in the 1920s by Budd Manufacturing and Morris* (British Leyland).

*After Len Lord had master-minded the modernisation of Cowley, Morris cars were built in a much more logical manner, on moving production lines. This appears to be 1935, with Morris Eights nearest the camera, Series II 10s/12s behind them and six-cylinder models behind the row of roof supports* (British Leyland).

By 1935 Morris were the sixth largest motor car company in the world (behind Ford USA, Chevrolet, Plymouth, Dodge and Oldsmobile) and the biggest in Europe. It was hardly surprising that they could boast of building cars by 'Specialisation', or of being able to sell 65,000 of the new Morris Eights by November 1935, only 14 months after the new model had been announced. The whole re-organisation at Cowley cost half a million pounds, which was no mean sum for its day and it was to reap the reward he thought he deserved for the job that Len Lord demanded even more than the managing directorship he already had. The result, as already mentioned, was that he and Lord Nuffield quarrelled, that Lord eventually left, joined Austin in 1938 and intensified a bitter rivalry which did not end for more than ten years.

With the help of supplies from a brand-new engines factory at Courthouse Green, Coventry, in 1938, Morris reached its pre-war peak. The millionth Morris car was produced in May 1939, when it was said that the plant was capable of building up to 150,000 cars every year, though it was also admitted, *sotto voce*, that actual production had not exceeded 100,000.

Austin's success story in the 1930s was just as pronounced, though they did not quite suffer as badly in the Depression as Morris had done. Austin ended the 1920s well placed for their future, especially when one remembers how nearly they had been bankrupted by the wrong 'one model' policy at the beginning of the period. In time, however, the famous Austin Seven had transformed their standing and, aided by the long-established Twelve, it helped Austin into 1930 with a 23 per cent market share. The Ten which arrived in 1932 added to the company's prospects and to the complexity of the range.

*One way to publicise the product was to invite a show-business personality to sample it. That familar face behind the wheel of a new Morris Eight chassis belongs to Sir Harry Lauder and flanking him are Len Lord and Nuffield's M. Seaward* (Autocar).

By then Longbridge sprawled to 220 acres and manufactured almost everything – engines, transmissions and bodies – on the site. Whereas Morris was only a car *assembly* plant, Longbridge was definitely all about car *manufacture* as its 12,000 work force makes clear. For 1934, for instance, Austin offered no fewer than 50 different models in only six basically different ranges, with prices ranging from £105 to £595. That was the year their sales exceeded 60,000 for the first time and by 1937 this had risen to nearly 90,000. The fact that the cars were technically backward and their styling rather stodgy for much of the time, did not deter the customers. Their advertising made much of falsely snobbish model names like 'Ascot', 'Goodwood' and of course 'Cambridge', talked of dependable Austins, of the 'Penny a Mile' cost of running an Austin Seven and was highly successful with the theory that 'You Invest in an Austin'.

Ford, however, were bravest of all, by building and commissioning an entirely new factory at Dagenham in Essex during the Depression. The first Dagenham-built machine – a truck – was ready in 1931 when industrial prospects could not possibly have been more gloomy and examples of the very important 8 hp Model Y saloon (announced in February 1932) were being delivered in autumn 1932. By then more than 7,000 people were at work at Dagenham.

By 1934 the Model Y had captured more than half of the entire 8 hp market, but it was badly hit by the arrival of the new Morris Eight later that year, which was one good reason for Ford's decision to start marketing a £100 version of the car – the 'Popular'. Although Ford 8s and 10s were not at all technically advanced, they were both cheap to buy and reliable to run; about a quarter of a million 8 hp models and more than 200,000 10 hp cars

**Above** *All the battle of the Austin assembly lines in 1939, caught by the unique talents of* The Autocar's *F. Gordon Crosby* (Autocar).

**Right** *Hillman advertising of 1939. Could they* really *have been serious?* (Autocar).

were built before the end of 1939 and cars based on their layout were built until 1959. It was no wonder that Ford (Henry Ford, in fact) could continue to object to the SMM & T, or any such associations and refuse to show his cars at London motor shows. Until 1937 there were annual Ford exhibitions in London at motor show time, latterly at the Albert Hall, with a lot more space than would have been available at Olympia. By 1939 Ford's Dagenham workforce had risen to 12,000.

Dagenham itself was a Utopian manufacturer's dream. Once the problems of building a factory on marshy ground had been solved, it was possible to erect an ideal site on virgin land, where iron ore for making castings came in from the sea (the lower reaches of the Thames) at one end and where complete motor cars left at the other. Yet, for all that, Dagenham in the 1930s was only a fraction of its present size, as the aerial picture on page oo confirms.

In Coventry it was Standard and the Rootes Group who made all the headlines. Standard, under John Black, expanded enormously throughout the period, not even being deterred by the Depression. Their Canley site had originated as an aircraft factory in 1916, but progressively took over from the city centre properties in importance in making cars. It was blessed with a great deal of land on which to expand (not all of which, even today, has been fully developed, though government policies have had something to do with this), an ambitious managing director and a logical and attractive range of models. By 1938, when the Flying Eight was being prepared for production, Fisher & Ludlow thought Standard an important enough customer for an entirely new body-building factory to be erected at Tile Hill, a building which Standard-Triumph eventually bought for their own use in the 1950s.

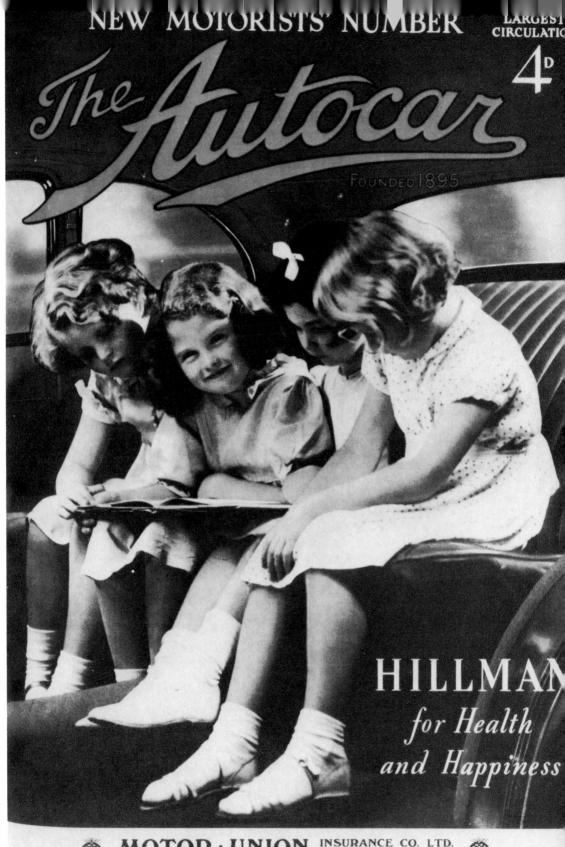

# NEW MOTORISTS' NUMBER

LARGEST CIRCULATIO

# *The Autocar*

4D

FOUNDED 1895

HILLMAN
*for Health
and Happiness*

While Standard had a great deal of elbow room in which to build new production workshops in the 1930s, the rapidly-developing Rootes Group did not. Although the Rootes brothers were anxious to expand their empire by acquiring other firms, they first of all had to gain complete control of the Humber-Hillman combine, which had joined together in 1928. By a most felicitous coincidence, Humber and Hillman (when independent firms) had developed factories literally next door to each other in Humber Road, Stoke, Coventry (the Hillman works being that nearest to the Coventry-Rugby railway line) so that when Rootes gained financial control in 1932, speedy rationalisation was possible.

Even before this, however, rationalisation was in progress in 1930 and 1931 when (with the Minx in mind, no doubt) it was suggested that more than 100 cars a day – equivalent to perhaps 25,000 cars a year – could soon be built. By 1935, with the empire expanding mightily (Talbot and Sunbeam had both been taken over at the beginning of the year), a smooth new Minx (advertised as a 'Minx Magnificent' by the company) was almost bound to give the company a boost.

It did. The 10,000th example was built in January 1936, only a few months after its release the previous autumn and more than 700 a week were being built by the summer of that year. The 100,000th Minx (of two distinct model series, since spring 1932) was built in July 1937, by which time Rootes were vying with Standard for 'leadership' in the Coventry prestige stakes. Although this was not at all due to capitalising on the famous names of Sunbeam and Talbot, it was certainly due to rapid and ruthless rationalisation. It was an enormous insult to fans of famous marques like Sunbeam and Talbot to merge them into a 'new' name for 1939, but the permutations then possible were quite remarkable.

When war broke out on 3 September 1939, the Rootes Group's 1940 range was to have comprised a new unit-construction Minx, a Hillman 14, Sixteen, Snipe, Super Snipe, Imperial and Pullman Humbers and four Sunbeam-Talbots – all based on two engine families, two transmissions, three chassis frames and three different body shells. Tourer, drop-head coupé and coachbuilt versions were also sold as production-line Rootes models, in what was a most impressive and (to their customers) attractive range. But as for advertising Hillmans as being 'For Health and Happiness' – surely they could not have been serious!

The last, and most reticent, of the 'Big Six' was Vauxhall, another marque now reviled by vintage enthusiasts because of the way a small concern selling hand-built machines in mid-1920s had been turned (under General Motors control) into one rivalling Standard and Rootes in terms of production achievements, if not in style. Although they retained their original factory site in Luton, it expanded, needed a by-pass to keep traffic flow in reasonable shape and eventually spilled over to the other side of the road. Vauxhall, more than most British firms, thoroughly understood the value of product-cocktailing and, inside the styles laid down for them by General Motors in Detroit, produced a comprehensive range of 'look-alike' models (Vauxhall did almost none of their own styling until the end of the 1930s and then only on special-bodied versions of a standard car).

It was not only in sales that Vauxhall were so successful. They were the first to introduce synchromesh gearboxes to Britain (with the Cadet in 1931), the first to introduce unit-construction bodywork (the Ten in 1937) and among the series-production pioneers of independent ('Knee Action') front suspension.

Even among the middle class car makers, there was still a great deal of progress in regard to the way their cars were built and in the number of different models which could

**Opposite** *In the 1930s Austin often filled their advertising space with short and telling little parables, like this chat between 'The Major' and his young protégé. Austin also invented one of the most famous slogans of all: 'You buy a car – but you invest in an Austin' (Autocar).*

BRITAIN'S . DEPENDABLE . CAR

# "You young fellows never look two days ahead!"

# "I've just looked a good few years ahead, Major—invested in an Austin."

"H'M, there's hope for your generation, after all."

"We're not so crazy as some would make out, Major. Notice the men I had lunch with? Both my age and both Austinites. One by nature and one by necessity!"

"I didn't think your lot could tell a good investment from a gamble."

"Some of us couldn't till we had to. Take one of the two men you saw at my table. A rich uncle gave Millington a car for his twenty-first birthday. Unfortunately, Rich Uncle never had to consider running costs. Imagine what *that* meant!"

"Shouldn't have got cars out of his elders! Ought to have changed to one he could afford to run."

"He did. Invested in an Austin. Same horse-power, 'all-in' bills twenty per cent down."

"And t'other fellow?"

"Oh, William's one of your Austinites by nature. Wanted a car without trouble—and got it. Said his car must run smooth while he treated her rough. Now he's done 20,000 in his Austin without so much as dirtying his trouser-knees."

"Like my niece, pesterin' me for an Austin because it won't need tinkering with."

"All comes round to investment—in time or money. Might as well invest 'em both well, don't you think, Major?"

READ THE AUSTIN MAGAZINE: 4d. every month.

*For list of Austin Dealers see following pages.*

**THE LIGHT TWELVE-FOUR DE LUXE SALOON**
*A spacious 4-5 seater. Selected hide upholstery. Pytchley sliding roof. 4-speed Twin-Top gearbox. 11.9 h.p. 4-cylinder engine developing 26 b.h.p. at 2,600 r.p.m. Engine insulation at 3 points by rubber bushes. Semi-elliptic springing; zinc interleaved. Silentbloc shackles. Hydraulic shock absorbers. 12-volt electric lighting and starting. Chromium finish, Dunlop tyres.*

YOU BUY A CAR—BUT YOU INVEST IN AN

# AUSTIN

The Austin Motor Company Limited, Birmingham and 479 Oxford Street, London. London Service Depots: 12, 16 & 20 h.p. Holland Park, W.11. 7 & 10 h.p. North Row, W.1.

OVERHEAD AT THE GOLF CLUB:

*"I always feel a bit uneasy here. We seem to be the only people with a foreign car"*

# buy a car made in the
# UNITED KINGDOM

be offered from a restricted range of major components. On the SS Jaguar of the 1937–39 period, one basic saloon car body covered 1½-litre and 3½-litre cars. Every Triumph of the 1937/39 period was concocted from the same basic chassis/engine/transmission family, though at times there seemed to be dozens of different body styles and two or three separate ranges. As for Riley in mid-1930s and late-1930s, their engines, body shells and model names were combined in a most energetic way, which (considering that they built their own engines and many of the body shells) must have contributed something to the financial problems of 1938. Even Daimler, who were so proud of their Royal patronage, could produce a staggering variety of cars badged as Daimlers, Lanchesters *and* BSAs between 1933 and 1936. In 1934 for instance, at the Olympia Show, there were BSAs and Lanchesters looking virtually alike, with near-identical mechanical specifications, both with larger and more powerful Daimler relatives carrying the same family resemblance. By the end of the 1930s BSA had reverted to building front-wheel drive Scouts in Birmingham, but Lanchester and Daimler were yet more inextricably linked; all this, mark you, on a total annual production of little more than 5,000 units.

By comparison with the way production methods were revolutionised, cars were still being advertised in a most discreet and detailed manner. Marketing gimmicks abounded (surely everyone knows of the cars being given away as prizes in cigarette card competitions?) but precious few really deathless slogans, or striking displays were developed. On the contrary, Austin, for instance, developed a whole series of display advertisements on the theme of 'You Invest in an Austin' which contained as much light reading as the average full-page article.

The British attitude to selling their cars altered considerably in only a few years. Sir William Morris's remarks in South Africa in 1930 typified the smug self-satisfaction of many people:

'The reason why British motor car manufacturers do not manufacture cars suitable for Dominion markets was that it was only recently that they have caught up with home demands . . ..'

– but after financial storms had swept through Britain, almost every source turned to urging the British to buy more cars. Supply, all of a sudden, was well ahead of demand and publicity was aimed at changing this. One magazine editorial of October 1931 said that people should 'Buy Cars Now. They are investments that are intrinsically sound.' Only weeks later, Morris were writing: 'You chose a National Government. Now choose the National car – Morris.' For years afterwards Morris adverts always seemed to include a separate exhortation to 'Buy British and be proud of it'.

The 'Buy a car built in the United Kingdom' advertising, made without reference to any make and jointly financed by companies in the motor industry, went ahead in 1936 and later in the year it became more pointed. A whole series of adverts showed middle class people in potentially embarrassing social positions. There was the young couple coming away from the golf club ('I always feel a bit uneasy here. We seem to be the only people with a foreign car') or the two bankers talking in the City, ('surprised at a man like Charles running a foreign car').

There was little enterprise among manufacturers in the way they advertised their own new cars, though a strong theme of snobbery and the appeal to social climbing values usually shone through. Even Ford fell foul of this at times, as instanced by their 1939-model 8 hp recommendations: 'Back at school again, the youngsters will get lots of surprise

*Opposite The British motor industry was worried about imports of foreign cars even in the 1930s, when the numbers involved were tiny. From time to time they resorted to a series of snide advertising campaigns in which snobbery and class distinction usually played a part (Autocar).*

**Above** *Somewhere in there, behind the foliage, is a car showroom (Heath and Wiltshire's) and a line-up of new Rootes models. But the flags, potted palms and the drapes were all typical of 1930s gimmickry* (Autocar).

**Left** *How much did used cars cost in 1936? Not a lot – but remember the much lower level of salaries too. Isn't that rather a famous Bentley for sale from France, Radford and Co for a mere £345? Hugh Harben restored it only a few years ago. The 'world-famous racing motorist' was Woolf Barnato, one-time Chairman of Bentley Motors* (Autocar).

visits, now that the Mater has a Ford "Eight".' Were there really a lot of people who still called their mothers 'Mater'?

Selling cars, it seemed, was still quite a discreet business, even if the products themselves were often very plebeian. But traders mainly dealing in the more expensive cars could be almost embarrassingly reserved. How about this one from 1934: 'Whitney Straight Ltd have for disposal Mr Whitney Straight's private 8-litre Bentley . . . £1,200. (A Wilson self-changing gear-box is optional)'.

Part of the selling process, if never openly admitted, though rather plain on hindsight, went into the cultivation of the motoring press, who for their part, responded in kind. Both *The Autocar* and *The Motor* were well-respected in the motor industry and both were privy to its secrets. The two, incidentally, were deadly rivals in every way and new staff men were solemnly instructed not to talk to their rivals, nor to help them in any way. The magazines' advice was often solicited about features of new models under development, but in return they were never known to betray a confidence, break a deadline, or carry consistently anti-industry views. Both held the view that British cars were best for British buyers (which in truth, they usually were, because of the taxation and social conditions) and both made every attempt to promote the sales of British cars. Perhaps we could even do with a dash of this approach today, when imported cars take such a slice of the market?

Their road tests, in retrospect, appear to be masterpieces of 'double-speak', especially by modern standards and particularly in comparison with the fringe press where bias and opinionated testers often get in the way of a balanced judgement; in reality the 1930s tests preserved an impartiality that bordered on the meaningless. Their technical analyses, on the other hand, were masterpieces of detail and every historian's task has been made easier because of this. It was *The Autocar*, of course, which invented and refined the technique of cutaway drawings, some of which grace these pages.

Both did their best for the industry and sought to present new models in the best light. Even when Rolls-Royce were involved, the superlatives were not muted:

'Certain cars have acquired a prestige so great that any radical change in their design is a great moment for the industry as a whole. That is why the decision to give the latest model Rolls-Royce Phantom a twelve-cylinder V engine and independent suspension for its front wheels, is so very interesting. Today, what used to be called complication is of no moment; the multiplication of parts, provided it ensures their better functioning, is definitely of advantage . . ..'

Or how about this, when Morris revised their smallest model in 1934:

'In the new Eight the Morris firm undoubtedly are offering the all-round best small car they have produced. It is better almost beyond comparison than any of its predecessors of this make in point of roominess of the bodywork, lightness and facility of control, liveliness of performance on the road, and not least, in appearance.'

On the other hand, any historian looking for serious comment on the effects of the Depression, the reasoning behind many industrial moves or for the story behind some of the more spectacular failures and mergers, had a very thin time. The motoring press were not anxious to rock the boat. Bankruptcies happened to someone else, no reader was ever out of work and the exigencies of public transport were rarely considered. Motoring was always a pleasurable pursuit, hotels were usually large and welcoming and everything new was thought to be an advance on the old. Gossip columns were only spicy or pointed if an industrial source had primed the writer, the Captains of Industry were all fine fellows until or unless they were deposed and their failings were classed as misfortunes. Success, of course, was only to be expected and everyone cheered.

It all sounded very serene and orderly in contrast with a world and a nation which demonstrably was not. Yet, in many ways, the 1930s in Britain was a very serene period in which to go motoring. Looking back, even from the depths of inflationary and industrial gloom, it is plain to see that the cars were relatively cheap and that many more pleasures were available than now remain. The pace of motoring – indeed, the pace of living – was more gentle. In spite of the harsh realities of European politics, 'This England' was still worth living in. As motorists, and as private citizens, there was much of which to be proud. Most of us can look back on the 1930s with nostalgia and with pleasure.

# Appendices

# Who made what? How many were made?

It is not my intention to drown the reader in a final sea of statistics, but I think it is necessary to draw together a few facts and figures summarising the changes in the motor car market and the industry which served it, throughout the 1930s.

## 1 The British car makers

At the time of the Olympia Motor Show of October 1930, *The Autocar* listed the following makes of British car in its authoritative Buyer's Guide:

| | | | |
|---|---|---|---|
| AC | Calthorpe | Jowett | Singer |
| AJS | Crossley | Lagonda | Standard |
| Alvis | Daimler | Lanchester | Star |
| Argyll | Ford | Lea-Francis | Sunbeam |
| Armstrong Siddeley | Frazer Nash | Marendaz Special | Swift |
| Arrol-Aster | GWK | MG | Talbot |
| Aston-Martin | Hampton | Morris | Triumph |
| Austin | HE | Rhode | Trojan |
| Bentley | Hillman | Riley | Vauxhall |
| Beverley | Humber | Rolls-Royce | Whitlock |
| Burney | Invicta | Rover | Wolseley |

– a total of 44 marques

This list looks relatively impressive. However, there is no doubt that several makes were listed merely out of bravado by their tottering companies, or out of 'old time's sake' by the magazine's editors. Within a year Argyll, Arrol-Aster, Beverley, GWK, HE, Rhode, Swift and Whitlock had all disappeared permanently from the motoring scene; Calthorpe, Hampton and Star were not far behind them.

Nine years later, immediately before the outbreak of the Second World War, *The Autocar* produced a price list of all current British cars, which comprised the following marques:

| | | | |
|---|---|---|---|
| AC | Brough Superior | Jowett | Rolls-Royce |
| Alta | BSA | Lagonda | Rover |
| Alvis | Daimler | Lanchester | Singer |
| Armstrong Siddeley | Ford | Lea-Francis | SS Jaguar |
| Aston Martin | Frazer Nash | MG | Standard |
| Atalanta | Hillman | Morgan | Sunbeam-Talbot |
| Austin | HRG | Morris | Triumph |
| Bentley | Humber | Railton | Vauxhall |
| British Salmson | Jensen | Riley | Wolseley |

– a total of 36 marques in all

In nine years, therefore, only 27 marques had survived, although two of them had been merged (Sunbeam and Talbot) and one – Triumph – was in the hands of a receiver when the lists were compiled. Of these 27 marques, no fewer than 17 were either members of the 'Big Six', or part of multi-marque combines.

In the intervening period, several other makes of car had been born, flourished briefly, then disappeared again. Most of them produced models sporting in character, and all built and sold cars in extremely limited quantities. The only marque to establish itself permanently, to sell cars in any numbers and to achieve financial stability, was William Lyons's SS concern. The first SS car was announced in 1931 and the first SS Jaguar in 1935. Incidentally, identical cars to the relatively rare 1940 SS models were to be built immediately after the war, but the 'SS' part of the title was dropped.

During the 1930s, several substantial companies fell on hard times or were bankrupted by their creditors and were subsequently re-born in considerably altered forms, sometimes after a takeover. Among these were: Bentley, Lagonda, Lanchester, Lea-Francis, Riley, Sunbeam, Talbot – and the same fate was awaiting Triumph, if war had not intervened.

In addition, several makes of car – American or European – were built under licence in Britain, often with a considerable proportion of British-made components. Until Ford's Dagenham factory started producing cars, Fords built in Manchester really qualified as 'imported cars' and their large V8 engines continued to be brought in from Canada until 1935. The most notable 'built in Britain' marques were Chrysler and Dodge (built at Kew) and Citroën (built at Slough).

## 2 Production, sales, exports and imports

As I have already pointed out in the main body of this book, the British motor industry hit its 'vintage' production peak in 1929. Economic effects of the Depression then caused a decline in sales until the bottom of the trough was reached in 1931. After that there was a remarkable recovery, which peaked out in 1937 and a minor decline leading up to the outbreak of the Second World War.

These were the details, including the last two 'vintage' years for comparison:

| Year | British cars produced | Year | British cars produced | Year | British cars produced |
|---|---|---|---|---|---|
| 1928* | 165,352 | 1932* | 171,244 | 1936 | 367,237 |
| 1929* | 182,347 | 1933* | 220,779 | 1937 | 379,310 |
| 1930* | 169,669 | 1934* | 256,866 | 1938 | 341,028 |
| 1931* | 158,997 | 1935 | 325,192 | 1939 | 305,000 |

*Note: These figures are as supplied by the SMM & T and there is a minor hiatus between 1934 and 1935. Figures marked with an asterisk (\*) refer to the year ending in September (roughly equivalent to the model year); others refer to the calendar year.*

Although neither imports nor exports took up such an important part of the motoring scene in the 1930s, it is interesting to see how these lined up, alongside actual British registrations and the number of cars on our roads. I hope the following table is simple enough to understand:

| Year | New cars registered during year | Imported cars that year* | Total number of cars on British roads | British cars exported* |
|---|---|---|---|---|
| 1928 | 161,493 | 32,121 | 900,557 | 26,180 |
| 1929 | 169,355 | 21,520 | 998,489 | 33,792 |
| 1930 | 156,460 | 9,751 | 1,075,081 | 23,210 |
| 1931 | 144,212 | 2,118 | 1,103,715 | 19,032 |
| 1932 | 145,874 | 2,762 | 1,149,231 | 32,043 |
| 1933 | 186,543 | 3,619 | 1,226,541 | 40,308 |

| Year | New cars registered during year | Imported cars that year* | Total number of cars on British roads | British cars exported* |
|---|---|---|---|---|
| 1934 | 230,866 | 10,811 | 1,333,590 | 43,907 |
| 1935 | 281,388 | 13,471 | 1,505,019 | 54,520 |
| 1936 | 310,091 | 12,143 | 1,675,104 | 64,765 |
| 1937 | 318,461 | 18,560 | 1,834,248 | 78,113 |
| 1938 | 280,217 | 9,180 | 1,984,430 | 68,284 |
| 1939 | 235,795 | **5,750 | **2,150,000 | 53,983 |

**\*\* Accurate figures not issued by SMM & T because of outbreak of war.**
*\*Includes complete cars and rolling chassis.*

Imported cars never captured a serious proportion of the British market, compared with the inroads they had made in the 1920s. In 1928 imported cars had taken no less than 20 per cent of the market, but by 1931 this had plummeted to a miserable 1.5 per cent. Even in 1937, when the new-car sales boom was at its height, that share only rose to 6 per cent, and it makes me wonder whether all the 'anti-foreign-car' propaganda was necessary? Or did this, in fact, keep numbers down at a time when a bigger market could have been opening up for the imported car?

A study of the industry's export achievements is even more instructive, for it goes some way to disproving the old belief that British cars of the 1930s could not be sold on world markets. Exports dipped to 19,032 in 1931, but then surged impressively ahead to a peak of 78,113 in 1937. Although the absolute figure was well down in 1939, it was achieved in only the first eight months of the year and the SMM & T (as custodians of the industry's statistics) rightly claimed that this was a record *rate* of exports. In that peak year of 1937, 20 per cent of all British private car production was exported, mainly to 'The Empire'; even at the low point of 1931, when international trade was at a low ebb, we exported 12 per cent of our production.

Figures also show, incidentally, that private car sales by no means stopped dead after the outbreak of war. Although only 1,949 cars were actually built in 1940 (which makes a mockery of all the bright advertisements placed by our car makers to reassure their old customers that production was continuing in spite of the war) no fewer than 31,988 cars were registered in that year; in the case of both those figures, a substantial proportion must have been 'Official' or military cars, for the figures changed in 1941 to 5,117 and 3,091 respectively.

## 3 What we bought and when we bought it

Changing social and financial conditions affected the types of car we bought throughout the 1930s to a considerable degree and the evolution of new baby cars, taxation changes, the price of petrol and our general prosperity all had their effects.

By splitting British new car registrations in horsepower groups (using the RAC taxation rating) it has been possible to produce this very interesting table. Figures quoted are percentages of the total year's sales:

**Percentage of total home sales**

| RAC hp group | 1927 | 1928 | 1929 | 1930 | 1931 | 1932 | 1933 | 1934 | 1935 | 1936 | 1937 | 1938 |
|---|---|---|---|---|---|---|---|---|---|---|---|---|
| 8 or less | 16 | 18 | 25 | 27 | 28 | 24 | 26 | 23 | 30 | 27 | 27 | 30 |
| 9 and 10 | 7 | 8 | 10 | 9 | 14 | 24 | 34 | 34 | 31 | 33 | 32 | 33 |

**Percentage of total home sales**

| RAC hp group | 1927 | 1928 | 1929 | 1930 | 1931 | 1932 | 1933 | 1934 | 1935 | 1936 | 1937 | 1938 |
|---|---|---|---|---|---|---|---|---|---|---|---|---|
| 11 and 12 | 27 | 24 | 18 | 17 | 13 | 16 | 15 | 17 | 13 | 16 | 15 | 16 |
| 13 and 14 | 28 | 23 | 13 | 7 | 9 | 15 | 8 | 8 | 8 | 9 | 11 | 9 |
| 15 and 16 | 6 | 10 | 16 | 25 | 21 | 12 | 9 | 9 | 5 | 3 | 2 | 2 |
| 17 and over | 16 | 18 | 12 | 15 | 14 | 10 | 9 | 9 | 13 | 12 | 13 | 11 |

This simple table shows, in the clearest possible way, how the market was changing at the end of the 'vintage' period of the 1920s and how the Depression of 1931 and 1932 had its own effects.

Even by 1927 the 'baby car' boom had begun, with one car in every six having nothing larger than an 8 hp engine. Small 'eights' increased their share to 28 per cent by 1931 and – after a pause in the next few years – to 30 per cent by the mid-1930s.

Without any doubt, however, *the* winner in sales terms was the 9 hp/10 hp bracket. Starting from only a 7 per cent share in 1927, they forged ahead to 34 per cent as sales began to climb out of the Depression and retained that share for the rest of the decade. Nor were they winning sales from the really small cars. They sold in the sector most popular to the new motorist, who often progressed beyond his first 'baby' and never troubled to push ahead any further.

The 11 hp/12 hp cars suffered sharp losses during the Depression (losing half of their sales compared with 1927) but came back slightly by 1934. The slightly larger 13 hp/14 hp cars, which had been so popular in the 1920s, slumped badly at the end of the 1920s and never really recovered.

As one would expect, buyers of large cars managed to keep their heads above the financial whirlpools of the early 1930s and through the proportion of cars sold halved between 1928 and 1933, it edged back before 1937 due to the lower tax imposed after 1934. The real losers, of all groups surveyed, were the 15 hp/16 hp cars. They had actually gained sales as the 1920s drew to a close, but once the Depression began to hurt business and industry, sales fell sharply away. By 1936 this sector was of an almost negligible size, which might explain why firms like Morris and Austin tended to by-pass it – selling cars below the 15/16 hp bracket in great numbers and always having one large-engined car to shoot for the '17 hp and over' market sector.

Summing up the trend of the 1930s, it seems that many 'new motorists' bought cars in the lower horsepower sections, as might have been expected and that below the really wealthy classes there was considerable 'trading down' in engine size, if not in terms of the marques actually favoured, as the decade progressed.

In 1930, for instance, cars of 12 hp or less captured 53 per cent of the total market of 156,460 – in other words a total of about 83,000 cars. In 1938, on the other hand, the same types of cars held no less than 79 per cent of the total market and sold to the tune of 221,000 cars.

# 4 Individual achievements

Accurate and authoritative production figures for individual marques are difficult to find and would in any case be very turgid if quoted at enormous length. The SMM & T destroyed its records many years ago. The Second World War, takeovers and mergers, production 'years' which differ considerably from company to company and plain indifference to their heritage mean that a synthesis has been needed even for what follows:

Throughout the 1930s, Austin and Morris were always the market leaders. Except for 1933 and 1934, when Nuffield's policies were in some confusion, Morris were always market leaders and when we consider that Wolseley were also making up to 30,000 cars a year by 1938, it is obvious how the Nuffield Group dominated the British motoring scene.

With the proviso that accurate Morris figures are not available for the years 1936-1939, the following shows just how the two big rivals matched up:

|  |  |  | Cars sold | | |
| --- | --- | --- | --- | --- | --- |
| Year | Total | Austin | % of Total | Morris | % of Total |
| 1929 | 182,347 | 43,287 | 24 | 63,522 | 35 |
| 1930 | 169,669 | 38,437 | 23 | 58,436 | 34 |
| 1931 | 158,997 | 42,817 | 27 | 43,582 | 27 |
| 1932 | 171,244 | 36,326 | 21 | 50,337 | 29 |
| 1933 | 220,779 | 53,186 | 24 | 44,049 | 20 |
| 1934 | 256,866 | 62,292 | 24 | 58,248 | 23 |
| 1935 | 325,192 | 77,171 | 24 | 96,512 | 31 |
| 1936 | 367,237 | 70,458 | 19 | approx 90,000 | — |
| 1937 | 379,310 | 89,745 | 24 | approx 90,000 | — |
| 1938 | 341,028 | 64,058 | 19 | approx 90,000 | — |
| 1939 | 305,000 | 76,482 | 25 | na | — |

At the beginning of the 1930s, therefore, Austin and Morris accounted for more than half of all car production in Britain in a particular year. Though this share dropped away to 44 per cent in 1933 – the infamous Nuffield 'year of the traffic light' – it bounced back again to well over 55 per cent in 1935 and if the MG/Wolseley contribution was added in (for Nuffield), the two giant corporations must have been responsible for 60 per cent of the industry's production in that year.

It is also worth noting that all the future members of the 'Big Six' expanded their production most impressively during the 1930s. Ford's achievement is already documented earlier in this book (only Morris, with their 8 hp cars, could challenge Ford's 8 hp sales in mid and late 1930s) but their American-owned rivals, Vauxhall, who had sold only 3,927 cars in 1931, pushed this up to 11,106 by 1933, to 26,240 by 1935 and to 35,415 in 1938, by which times they had cornered 10 per cent of British car production. Rootes, as already noted, had consolidated and improved on the base left for them by individual Hillman and Humber managements and were certainly capable of building 1,000 cars a week by the end of the decade. Standard, guided by Captain John Black, performed remarkably well and were selling as many cars at the end of the 1930s as anyone except Austin, Morris or Ford. They built only about 7,000 cars in 1930, but 21,000 in 1933, 34,000 in 1937 and no fewer than 50,700 in their financial year 1938/39, which ended neatly just before the outbreak of war. That last achievement was equivalent to nearly 17 per cent of all British production, which had both Austin and Morris very worried indeed.

I would also like to show, by means of production figures, why two Coventry-based companies – Rover and SS – did so much to upset the balance of power and popularity among the middle class car makers of this country in the period. Their production achievements were as follows:

| Year ending in Autumn | Rover cars built | *SS and SS Jaguar cars built | Year ending in Autumn | Rover cars built | *SS and SS Jaguar cars built |
| --- | --- | --- | --- | --- | --- |
| 1931–31 | 10,144 | — | 1935–36 | 8,335 | 2,469 |
| 1931–32 | 6,400 | 776 | 1936–37 | 10,183 | 3,554 |
| 1932–33 | 4,960 | 1,525 | 1937–38 | 10,516 | 2,154 |
| 1933–34 | 5,964 | 1,793 | 1938–39 | 11,103 | 5,378 |
| 1934–35 | 7,253 | 1,720 |  |  |  |

*SS production, as opposed to the building solely of special bodies, did not begin until the winter of 1931–32.

In view of the above, perhaps it is no wonder that Riley gradually drifted down into bankruptcy in 1938, that Triumph followed them in June 1939, that the smaller-engined Armstrong Siddeleys, Lanchesters and Alvis models could make little impact on the motoring scene – and that Rover and Jaguar were among the strongest to face up to post-war austerity in 1945.

Finally, I am enormously indebted to that eminent historian, Michael Sedgwick, against whom no other motoring scribe can possibly compete, for his comments on other firms' production. His knowledge, and some of my own, go to add a few snippets on the rest of the industry of the period.

Of the other 'middle class' manufacturers of the period, it seems that the BSA/Daimler/ Lanchester combine, for all their great and complex model ranges, never produced more than 5,500 to 7,000 cars a year up to the mid-1930s and that this figure even declined to-wards the end of the decade; this also goes some way to explaining why all their body shell production (even of 'standard steel' models) was contracted out to firms like Holbrooks, Mulliners and Charlesworth. Armstrong Siddeley, who relied rather less on car pro-duction for their profits, probably had a peak production year in 1937, of between 4,000 and 4,500 cars. During the decade they made a total of 31,167 cars, of which about half were 12s and 14s, but of which only 70 cars were 30s and only 253 were Siddeley Specials.

Up to the end of 1939, MG built about 20,000 cars in the decade but did not expand as well as might have been expected. More than 1,800 cars were built in 1930 when the little M-Type was at its peak of popularity, only 1,250 in 1935 when the racing activities had to be cancelled and a peak of 2,900 cars in 1937 after the SA range had gone into production. Accurate figures do not exist for Triumph's pre-war production achievements, but a study of chassis numbers suggests that their peak was in the early 1930s when the Super Seven/ Eight models were selling well (up to 100 cars a week was mentioned) but that later in the decade the Glorias and Dolomites, for all the nice things said about them in print, were always struggling to sell at more than 1,000–1,500 cars a year.

The really specialised cars sold in tiny numbers, as marque histories and club register records prove. For instance, there would certainly be less than 500 British Salmsons in all, probably little more than 150 1930s Invictas, Lagonda production measured in tens rather than hundreds per month, and mere penny numbers of famous sporting marques like Frazer Nash, Railton, Talbot and Morgan. Then, as now, the enthusiasm for a particular marque was rarely supported by a rush of customers. Then, as now, the bank manager and the benevolent proprietor was of more value than the cash buyer. Then, as now, bread and butter cars were often vilified by the enthusiasts, but contrived to make big profits and ensure financial stability for their makers. That aspect of the motoring scene, at least, has not changed.

# Index